# WOMEN IN
# DEVELOPING
# COUNTRIES

# WOMEN IN DEVELOPING COUNTRIES

## Assessing Strategies for Empowerment

edited by
Rekha Datta and Judith Kornberg

LYNNE
RIENNER
PUBLISHERS

BOULDER
LONDON

Published in the United States of America in 2002 by
Lynne Rienner Publishers, Inc.
1800 30th Street, Boulder, Colorado 80301
www.rienner.com

and in the United Kingdom by
Lynne Rienner Publishers, Inc.
3 Henrietta Street, Covent Garden, London WC2E 8LU

**Library of Congress Cataloging-in-Publication Data**
Women in developing countries : assessing strategies for empowerment /
    edited by Rekha Datta and Judith Kornberg.
        p.  cm.
    Includes bibliographical references (p.  ) and index.
    ISBN 1-58826-014-3 (alk. paper)
    ISBN 1-58826-039-9 (pbk. : alk. paper)
    1. Women in development—Developing countries. 2. Women—Government
policy—Developing countries. 3. Women's rights—Developing countries. I. Datta,
Rekha. II. Kornberg, Judith F., 1954–
HQ1870.9 .W65286 2001
305.42'09172'4—dc21                                                    2001048638

**British Cataloguing in Publication Data**
A Cataloguing in Publication record for this book
is available from the British Library.


Printed and bound in the United States of America

The paper used in this publication meets the requirements
of the American National Standard for Permanence of
Paper for Printed Library Materials Z39.48-1984.

5  4  3  2  1

*To my mother, mother-in-law,*
*and the millions of women in the developing world*
*who have silently, courageously, and cheerfully*
*borne the burden of household and community*
*and thereby raised the self-esteem of their daughters.*

*To the memory of my father*
*and to my father-in-law,*
*who have instilled in me the belief that*
*education is the greatest source of empowerment.*
*To my husband, Subrata, and my daughter, Amrita,*
*for their cheerful patience,*
*which helped me endure the long process.*
*—R. D.*

*To those who have worked on*
*international, national, and local levels*
*to empower women and*
*who have inspired the authors of this text.*
*—J. K.*

# CONTENTS

# ACKNOWLEDGMENTS

Before reaching publication, every book travels a long way and benefits from numerous contributions. This book is no exception. The journey has been long, sometimes arduous, but eventually joyous! We would like to thank each other and the authors for patiently working over the last few years to make this book possible. We would like to especially thank Bridget Julian and the staff of Lynne Rienner Publishers for not giving up on us. Special thanks to the Grant-in-Aid for Creativity and the Stanley Fellowship of Monmouth University for partial funding for this project. To members of the Self-Employed Women's Association in India, other nongovernmental organizations, and millions of women around the world who are tirelessly working to improve the conditions of women and contributing to empowerment, thank you for the inspiration to conduct this study. Sincere appreciation to all our colleagues and friends at Monmouth University and Purchase College for all their support and help. Finally, to family members, Subrata, Amrita, Suheeta, Debashis, and our friends who have given up numerous weekends and much family time, thank you!

— *Rekha Datta*
— *Judith Kornberg*

# 1

## Introduction:
## Empowerment and Disempowerment

### Rekha Datta & Judith Kornberg

Since the 1970s, researchers and policymakers have examined the impact of development on women in developing countries. Ester Boserup's path-breaking 1970 study inspired academics and practitioners to address the problems of gender discrimination that exist in the development process.[1] With such impetus, many studies have demonstrated the extent of gender discrimination in development. These efforts have resulted in policy changes at local, national, and international levels to ensure more gender equity. Women's organizations are empowering women in developing countries to play a more active role in the development process. Women are adopting strategies to confront discrimination and deprivation in the workplace, community, and society.[2] Consequently, the question of how development policies affect women's control of resources and decisionmaking capacity has initiated great interest in empowerment studies.

## EMPOWERMENT AND DISEMPOWERMENT

Empowerment is a widely used but complex and contentious concept. Since the 1970s, the feminist literature and the gender and development (GAD) discourse have shed considerable light on the concept of empowerment. The dialogue has addressed several important questions. What constitutes empowerment? Who empowers whom? What are the goals and strategies of empowerment as well as the process of disempowerment?

To be sure, the notion of empowerment is multifaceted, a process eluding simple definition. Perhaps a helpful way of organizing the literature would be to examine empowerment as a *process* and as an *outcome*. Even though conceptually separable, there is a great deal of overlap between these two aspects of empowerment.

As a process, empowerment addresses the policies and strategies of decades of development in the third world that affected women. It provides a framework for feminist scholars, activists, and nongovernmental organizations (NGOs) to understand social relationships (gender equality) and the impact of social and economic processes. Such processes include, for example, colonialism and development policy, as they shaped and transformed women's position in national and international contexts.[3]

In the 1970s and 1980s, third world feminists used the concept of empowerment to address the issue of the gender differences that exist in the control and distribution of resources. Embedded in the notion was the idea of power, in a relational context (i.e., "power over [whom]" and "power to [influence whom/what]"). Nancy Hartsock distinguished between "power over," meaning control, and "power to," meaning the ability to influence change. She considered the latter notion more useful.[4] The reference is to strategies of change that women can bring about.

Following that trend, subsequent studies manifest the importance of the phenomenon of "power to"—that is, power to bring about change in situations of inequity and discrimination in which women find themselves. Essentially, the reference is to the strategies that women use to increase their control of resources and generate decisionmaking capacity. Gita Sen and Caren Grown argue that women's organizations are central to these strategies. Thus, women must not only "strengthen their organizational capacity [but also] crystallize visions and perspectives that will move them beyond their present situation."[5]

The 1990s witnessed the use of the concept in a more inclusive sense. The focus on power to, which began in the 1970s, was included with the notion of power over, thus expanding the meaning of empowerment. For example, Srilatha Batliwala defines "power" as "control over material assets, intellectual resources, and ideology" and "empowerment" as "the process of challenging existing power relations, and of gaining greater control over the sources of power."[6]

Thus, the current effort is toward reconciling the issue of empowerment as a process and as an outcome of that process:

> Empowerment is manifested as a redistribution of power, whether between nations, classes, castes, races, genders, or individuals. The goals of women's empowerment are to challenge patriarchal ideology (male domination and women's subordination); to transform the structures and institutions that reinforce and perpetuate gender discrimination and social inequality (the family, caste, class, religion, educational processes and institutions, the media, health practices and systems, laws and civil codes,

political processes, development models, and government institutions); and to enable poor women to gain access to, and control of, both material and informational resources.[7]

These components outline the inclusive elements of empowerment. In general, these elements work in a complex continuum, resulting in changes that ensure more power to women. The process can also produce an erosion of power, resulting in disempowerment.

## DISEMPOWERMENT

Empowerment studies often address a central question: As a result of empowerment, have women achieved more power compared to men and compared to women in previous decades? Alternatively stated, Are women empowered or disempowered as a result of organizational, structural, and policy changes? The GAD literature has demonstrated many cases where women have actually lost power as a result of development initiatives. Institutions have manifested male biases, and capitalist development strategies have eroded women's power compared to men's.[8] Many of these studies demonstrate that women have lost a lot of ground compared to men, especially in economic development. Examples of disempowerment would thus include women's increased dependence, reduced access to resources and decisionmaking, worsening quality of life, and compliance with policies and practices that circumscribe women's rights.

A related issue is whether women's empowerment led to men's disempowerment. One researcher argues that "women's empowerment does mean the loss of the privileged position that patriarchy allotted to men," yet "women's empowerment also liberates and empowers men." When men recognize women as equal partners, there is a qualitative change in gender relations; renewed energy and skills are brought to social and political movements and institutions.[9] Thus, it no longer remains a zero-sum game in which women's gains become men's losses.

Furthermore, it is important to note that even though the process of empowerment will hypothetically lead to outcomes, it is not a simple, unidimensional path. There is no "straightforward cause and effect relationship between process and outcomes. Nor is it always clear when a change is cause and when effect, when process, and when outcome."[10] Thus, when evaluating the empowerment outcome of any particular process (individual skill enhancement, community organization enterprise, policy impact), one has to consider the complex nature of the empowerment process and the effect it may have directly or indirectly in enhancing power. In a recent study of credit programs for rural women in Bangladesh, Naila Kabeer finds that a growth of women's self-confidence, in their knowledge of their rights, their willingness to participate in public action and even the reduction of domestic violence may have occurred as a result of women's participation in the new forms of social relationships embodied in credit organizations; they bore little relationship to the productivity of their loans.[11]

Evaluating the impact of empowerment also raises the question of *which* women are being empowered, whether the empowerment of some women means the disempowerment of other women, and how the struggle for women's empowerment interfaces with struggles around racial, class, religious, and ethnic oppressions. Sen and Grown argue that it is the vantage point of poor and oppressed women that should be taken into consideration. They recognize that empowerment must address the multiple layers of the subordination of poor women: "We want a world where inequality based on class, gender, and race is absent from every country; and from the relationships among countries."[12] The extent to which the empowerment of poor women leads to resistance by women privileged in terms of class, race, and nationality in specific contexts is an empirical one that requires further research.

## THE CASE FOR A MULTILEVEL APPROACH

Critics have pointed out that the concept of empowerment is rooted in the Western culture of individualism and personal achievement.[13] Despite its Western origins, however, as we have already discussed, empowerment is now a widely used term in the field of GAD.[14]

Empirical analyses using an empowerment perspective, though, are at the very beginning stage. Some studies have characterized empowerment as a multilevel process involving the individual, organizational, and policy levels. At the individual level, the process involves raising consciousness and developing skills; at the organizational level, women learn collaborative skills to work in collectivities; and at the policy level, women partake in drafting, enacting, and enforcing legislation that seeks to redress gender discrimination.[15]

In addition to the different levels of empowerment, the 1990s trend was also toward a synthesis of power over resources and power to make decisions. This definition of empowerment is captured effectively in the definition of empowerment used in the United Nations (UN) system. It includes the following components: women's sense of self-worth; their right to have and to determine choices; their right to have the power to control their own lives, both within and outside the home; and their ability to influence the direction of social change to create a more just social and economic order, nationally and internationally.[16] How do these efforts translate to empowerment as it is occurring in different developing contexts? This book seeks to contribute to that perspective by demonstrating the multifaceted aspects of empowerment at all these levels. In addition, it presents case studies from various regions of the world in order to manifest the different meanings that empowerment can take when examined from the perspective of the needs of women in particular situations (development, social change, war).

Hence, our perspective of empowerment is that it occurs when individual and group efforts correspond with those of agencies. Policies and programs that states and international organizations undertake to alleviate the adversities that women face every day are well within the purview of empowerment. They do this by enabling women to have more power over resources and decisionmaking. These policies include legislation addressing economic reforms, domestic violence, cultural constraints such as divorce legislation, inheritance issues, and the like. Eventually, this sense of empowerment addresses the issue of "power relations" (i.e., how are women able to address and redress power inequities in gender relations?).

Therefore, agencies—along with international laws and policies addressing issues of discrimination—go a long way in empowering women. Grassroots movements and women's organizations also play an important part in the process. Women become conscious of their power relations and decisionmaking ability by actively participating in the process of development. Thus, empowerment constitutes women's feeling of empowerment as achieved through activism and grassroots movements.[17]

Using this empirical, multidimensional perspective to understand empowerment, we maintain that empowerment occurs most definitely when women mobilize themselves and take leadership positions in work settings and in the community. Indigenous groups, NGOs, and international intergovernmental organizations such as the United Nations have been at the forefront of evaluating the status of women and making recommendations to governments about the need to alleviate discrimination at all levels. This has empowered women and has had an impact on policymakers at each of these levels as well.

At the macro level, Chapters 2 and 3 discuss how international organizations are addressing the problem of women's rights and inequality. In Chapter 2, Charlotte Patton takes note that the United Nations has been godmother to the global women's movement through four UN world conferences on women (1975–1995), as well as the follow-up Beijing +5 (June 2000). The subject of her chapter is that women have taken greater prominence as activists, policymakers, and critics and, further, have promoted a reconceptualization of population policy.

Do cultural and systematic violations of basic rights of women constitute a violation of human rights? Can there be international law addressing issues of female mutilation, sex trade, prostitution, and so on? In an effort to address these issues, are international agencies and conventions such as the Convention on the Elimination of All Forms of Discrimination Against Women able to empower women against violence and discrimination? That is the focus of Chapter 3 by Kathleen Suneja.

Chapters 4 and 5 examine national government policies in two very significant countries in the world: China and India, the world's two most populous countries. They also share the distinction of having a negative female-to-male ratio. Despite pledges to the contrary, national government policies in both these countries have not resulted in women's empowerment in economic and social well-being (i.e., education, health, and economic activity).

An essential element of empowerment is self-empowerment and grassroots activism. National policies and ideologies often declare their commitment to equality for women and men. In reality, how much of this is practiced, and does it lead to empowerment of women? Kellee Tsai examines whether the post-1949 communist ideological commitment to gender equality has resulted in transforming gender relations within patriarchal institutions and family structures in China. India, in contrast, is a parliamentary democracy. The constitution of India makes express commitment not only to equality but also to providing special opportunities for the advancement of women. Rekha Datta examines whether that commitment, after five decades of Indian independence, has translated into the empowerment of women.

Chapters 6 and 7 examine the complexities of West African and Latin American countries, looking at structural adjustment policies and microenterprise projects that have in fact reversed the socioeconomic status of women. Likewise some governments have implemented structural adjustment policies (SAPs) to generate greater economic development. Based on field research, the case study on Niger and Senegal (Chapter 6 by Lucy Creevey) explores the outcomes of economic and political effects that women have encountered as a result of government downsizing, reductions in government spending, and SAPs adopted by these governments in the 1980s and the 1990s. In this study, Creevey raises a very important question: Have these policies resulted in the empowerment or disempowerment of women? Her conclusion is that SAPs cannot be blamed for all the hardships poor women now face in both countries. Poor women were already being forced into work in the informal sector, or "proletarianized," to fulfill their family obligations. SAPs worsened the situation initially, reduced their already scarce incomes, and thus disempowered them. But there are signs that at the upper economic level women are beginning to profit from improved terms of trade, and some of this benefit is trickling down through the traditional informal female financial network. In Chapter 7, Kiki Anastasakos examines whether SAPs in Mexico and Costa Rica have produced comparable results, leading to empowerment/disempowerment. Interestingly enough, even though women in both countries felt the severe impact of

SAPs, Costa Rican women were relatively less disempowered compared to Mexican women. These studies make the case for more concerted efforts by governments to evaluate the effects, especially on women, of SAPs and policy changes before they launch what are generally advocated and accepted as models of development elsewhere.

Chapters 8 and 9 focus on areas of the world that are just beginning to receive attention from researchers, namely, the Caribbean and Palestine. Women in these regions are initiating waves of social consciousness and protest to improve their socioeconomic status and overall empowerment and leadership in the community. A basic thrust of empowerment is self-empowerment. Caribbean women's groups have taken upon themselves to promote a more people-centered development model. In Chapter 8, Marian Miller examines their successes and challenges of these women's groups as they are "making waves."

In war-torn countries, women have a special role to play. Saliba Sarsar's analysis of Palestinian women on the West Bank and the Gaza Strip (Chapter 9) reflects the multidimensional nature of empowerment. Here, women are caught in the conundrum of conflict, nationalism, activism, state-building, and peace. They have begun to formulate their demands and rights through movements and organizations.

The collection of essays in this volume thus approach the multilevel and complex nature of empowerment by looking at the international, national, and subnational levels and the various strategies of empowerment used at these levels. They highlight the different implications of empowerment for women in unique contexts of development and social change. International organizations take a broader perspective to address systematic gender violence issues. Although they may or may not generate economic development, these laws and policies enable women to have greater self-confidence and freedom from violence and oppression and also empower women to take leadership in other spheres of their life.

Thus, the volume does not seek to offer a definition or meaning of empowerment that will be effective and applicable globally. The case studies provide an opportunity to recognize the differences in empowerment experiences in different regions of the world and the levels at which they occur. They recognize the effect of scholarship as well as policies, laws, regulations, and movements that affect the status of women. "To succeed, women must become active both at the level of discovering strategies and implementing them at the level of national politics. They must continue to fight to maintain the language of equality and translate it into practicable measures."[18]

We hope to reinforce the emerging notions of assessing empowerment is all its richness, variety, and complexity. The meaning of empowerment for this book is therefore broad, inclusive, and flexible. In order to understand empowerment we must recognize the unique experiences of women in developing countries. Likewise, the strategies and policies that bring empowerment will vary in different contexts. The vicissitudes of the development process are already established. Studies such as these underscore the complex and varying degrees and nature of empowerment.

## NOTES

1. Ester Boserup, *Women's Role in Economic Development* (New York: St. Martin's, 1970).
2. Some of these studies include Lucy Creevey, *Women Farmers in Africa: Rural Development in Mali and the Sahel* (New York: Syracuse University Press, 1986); and Aihya Ong, *Spirits of Resistance and Capitalist Discipline: Factory Women in Malaysia* (Albany: State University of New York Press, 1987). Others include Kathryn March and Rachelle Taqqu, *Women's Informal Associations in Developing Countries* (Boulder: Westview, 1986); Christine Oppong, *Seven Roles of Women: Impact of Education, Migration, and Employment* (Geneva: International Labour Office, 1987); and Vidyamali Samarsinghe, "Puppets on a String: Women's Wage Work and Empowerment Among Female Tea Plantation Workers of Sri Lanka," *Journal of Developing Areas* 27, no. 3 (April 1993): 329–340.
3. This perspective is discussed in Gita Sen and Caren Grown, *Development, Crises, and Alternative Visions: Third World Women's Perspectives* (New York: Monthly Review, 1987).
4. Nancy Hartstock, *Money, Sex and Power: Towards a Feminist Historical Materialism* (Boston: Northeastern University Press, 1985), pp. 223 ff.
5. Sen and Grown, *Development, Crises, and Alternative Visions*, p. 89.
6. Srilatha Batliwala, "The Meaning of Women's Empowerment: New Concepts for Action," in Gita Sen et al., eds., *Population Policies Reconsidered: Health Empowerment and Rights* (Cambridge: Harvard University Press, 1994), pp. 130–131.
7. Ibid., p. 130.
8. Boserup, *Women's Role in Economic Development;* Irene Tinker, "The Adverse Impact of Development on Women," in Irene Tinker and Michelle Bo Bramson, eds., *Women and World Development* (Washington, D.C.: Overseas Development Council, 1976); Lourdes Benería, ed., *Women and Development: The Sexual Division of Labor in Developing Societies* (New York: Praeger/ILO, 1982); Naila Kabeer, *Reversed Realities: Gender Hierarchies in Development Thought* (New York: W. W. Norton, 1994).
9. Batliwala, "The Meaning of Women's Empowerment," p. 131.
10. Naila Kabeer, "Conflicts over Credit: Re-Evaluating the Empowerment Potential of Loans to Women in Rural Bangladesh," *World Development* 29, no. 1 (2001): 81.
11. Ibid., p. 81.
12. Sen and Grown, *Development, Crises, and Alternative Visions*, p. 80.
13. Jo Rowlands, "A Word of the Times, but What Does It Mean? Empowerment in the Discourse and Practice of Development," in Haleh Afshar, ed., *Women and Empowerment: Illustrations from the Third World* (New York: St. Martin's, 1998).
14. Caroline Moser, *Gender Planning and Development: Theory, Practice, and Training* (New York: Routledge, 1993).

15. Jorge Arditti, "The Feminization of Etiquette Literature: Foucalt, Mechanisms of Social Change, and the Paradoxes of Empowerment," *Sociological Perspectives* 39, no. 3 (1996): 3.

16. See http://www.undp.org/popin/unfpa/taskforce/guide/iatfwemp.gdl.html, p. 2.

17. See, for example, the work of noted gender planner Caroline Moser, esp. *Gender Planning and Development*.

18. Haleh Afshar, "Introduction," in *Women and Empowerment: Illustrations from the Third World* (New York: St. Martin's, 1998), p. 6.

# 2

# Women and the United Nations: Norms, Reproductive Health and Rights, and Population Policy

## CHARLOTTE GRAVES PATTON

Women and population issues now command attention on the global agenda. Although there has been an intergovernmental commission focusing on the status of women since 1947, the salience and high visibility of gender issues emerged only with a decade for women sponsored by the United Nations (UN).[1]

The end of the Cold War has allowed focus on pressing global issues through major conferences, including the environment, human rights, social development, population (International Conference on Population and Development, 1994), and women (Fourth World Conference on Women, 1995), followed by the Habitat Conference (1996). The attention given to women's issues varied from conference to conference. Nevertheless, the expanding role of nongovernmental organizations (NGOs) and more integrated thinking and experience among a growing set of players has resulted in normative development and expansion in women's issues. How the United Nations proceeds to clarify and define the rules, to incorporate the latest norms into programming, and to institutionalize these global commitments therefore calls for increased attention.

In this chapter I begin with a brief overview of the United Nations as well as some norms and rules on women as they were articulated in UN conferences of the 1990s. I also consider how the United Nations has contributed to the empowerment of women. Finally, I analyze and critique the roles and activities of several specific UN units in the context of empowering women.[2]

## INTRODUCTION

The United Nations has a long history of involvement with women and women's issues.[3] Article 8 of the UN Charter forbids any restrictions on the eligibility and participation of women and men *in any capacity and under conditions of equality in its principal and subsidiary organs.* Established in 1947, the intergovernmental Commission on the Status of Women (CSW) initiated major normative policy on behalf of equality for women, including declarations and treaties (on nationality, marriage, and political rights), as well as the very important 1981 Convention on the Elimination of All Forms of Discrimination Against Women. These CSW declarations and treaties contributed to the expansion of the women's movement and its search for equality between men and women. During the UN Decade for Women (1976–1985), political negotiations among the then competitive international forces forced UN political, institutional, and normative development for women, as well as interaction on issues in which women claimed interests and roles: development and peace.[4]

The three UN conferences related to the UN Decade for Women— Mexico City (1975), Copenhagen (1980), and Nairobi (1985)—not only interlinked these issues as necessary conditions for the improvement of women's status and lives, but the Nairobi Forward-looking Strategies (FLS) culminated in strategies to carry out those interrelated norms. The UN role to carry out these strategies has remained modest, with minimum funds, although the United Nations Development Fund for Women (UNIFEM), with an annual budget of about $13 million in 1993, was one outcome of the Decade for Women. Hopeful signs of progress included patterns of interaction at the global level, such as contacts made by women across national, ethnic, and class barriers at the Nairobi NGO Forum. Furthermore, national governments established national machineries for implementation of the FLS.

According to a Nairobi conference document, women had made progress toward equality during the Decade for Women in many areas (e.g., legal equality, participation in the labor force, and government expansion of basic health services).[5] But along with progress came unfulfilled expectations, programs that were not extended, and machinery that was not utilized to deal with women's issues. Also, new issues arose, for example, abuses against women and children. Women continue to be paid less than men for work of equal value, and too few programs have been implemented to eliminate discrimination against women. Women have remained undereducated, underpaid, and overworked in comparison to men. Women themselves have neglected their own health. Obstacles to overcome if women are to advance in equality include attitudes that legitimate women's position of inferiority; the praise of childbearing and childrearing responsibilities without role accommodation; the lack of data and knowledge about existing contributions of women and their potential for other contributions; and, always, lack of resources. Women face *real* problems, including lower literacy levels and discrimination.[6]

Women's roles in the political process are not exempt. In the answers to the extensive questions in the UN questionnaire on women's political participation, governments for the most part failed to include solid data, for example, on *gender-specific* voting statistics.[7] The Secretary-General's report presented selected percentages of women legislative representatives and deputies for selected countries, but not total composite figures for all countries.

Thus, some feminists have asserted that conditions for many women worsened during the Decade for Women and that not enough was being done to counter the effects of structural adjustment, worldwide expenditures on the military, and the consequences of local wars. Women were the faces of poverty and were being forced back into the informal sector. Hence, feminist academics and activists set out to substantiate some of these contentions. Others were added to the list, directing attention to grassroots, poverty-stricken, or head-of-household women. Scholars and activists did research on, organized around, lobbied for attention to, and joined forces with expanded networks and caucuses on a variety of issues: health, credit, education, employment, and violence against women, to name a few. After the end of the Cold War, with the focus now on globalization and the entry of more women into formal politics and NGOs, these issues have become increasingly significant.

The question of empowerment of women raises several questions. How is the concept being used in this book? This chapter advances the definition of power as the capacity to influence behavior of others as relative, relational, and situational. When assessing the power of women, while the other components are important, the relational aspect of power seems to be the most important. Power is a social relationship. Increased power of women will be reflected in their increased decisionmaking authority in the family and in community affairs.

Power for a woman, then, has been defined not as an end in itself but as an instrumental mechanism for a change in relationships, to herself and to others around her, especially authoritative males, in public and private institutions. Women themselves will exercise more authority.

Empowerment also means greater self-reliance on the part of women, that is, challenging a subordinate position in order to change roles and by striving and persisting to gain leadership. Empowerment includes a focus on those who needed help the most as well as on developing a consciousness of new ways and new behaviors to achieve what was desired. Whether an end or a process, presumably the conditions of the lives of more (or even most) women would be better.

New standards for women's empowerment emerged from the 1990s conferences. The 1985 UN Nairobi Women's Conference had asserted that all issues are women's issues. Women are concerned about and have emerged as potential players in many issues on the global agenda, not because they are decisionmakers (in many instances, they are not) but because they have begun to identify how political, social, economic, and cultural forces shape their lives. That particular consciousness has put some of the control of women's lives into their own hands.

In the 1990s, women's rights were human rights, and reproductive rights were human rights. For example, women's health mattered because those who gained health care might better responsibly decide the number of children to have *free of discrimination, coercion, and violence.*[8]

Some feminist scholars and activists have argued that women should be defined as a group based on a commonality of experiences, whether oppression or discrimination or some other gender construct. Others argue that women are expressly separated by class, education, race, or ethnic identity, sometimes experiencing privilege but more often marginality.[9] The world we live in is the world of groups in a planetary global village. What happens to the most marginal of us happens to the most privileged. The affirmation of women as a group declares the *possibility* of a relational change. Politically, to define oneself as a group provides a foundation for action. Even such a designation can be action itself.

Choices to be made by women are sometimes dichotomized in the literature: to reform politics by increasing women's participation in politics, or to transform politics by working outside conventional political institutions, raising consciousness, and expanding women's personal and social relations.[10] One answer might be that the understanding of the concept of empowerment has moved beyond this to identify a lengthy and multilayered process whereby women struggle with consciousness and policy simultaneously.

Thus, a particular interest is seen in the activation of UN Secretariat staff and their efforts to establish programs and projects to carry out the agreed-upon goals of Cairo and Beijing. In this chapter I focus on UN action related to the empowerment of women.

## THE UNITED NATIONS AND THE WOMAN ISSUE

Any writing on the United Nations and women acknowledges the United Nations as an international intergovernmental organization established by international treaty (i.e., the UN Charter). The name "United Nations" generally refers to UN Headquarters, comprising the General Assembly

(GA), the Economic and Social Council, the Security Council, and the Trusteeship Council, four of the five principal UN organs; the fifth is the Secretariat, headed by the Secretary-General, with Secretariat officials supporting the intergovernmental units.[11] Over the years, Secretariat functions have changed, new tasks have been added, and technical assistance has expanded beyond advisory missions and training programs to grants (supplies and local salaries) directly to governments. The United Nations, as an international intergovernmental institution, is policy-oriented, sometimes itself serving to influence policies of governments. It can also be a pressure point from which NGOs lobby governments.

The main players in the United Nations are government delegates who are generally instructed (although not always) about positions they are to take in the deliberative bodies. Normative rules are articulated in the legislative enactments of these bodies. Some are confirmed in legal treaties, such as the Convention on the Elimination of All Forms of Discrimination Against Women (CEDAW). Governmental control has been inexactly exercised by the power of the purse, a substitute for well-designed policy. Governments active in population policy since roughly 1970 have included the major donors (Canada, the United Kingdom, Germany, Sweden, Norway, Finland, and, depending on domestic politics, the United States). The major recipients of UN population policy funding have been India, China, Pakistan, and other Asian countries practicing family planning, some Latin and African countries, as well as almost all others for censuses and demographic research and evaluation.

In the 1990s, reform of the United Nations was a driving political force, publicly demanded by the U.S. government (part of the reassertion of the role of the U.S. Congress, in particular the Senate under Jesse Helms, former chair of the Committee on Foreign Relations, in the making of U.S. foreign policy), and quietly supported by other governments. Even before Secretary-General Kofi Annan's *Renewing the United Nations: A Programme for Reform* was introduced to the General Assembly on July 16, 1997, budgetary constraints, NGO complaints about failing adequately to consider issues, and criticisms within intergovernmental bodies had already encouraged some UN units to cooperate more fully on women's issues.[12]

In both women's and population issues, NGOs have been significant players. The women's movement, discussed below, and the so-called population club (variously, the International Planned Parenthood Federation, the Population Council, the Rockefeller Foundation, the Ford Foundation, and the International Union for the Scientific Study of Population) have worked with various UN units, encouraged new endeavors, and have received monies for programming from the United Nations Population Fund (known by the acronym UNFPA). Some NGOs have even become enmeshed with the United Nations and shared an insider's role at the United Nations.

In this chapter I take note of Secretariat units located at UN Headquarters in New York, in particular the Division for the Advancement of Women (under the CSW), the expert committee reviewing CEDAW, and the UNFPA, a funding agency substantively supporting and promoting family planning to lower the birthrate in third world countries and, since Cairo, reproductive health.

### FROM THE NORMATIVE TO EMPOWERMENT: THE UNITED NATIONS, GENDER POLITICS, AND HEALTH

By 1995, the United Nations could present a more optimistic picture of the world's women—at least in a general way.[13] Summarizing and analyzing on a regional basis, the United Nations reported many improvements despite continuing divergence in conditions between women and men. For example, literacy in Latin America was at 75 percent across the region, with more girls than boys in school at the secondary and tertiary levels. In sub-Saharan Africa, only minimal progress has been made, with literacy rates among the lowest in the world, only 43 percent for women and 67 percent for adult men. In northern Africa and western Asia, increased enrollment of girls has raised female literacy to 44 percent. In southern Asia, two-thirds of women are illiterate, with primary and secondary enrollment of girls below that of all other regions except sub-Saharan Africa. In East Asia, literacy is not yet as universal for women as for men.[14]

Translating the basic advantages that women have earned into advancement has been slow. Women's participation in management and administration (including middle levels) rose in all regions but one. In Western Europe, the rise was from 16 to 33 percent, whereas in Latin America it rose from 18 to 25 percent. Women's participation at the top levels of government remained exceptional. At the time of Beijing +5 (June 2000), only Norway had as many as one-third women ministers or subministers.

With respect to health, women continued to live longer than men. Life expectancy for women made the greatest gains in northern Africa, eastern, southern, and western Asia, and Central America (by ten to eleven years). The mortality rates for men and women also reflected different biological and socioeconomic factors. In the developing world, women's major health risks were related to pregnancy. In the developed world, after age sixty-five, heart disease has overtaken cancer as the first cause of women's death. In developing countries, maternal mortality has remained a leading cause of death for women of reproductive ages (nineteen to forty-four). The World Health Organization (WHO) estimates that 500,000 women die each year in childbirth.[15] Sub-Saharan Africa has the highest maternal mortality rates in the world, followed by southern Asia. Maternal mortality has been especially high where maternity care has been low.[16] According to the UN report, where childbirth is a woman's event, pregnancy commanded neither extra expenses nor emergency transport for a woman in crisis during labor.

Health had not been a major topic at the United Nations but had been dealt with primarily by the WHO. But prior to the 1990s, two major initiatives by the WHO (in conjunction with others) had begun to link health issues with development. The Alma Alta Conference (1978) and its Declaration on the Right to [Good] Health for All and the Safe Motherhood Initiative (1987) emphasized improvement in the health and wellbeing of mothers, part of the maternal and child-health (MCH) operational programming formula in the United Nations Children's Fund and the WHO.[17]

Health had become salient because health-related conditions and initiatives impinged on population policy. Driven only by demographic imperatives, a program began in the 1960s to distribute contraceptives in order to lower the birthrates among women of third world countries. Since the Bucharest UN World Population Conference (1974), directives and linkages to development had placed population and family-planning services within MCH, within primary health care programs, or within community development programs. Hence, when later changes in population/family-planning programming led to a focus on the quality of services and the need for better access by those being served, such issues as high maternal mortality rates and contraceptive acceptability had become factors critical to the delivery and distribution of contraceptives. And in the 1980s, critics of a demographically driven population policy asserted a development framework to take account of women's reproductive health. This led Dr. Nafis Sadik, the second executive director of UNFPA, to become aware of her women's constituency, particularly after the 1985 Nairobi Conference.

By the time of the preparations for the International Conference on Population and Development (ICPD) held in Cairo, Egypt, in 1994, women's groups worldwide and at the United Nations had been organizing to lobby and make an impact on the conference agenda, particularly the final document. As an example, the Women's Environment and Development Organization, organized by Bella Abzug in New York and with members worldwide, as well as the International Women's Coalition, which served as the Secretariat, convened the January 1994 Conference on Reproductive Health and Justice, International Women's Health Conference for Cairo in 1994.[18] Since the UN Conference on the Environment and Development in Rio de Janeiro (1992) had been opened up on an ad hoc basis to nonconsultative-status NGOs, national and local groups, research institutes, and smaller groups of activists had access to the preparations for the conferences themselves.

*Cairo and the Politics of
Reproductive Health and Reproductive Rights*

The Cairo *Programme of Action of the International Conference on Population and Development* (1994) reflected efforts at compromise on two significant conflicts: (1) a continued focus on demographic outcomes, or an increased focus on improving women's reproductive health; and (2) an extension of reproductive rights, including how abortion would be characterized.[19] At the third preparatory meeting for the conference, the Vatican delegation had asked that any such language be in brackets so that it could later be negotiated at the full conference. The United States and others staved off demands by some Latin American and Middle Eastern delegations actively supported by the Vatican's delegation for extensive restrictions. The document (paragraph 7.2) therefore acknowledges the right of men and women to all methods of fertility regulation not against the law. Using language drawn from the International Conference on Population (held in Mexico City, August 6–14, 1984), a compromise was reached. Abortion was not to be promoted as a method of family planning, but it was acknowledged that population growth was indeed a serious public health problem to be reduced through expanded and improved family planning services (paragraph 8.25).

The Programme of Action was the most important outcome of the conference. Its preamble, as well as chapters on population growth and structure (Chapter 6); on health, mortality, and morbidity (Chapter 8); on population distribution (Chapter 9); and on international migration (Chapter 10) reflected the demographic focus of the Programme of Action. In contrast, the earlier Mexico City Population Conference had produced the *Recommendations for the Further Implementation of the World Population Plan of Action*—strictly a demographic-oriented document. The largest section, on population goals and policies, was itself the result of more than twenty years of policy efforts to affect birthrates directly. Reproduction and the family (the locus of statements on family planning), as well as migration (international and internal) and population structure were discussed in 1984. The role and status of women gained a separate heading in the 1984 document (especially influential for 1994), having been shifted out of the section on reproduction and the family by an ad hoc coalition of knowledgeable NGOs, government delegates, and UN Secretariat staff.[20]

The 1994 ICPD's Programme of Action was longer, more focused on health and health-related issues than the 1984 Recommendations, and contained chapters on gender equality, equity, and the empowerment of women, reproductive rights and reproductive health, and health, morbidity, and mortality. What pervaded the Cairo conference document was an enlarged acknowledgment of individual options and choices. A wider assertion of human rights was emphasized: for example, user-centered services, helping couples, improving the quality of care, and the principle of informed free choice as an essential to long-term success of family planning. The Cairo document expanded its domain to all potential clients and, by implication, to everyone.

The new focus on better services and the improvement of people's lives, as well as on responsiveness to the needs of individuals, many of whom are women, should be called a new development strategy. The new concept of reproductive health (and rights) had to be integrated with demographic goals as well as women's health concerns. The prominence given to women in the Cairo document linked it to Beijing, which relied on the Cairo document for wordings on abortion as well as other issues. Linkages would be made in the later efforts by the UNFPA and the Division for the Advancement of Women to integrate reproductive health rights and the empowerment of women into existing population programs. Cooperation among UN units was to be a leitmotif in the last half of the 1990s.

## ICPD, the Fourth World Conference on Women, and Empowerment

The Cairo document remained in part a demographic document, even without targets recommended to governments wishing to reduce fertility. It emphasized population growth, the movements of people, new attitudes toward family planning, reproductive health and rights, and demographically focused features of the increased empowerment of women such as combining mothering with workforce participation. These are the 1990s versions of population issues related to the empowerment of women.

The demographic context of Cairo's Programme of Action seemed especially pervasive in contrast to the Platform for Action of the Fourth World Conference on Women (FWCW) in Beijing.[21] Both conference documents addressed the issue of poverty. The Cairo document considered population, economic growth, and sustainable development; women and poverty; and strategic objectives. The ICPD document placed poverty in a broad framework of challenge to development, where poverty was accompanied by unemployment, malnutrition, illiteracy, low status of women, and other features.

Slower population growth, according to the ICPD Programme of Action, could buy time for adjustment to continuing population growth (paragraph 3.14), a way of attacking poverty that did not focus exclusively on women. However, Cairo clearly said that human resources needed to be developed in regard to women. The conditions of women were important beyond their demographic impact; every problem has more than a demographic basis.

The women's document acknowledged that demographic changes do help explain the conditions women faced. For example, paragraph 30 (Global Framework) in the FWCW Platform for Action noted an additional 86 million people each year. The demographic trends of more young people and increased numbers of older people were changing the dependency ratio in families, to the detriment of women, because they remained the care-givers in conditions of poverty and unremunerated work. In another exam-ple, the FWCW Platform for Action asserted that the majority of the 1 bil-lion poor living in poverty were women (paragraph 47) but then cataloged a number of broad social, economic, political, and cultural factors in which specific gender discrimination contributed to this condition.

What would push for changes in social practices? Would it be larger numbers of people, or would they contribute to *demographic* inertia, that is, people overwhelmed by poverty and unable to change their lives for the better? In fact, it was not stated, either in Cairo's Programme or in Beijing's Platform, how a specific demographic contribution to the impoverishment of some women might occur. And along with the removal of demographic factors, what other critical factors needed to be remedied to empower women?

Population growth, in the global sense, catches the imagination, as it presents serious economic, social, cultural, and gender issues in the impov-erishment of women. At the micro level, the complexity of factors has made population growth a sufficient but not the single necessary factor in the im-provement of women's lives. Sorting out priorities bedevils population programming.

Both documents were political documents, drafted to the needs of a wide spectrum of influential political actors. The documents did not include careful directives from which defined actions necessarily would follow. In some sense, the documents served as justifications of existing sectoral and organizational structures. Nevertheless, cooperation and even collaboration would be important to expanded programming within the UN Secretariat. UNFPA much earlier had expanded its domain into women's issues, but not necessarily in ways known or of interest to the global women's movement. Population policy, reproductive health, and reproductive rights would now be issues new to the Division for the Advancement of Women.

## Engagement and Implementation: Beyond Cairo and Beijing

Cairo and Beijing focused on the empowerment of women. At least some women would no longer be passive subjects of policy; they had become ac-tive participants in their own future. Women had even become decision-makers in projects. These conferences themselves redefined empowerment to be a feature of political action by all women, which came about through and could contribute to transnational coalition-building. We see here that empowerment is a process and an outcome.

Conferences are happenings. They can be pressure points for innovation or legitimization of reorganization that is already under way. Both the Cairo and Beijing women's reproductive health and rights paragraphs could supply the basis for decisions by their respective UN intergovernmental bodies to put in place the next steps in implementation. On the recommendation of the UNFPA, its governing council approved UNFPA's approach to reproductive health, including family planning. The Commission on Population and Development called for reports on reproductive health, and the Commission on the Status of Women also adopted resolutions designating 1999 as the year for special focus on health. And CEDAW set out to adopt another general recommendation on health, including reproductive health and rights, to be available to the UN Human Rights Committees. Various NGOs continued their roles as lobbyists, advocates, researchers, and critical observers.

UNFPA (a funding unit turned substantive advocate) and the Division for the Advancement of Women (a Secretariat think-tank and UN bureaucratic counterpart of the intergovernmental CSW) began cooperation thematically on women and programmatic exploration and increased coordination. Some elements of coordination already existed. In place under the Administrative Committee on Coordination was an ad hoc subgroup on women established in the mid-1970s during the UN Decade for Women. UNFPA had a small suboffice on women, and in 1997 its annual publication *State of World Population* highlighted the fact that fertility decline may contribute to the improvement of women's status. Increased cooperation on programs for women emerged as a legitimized systemwide function in the first meeting of the Interagency Committee on Women and Gender Equality (October 1996) at UN Headquarters in New York City. Under the rubric of gender equality, issues of women's rights, including women's participation in decisionmaking and systemwide inclusion in programming, were to be given more salience. Very specifically, the meeting's agenda focused on mainstreaming of a gender perspective in the UN system. UNFPA was to support UNIFEM in its link with the Task Force on Basic Social Services for All. And UNFPA, as the Chair of the Women in Development Subgroup of the Joint Consultative Group on Policy, and the coordinator of the next meeting's three papers—on indicators; parameters for evaluating best practices; and policy enforcement and accountability—was to link efforts with the Division for the Advancement of Women.[22]

UNFPA's approach had begun with its programming as it existed before ICPD. It sought to incorporate this new approach of reproductive health and rights, including sexual health, into its programming. Expert meetings can serve to rationalize what a bureaucracy plans to do while also seeking broader public collaboration. Earlier recommendations to its executive board in 1995 and 1996 had laid the foundations of UNFPA's approach.[23] The approach was first based on its existing programs and projects, which were to be changed incrementally as additional funds became available or as earlier projects finished.

Acknowledging other UN units' role in the implementation of the ICPD's Programme of Action, UNFPA proposed a mission statement to serve as a framework for its activities over the coming twenty years.[24] The ICPD's new paradigm of population and development, according to UNFPA,[25] meshed the macro-level development/demographic goals with a recognition that their accomplishment depended on the attainment of individual goals and the inclusion of all groups in the efforts toward sustainable development. The three core areas selected by UNFPA within its new program framework were the following: reproductive health and family planning; population policy; and advocacy. Along with a commitment to universally accepted human rights, especially reproductive rights, and the monitoring of the implementation of the Programme of Action at all levels, UNFPA underlined its operational goals: to help countries attain the three quantitative goals specified in the ICPD Programme of Action—providing universal access to a full range of safe and reliable family planning methods and to related reproductive health services; reducing infant, child, and maternal mortality; and providing universal access to primary education.[26] In reproductive health, UNFPA had already established service delivery points for family planning at all levels and, in some instances, also providing treatment for reproductive tract infections. Post-ICPD planning included the expansion at the primary level of other components of reproductive health,[27] including Safe Motherhood as part of its core.[28]

New criteria for the allocation of UNFPA resources based on a quantification in the three numerical goals set for 2015 focused especially on Africa and the least developed countries. Assistance to countries beyond the new thresholds of the selected seven numerical indicators in favor of South-South cooperation was gradually limited.[29] Numerical indicators for access to reproductive health services were to be based on deliveries by trained health personnel, contraceptive prevalence rate, and access to basic health services. The targeted areas for other indicators included mortality reduction and universal primary education for young girls and adult females, with appropriate thresholds. On the basis of these indicators, UNFPA established new categories for countries' eligibility for UNFPA assistance.[30]

UNFPA had begun to address itself to women's reproductive health assistance, including but not limited to family planning services it provided (or might provide) directly to countries, or in collaboration with other UN agencies, or in some instances with NGOs. Along with other UN units,

UNFPA was responding to directives for gender mainstreaming at the United Nations.

A recent study presented at one of the many meetings held in conjunction with the special session of the General Assembly (Women 2000: Gender Equality, Development, and Peace for the 21st Century; the so-called Beijing +5 conference of June 2000) has suggested a diffuse quality to gender mainstreaming and to the inclusion of reproductive health and rights into UNFPA programming: guidelines existed but have not been fully incorporated into programming and budgeting. Specifically focused on the UN system and budgeting for gender equality, the reports noted two positive factors: strategic planning is being led by UN system budget offices, and the concept of mainstreaming gender had become more fully understood, moving beyond staffing to analysis of gender impacts. This combination suggested positive learning processes.[31]

After Cairo and Beijing, CEDAW proceeded to draft a new recommendation on women's health. Almost all the preceding twenty-three General Recommendations (the last one in 1997) had been short, one to two pages, designed to direct state parties on reporting, legislation, or further elaboration on particular issues, for example, violence against women. By contrast, two recommendations, General Recommendation No. 19, *Violence Against Women* (eleventh session, 1992) and General Recommendation No. 21, *Equality in Marriage and Family Relations* (thirteenth session, 1994, the GA-designated Year of the Family) contained extensive recommendations. Indeed, the *General Recommendation on Equality and Family Relations* urged close attention to issues of women's nationality (not to be lost by marriage or change in nationality by father or husband); equality before the law (the right to bring litigation, to enter into contract, and to choose her domicile); and, at length, elimination of discrimination in marriage and family relations (polygamous marriages, equal shares in inheritance between women and men, and other items).

## CEDAW and General Recommendation on Rights Related to Health and Well-Being

A pending draft General Recommendation—post-Cairo and post-Beijing—on rights relating to women's health and well-being has a lengthy format.[32] The initial draft asserted the right to a standard of living adequate for health (the Universal Declaration of Human Rights, which refers only to "him"). It also refers to WHO's constitution, which states that health is a state of complete, physical, mental, and social well-being, and not merely the absence of disease or infirmity. Although Vienna, Cairo, and Beijing focused on women's health, including sexual and reproductive health, the

General Recommendation explores possibilities of discrimination and of the impairment of the enjoyment of various rights and freedoms because of the failure of state parties to fulfill their treaty obligations. The following are highlighted: right to life; security of person; equality before the law; highest standard attainable of physical and mental health; safe conditions of work; privacy and confidentiality; medical information; informed consent in medical decisionmaking; reproductive and sexual health; and the right to benefits in scientific progress. Commentaries focussed on issues related to women's health under treaty articles such as prenatal sex selection, female infanticide, and son preference. These were called discrimination against the girl child and thus violations of: women' s rights to health; respect for integrity of women's bodies; and protection from discrimination in social, domestic, or employment spheres by reason of pregnancy and mother-hood.[33] Moreover, the focus on research on human reproductive capacity had unintended consequences. It ignored potential dangers to men, did not lead to the improvement of workplace conditions, and led to exclusion of women from places of work or higher-paying jobs.

The Recommendations for Government Action cited minimum core obligations: national policy to protect women's rights to health, health care, and well-being; creation of a system to monitor the status of those rights; and especially the identification of groups of women at risk with respect to discrimination in these rights. Also addressed to governments were collections of data on health status of women disaggregated by age, ethnicity, and race, urban, and rural locations:

1. Identification of serious health problems faced by women.
2. The adoption of affirmative actions where necessary.
3. Free reproductive and sexual health services to young girls.
4. A review of punitive laws against women who have had illegal abortions, in order to repeal them.
5. Working with communities to assure minimum age of marriage.
6. Monitoring and working with nongovernmental organizations and private groups in their health policies and programs.

Reporting guidelines were also expanded. Along with related treaties, CEDAW recommendations have on occasion been used to explore or buttress national legal standards upholding the equality of women.[34]

Possibly unique to this particular process were the published comments on this draft by a number of interested NGOs.[35] Extensive comments were made on each part of the draft, drawing out the consequences of discrimination against women. Various NGO groups wanted a life-cycle approach to women's health and care; greater emphasis on how women's health and related issues were different from those of men and needed recognition and care accordingly; and expansion of specific issues such as HIV/AIDS, violence against women, and poverty.

## CONCLUSION

The United Nations has framed the worldwide effort to empower women. Women and their allies worked for normative statements and developments on behalf of women. Increased UN cooperation on population and women's issues gained legitimacy from the UN conferences of the 1990s. Changes in programming have followed, but because UN units remain essentially separate—calls for reform, greater coordination, and collaboration notwithstanding—expansion has been slow. In view of the UN Secretariat policy approach of mainstreaming gender perspectives—difficult under the best of circumstances—the limited possibilities of increasing cooperation restrict the effectiveness of the United Nations. But, and this is very important, expanded institutionalization and policy expansion on behalf of women have been happening in national arenas. Civil society and NGO overlap/presence in these several arenas is a factor in that institutionalization.

The world looks different at the beginning of the twenty-first century. Countries face new and difficult problems: AIDS is increasing in Asian countries, and its devastation is already evident in Africa. These societies are beginning to recognize the critical role of full partnership with women; women realize their need to protect themselves and their children. The government of China has now begun a limited experimentation in a new approach to population policy—removal of permits for births in a given year, new choices for women when to give birth—in order to reduce the hostility among Chinese women to the implementation of Chinese population policy.[36] Termed a "client-centered approach," implementation is being financially assisted by the Ford and Rockefeller Foundations and the UN Population Fund. Women's educational achievements—one gender factor that research has established can clearly be correlated with lower fertility rates—grow in different ways from region to region. The ICPD's Programme of Action mentioned the role of men in fertility reduction. What changes improve relationships between men and women, thereby increasing possibilities of fertility control, remain unexplored.

The relationship between the global women's movement and population policy advocates will probably remain distant, if not unfriendly. The ICPD's Programme of Action is no longer a demographically defined policy. It is now a policy giving prominence to reproductive health and the empowerment of women while downplaying the demographic rationale for population policy.[37] Severe resource constraints remain. Now is the time for more collaborative efforts in population policy making and implementation and less focus on coercive rules.[38]

The UN remains the only global mechanism to record, monitor, and make public what women are doing worldwide. Its imperfections notwithstanding, it sets standards for empowerment of women and establishes the sites of later policy discussion about women. The treaty to eliminate all discrimination against women has 130 signatories, each of whose government makes reports to CEDAW about its compliance with the standards set forth in the treaty. The UN system has advantages not to be cavalierly dismissed or diminished. But the United Nations will need more expertise and more informal contacts at local levels if its programs are to respond to the real differences among women. At the political level, governments need to understand the serious issues in social and cultural policies. Civil society relationships may facilitate greater understanding. Regional exchanges may be useful, although politically difficult. More problem-solving on the status of women, including their reproductive health, poverty, and education, must be the focus of future UN discussions and formal meetings.

## DISCUSSION QUESTIONS

1. How does public policy empower women?
2. Is empowerment something to be given, something to be taken, or something to be created?
3. Is population policy collaborative or coercive?
4. Is empowerment a process or an outcome?
5. How do you think the United Nations has empowered women?

## NOTES

1. During the past twenty years, the United Nations has held four global conferences on women: Mexico City (1975), Copenhagen (1980), Nairobi (1985), and Beijing (1995). These conferences helped to define the obstacles to gender equality and action needed to overcome them. The Mexico City conference, which coincided with the observance of International Women's Year, "was the start of an international effort to right the wrongs of history," says the 1985 State of the World's Women. This led to the proclamation of 1976–1985 as the UN Decade for Women: Equality, Development, and Peace. The Copenhagen conference adopted an action plan for the second half of the decade. The Nairobi women's conference adopted a fifteen-year program for the advancement of women. About 120 governments have reported progress in meeting the targets set at that conference. In Beijing, at the Fourth World Conference on Women in 1995, representatives of 189 governments adopted a new five-year global action plan, aimed at equality, development, and

peace. More than 100 governments have made formal commitments to carry out such specific actions as allocating additional funds for education and health, changing laws, and increasing women's participation in decisionmaking.

2. Although an extremely troublesome issue, the status of women in the Secretariat will not be included because of space. A long history of efforts to improve the conditions of women in the Secretariat challenges the patriarchal UN political culture and the continued operation of the old boys' network. On the issue of discrimination against women in the Secretariat, the Group on Equal Rights for Women in the United Nations, an open-ended staff group dedicated to the elimination of that discrimination, celebrated its twenty-fifth anniversary in 1997. See the group's publication, *Equal Time* (March 8, 1997). On sexual harassment, see the op-ed in the *New York Times* (September 15, 1994); and *Catherine Claxton vs. the U.N.*, by Ciceil L. Gross, Esq., former president of the Women's Equal Rights Group, retired senior legal adviser and secretary of the UN Joint Appeals Board and Joint Disciplinary Committee.

3. For a comprehensive history focused on the UN Decade for Women, see Anne Winslow, ed., *Women, Politics, and the United Nations* (Westport, Conn.: Greenwood, 1995); also, Hilkka Pietila and Jeanne Vickers, *Making Women Matter: The Role of the United Nations* (Atlantic Highlands, N.J.: Zed Books, 1990).

4. Western European and others with whom the United States caucused, eastern socialist states, and third world governments, negotiating as the Group of 77, although they were about 120 in number.

5. "Review and Appraisal of Progress Achieved and Obstacles Encountered at the National Level," in *The Realization of the Goals and Objectives of the United Nations Decade for Women: Equality, Development, and Peace.* United Nations General Assembly, Report of the Secretary-General, A/CONF. 116/5 (Overview); Add. 1, Part I; Add. 2–14, Part II (New York: United Nations, 1984). The page citations in the text of this chapter are to the Overview unless otherwise noted.

6. United Nations, Report of the Secretary-General, pp. 5–7, 18–19.

7. Ibid., Add. 1, para. 38.

8. *Report of the International Conference on Population and Development,* United Nations International Conference on Population and Development, Cairo, Egypt, September 5–13, 1994, A/CONF. 171/13 (New York: United Nations, 10/18/94): para. 7.3.

9. For women, gender, and international politics, see special issue (Women and International Relations), *Millennium: Journal of International Studies* (1989); J. Ann Tickner, "You Just Don't Understand: Troubled Engagements Between Feminists and IR Theorists," *International Studies Quarterly* 41, no. 4 (December 1997); articles by Robert O. Keohane and Marianne Marchand, in *Dialogue* 42, no. 1 (March 1998), and by J. Ann Tickner in *International Studies Quarterly* 42, no. 1 (March 1998); for regional, national, and local politics, see Barbara J. Nelson and Najma Chowdhury, eds., *Women and Politics Worldwide* (New Haven: Yale University Press, 1994); and Cathy Cohen et al., eds., *Women Transforming Politics: An Alternative Reader* (New York: New York University Press, 1997).

10. For conflicts in meanings of empowerment and liberal rights versus lacking basis in collective struggles outside institutions, see Rina Benmayor and Rosa M. Torruellas, "Education, Cultural Rights, and Citizenship," in Cohen, *Women Transforming Politics,* pp. 187–204.

11. The UN system also includes the specialized agencies (the World Health Organization, the Food and Agriculture Organization, the UN Economic, Scientific, and Cultural Organization, etc.) and/or other units such as regional economic and

demographic commissions. Furthermore, there are yet other significant and voluntary funding/operational units such as the UN Development Programme (UNDP) or the UN Population Fund (UNFPA). The International Court of Justice, the sixth major organ (justices elected by the General Assembly and the Security Council), sits in The Hague.

12. See *International Documents Review* (IDR) (ed. Baskar Menon) 8, no. 27 (July 21, 1997), for a detailed overview and analysis. Earlier issues (May–July 1997) document the political process.

13. United Nations, *The World's Women: Trends and Statistics* (Social Statistics and Indicators, Series K, No. 12, ST/ESA/STAT/SER.K/12) (New York: United Nations, 1995). Pages below are from this document.

14. Ibid., pp. xviii–xix.

15. Ibid., p. 77.

16. Ibid., p. 75.

17. Family Care International serves as the secretariat for the Interagency Group for Safe Motherhood, including UNDP, UNICEF, UNFPA, World Bank, WHO, IPPF, and the Population Council.

18. A summary report of the conference attended by invitaton by 215 women from seventy-nine countries was widely circulated. The women drafted "Appendix II: Goals, Strategies, and Activities." Among others, women's right to safe, legal, accessible, and affordable abortion was to be nonnegotiable; population policies that only intended to control women's fertility and failed to address the broader conditions of poverty and livelihood were unacceptable.

19. I rely on C. Alison McIntosh and Jason L. Finkle, "The Cairo Conference on Population and Development," *Population and Development Review* 21, no. 2 (June 1995): 223–260, for a general overview of the Vatican's position as well as that of the U.S. government. See also Conor Cruise O'Brien, *On the Eve of the Millennium: The Future of Democracy Through an Age of Unreason* (New York: Free Press, 1994), esp. chapter 1, for a criticism of the Vatican's attempted alliance with Iran and Syria against safe abortion and contraception. O'Brien argues that the Vatican is trying to turn back the Enlightenment and that Americans will have none of it.

20. This is based on my personal observations and filled in with later informal discussions with Secretariat officials.

21. United Nations General Assembly, Fourth World Conference on Women, Beijing, China, September 4–15, 1995, *Report of the Fourth World Conference on Women*, A/CONF. 177/20 (New York: United Nations, 1995).

22. United Nations, Administrative Committee on Coordination (ACC), ACC/1996/22, *Report of the Inter-Agency Committee on Women and Gender Equality on Its First Session*, p. 4.

23. United Nations, Executive Board of UNDP and UNFPA, UN Population Fund, *Programme Priorities and Future Directions of UNFPA in Light of the International Conference on Population (ICPD)*, Report of the Executive Director, DP/-1995/28, April 18, 1995; and *A Revised Approach for the Allocation of UNFPA Resources to Country Programmes,* Report of the Executive Director, DP/FPA/1996/15, February 7, 1996.

24. Ibid., DP/1995/25, p. 3.

25. Ibid., p. 2.

26. Ibid., p. 3.

27. Ibid., p. 7.

28. Ibid., p. 11.

29. Ibid., DP/FPA/1996/15, pp. 7–12.

30. Ibid., pp. 13–16.

31. United Nations, UN Inter-Agency Committee on Women and Gender Equality, *Mainstreaming Gender Equality into Budget Processes Within the UN System* is two separate reports: Tony Beck for Carolyn Hannan, Phase I, *Inventory of Mainstreaming Gender in Budget Processes in Bilateral Donors, NGOs, Private Sector, and Others* (May 2000); and Tony Beck et al. for Carolyn Hannan, Phase II, *Overview of the UN System* (June 2000): Executive Summary, pp. vi–xiv. UNFPA is one of the specific subjects in Report Three, not yet available.

32. The Center for Reproductive Law and Policy in New York City circulated a fifty-four-page draft of the general recommendation containing paragraph-by-paragraph NGO comments: "Compilation of NGO Comments on CEDAW Draft General Recommendation on Rights Relating to Women's Health and Well-Being" (October 1997).

33. Ibid., pp. 13, 21, and 23.

34. *Advancing the Human Rights of Women: Using International Human Rights Standards in Domestic Litigation,* Papers and statements from the Asia/South Pacific Regional Judicial Colloquium, Hong Kong, May 20–22, 1996, ed. Andrew Byrnes, Jane Connors, and Lum Bik (London: Center for Comparative and Public Law, University of Hong Kong, for the Commonwealth Secretariat, October 1997).

35. Center staff has also authored *shadow reports* to parallel government reports presented to CEDAW.

36. Elizabeth Rosenthal, "For One-Child Policy, China Rethinks Iron Hand," *New York Times* (November 1, 1998), pp. 1, 20.

37. C. Alison McIntosh and Jason L. Finkle, "The Cairo Conference on Population and Development: A New Paradigm?" *Population and Development Review* 21, no. 2 (June 1995): 223–260. A critique of women's search for empowerment can be found in Dennis Hodgson and Susan Cotts Watkins, "Feminists and Neo-Malthusians: Past and Present Alliances," *Population and Development Review* 23, no. 3 (September 1997): 469–523.

38. Amartya Sen, "Population: Delusion and Reality," *New York Review of Books* (September 22, 1994), pp. 62–71.

# 3

## The Empowerment of Women Through International Law

### Kathleen Suneja

International law as a body of contemporary law has defined a new framework for women's rights. Gender-specific laws, as outlined by an international convention on discrimination against women, work in conjunction with domestic legal systems to create new bases to overcome discrimination. The Convention on the Elimination of All Forms of Discrimination Against Women (CEDAW), passed by the United Nations (UN) General Assembly in 1979, addresses in comprehensive form the root causes of *all* forms of gender discrimination: "Sex is a prohibited ground of discrimination under the international human rights covenants and the regional human rights conventions."[1] Leading scholars have argued that the prohibition of sexual discrimination is now a part of customary international law that binds states even without their express ratification and acceptance.[2] CEDAW develops the legal norm on nondiscrimination from a women's perspective. CEDAW moves from a sex-neutral norm that requires equal treatment of men and women, usually measured by how men are treated, to a recognition of the particular nature of discrimination against women as worthy of a legal response. CEDAW identifies the need to confront the social causes of inequality and discrimination against women.

Women have to strive for equality or parity with men and must also seek redress for past discrimination. States are required to show special sensitivity in situations where women are likely to face greater threats to their rights. CEDAW places an affirmative duty upon states to take positive measures to support innovative activities that directly benefit women. Among these measures are steps to end discrimination through gender-sensitive awareness-raising, capacity-building, literacy, training, and action-related research on women. In addition, states are required not to discriminate

31

by refraining from adopting policies that would infringe upon women's rights.

CEDAW has placed a duty upon signatory states to protect against gender-related violence. The result has been pathbreaking progress for women's rights under international law. International law has impacted women's rights in practical terms through the recognition by courts that women may be defined as a "group." As a group, they qualify for protection as refugees and asylum-seekers under international immigration laws. Additionally, international criminal tribunals have acknowledged crimes perpetrated against women are a means of controlling women's political participation.

The definition of "violence" includes physical violence, mental and health needs, and economic deprivation of women. The physical needs of women include the right to be free from threats of physical harm, including state-sponsored violence and private acts of violence against women. The mental health vulnerabilities are a part of women's right to have access to adequate resources to meet the physical needs *and* the emotional necessity to feel safe in her person to make informed decisions about her reproductive rights. The woman has to overcome traditional legal theories under which a woman was the property of a man, just as land. Included in this is the right to privacy and autonomy in regard to reproductive decisions, as they form the basis of the right to remain free from poverty.

## WOMEN'S RIGHT TO BE FREE FROM VIOLENCE: RECENT DEVELOPMENTS IN INTERNATIONAL LAW

International law has recognized the specific rights of women with the passage of CEDAW, as well as the Declaration of Violence Against Women. Both documents have increased sensitivity and awareness toward the special needs of women. The greatest benefit to women has come from instilling a greater awareness toward prosecuting crimes against women and the interpretation of international humanitarian law to include sexual violence against women as a crime. The International War Crimes Tribunal, which has heard matters stemming from the violence in the former Yugoslavia and Rwanda, has included crimes against women as war crimes and has successfully prosecuted perpetrators of these crimes who are now serving time in prison.

There are four possible charges under which sexual violence may be prosecuted: as a grave breach of the 1949 Geneva Conventions; as a customary war crime; as genocide; and as a crime against humanity.[3] Even a single act of rape or sexual assault is a customary war crime and may be prosecuted. Genocide and crimes against humanity require an intent to destroy or to persecute a racial, ethnic, national, or religious group. In this context, the violence against women in the form of rape in the former Yugoslavia has accorded new meaning to the act as a crime against humanity. Crimes against humanity are considered gross violations against a group; a member of a group has been singled out for the crime solely because the person belongs to that group. The UN Commission of Experts on the Former Yugoslavia found that sexual violence was "widespread" in the conflict and was "part of a policy of terror and violence designed to achieve ethnic cleansing."[4]

Most of the sexual violence was systematic and widespread, carried out in connection with efforts to displace the civilian population of a targeted ethnic group in a particular area. Sometimes field military and camp commanders explicitly ordered their subordinates to commit acts of sexual violence. In these cases, the individual commander's criminal responsibility is unequivocal. In other cases, field and camp commanders failed to prevent sexual violence and did not punish perpetrators when their crimes were exposed. This is a violation of a commander's duties and makes the commander criminally responsible under international law.[5]

Often the rape targeted community leaders and professional women, in an attempt to "break" their will. Victims of rape were frequently kidnapped, tortured, and executed on a mass scale. The victims were often held in custody after the rape and were told the women would have children of the perpetrator's ethnicity, a living reminder to what had happened to them.[6] The group rights of women under CEDAW has given them the opportunity to raise the crime of rape to an international crime of genocide. Force used in reproductive behavior made rape victims, if the member of an ethnic group, victims of "ethnic cleansing." Such crimes were perpetrated by groups of Serbs upon Muslim women held in detention facilities. These are crimes against humanity under current international law. Any deliberate attempts to enforce and encourage sexual assaults and violence by camp commanders were deemed to be part of the "simultaneous military activity . . . to maximize shame and humiliation of not only the victim, but also the victim's community."[7]

This documentation of violence against women is a reminder of the recent increase in the awareness and sensitivity toward women in international humanitarian law. In 1992, the International Committee of the Red Cross had declared that "willfully causing great suffering or serious injury to body or health" under Article 147 of the Fourth Geneva Convention covered rape. The U.S. State Department also concluded that rape could be prosecuted in the manner of a grave breach of customary international law or under the Geneva Conventions.[8] Public outrage and media coverage also indicate that women's rights and their violation thereof have begun to play an increasingly important role in the prosecution of international law. "Responsibility for gender-based violence resulting from political oppression in peacetime, where a state fails to protect women from violence, or condones or supports subjugation and persecution of women, is even less fully developed than responsibility for the use of violence against women during armed conflict."[9]

## WOMEN'S REFUGEE STATUS

The principle that women's rights are human rights dovetails with the development of international legal basis for granting women redress under the law, by prosecuting the offender, but also granting them the additional protection by their status as refugees. The recognition of refugee status for victims of sexual violence allows them to make a claim for "well-founded fear of persecution." Persecution through sexual violence or gender-related persecution is grounds for granting refugee status under the guidelines of the United Nations High Commissioner for Refugees.[10] According to the Declaration on the Elimination of Violence Against Women, "violence against women" is defined as:

> any act of gender-based violence that results in, or is likely to result in, physical, sexual or psychological harm or suffering to women, including threats of such acts, coercion, or arbitrary deprivation of liberty, whether occurring in public or private life.[11]

Gender-related claims for refugee asylum fall into four categories:

- where the method of persecution is gender-related;
- where the issue is one of punishment for having transgressed social mores and more generally laws that restrict the exercise of fundamental rights;
- measures used in carrying out a law or policy even if it has legitimate goals; and
- where the law, policy, or practice may in itself be persecutory.[12]

Whether a harm or a breach of a woman's human rights is serious enough to be regarded as persecution is to be determined by whether it is a grave breach or a serious violation of a fundamental human right. Violence includes forms of threats, assaults, interference, and exploitation, including rape, statuary rape, and molestation without physical harm or penetration.[13]

States have granted asylum in situations where the country of origin of the asylee has failed to protect the asylee due to any variety of reasons, including civil war, political violence, cultural reasons, and government inability to enforce the law. Where government authorities are involved in the persecution, the person is likely to have a greater claim to protection. In the U.S. case of *Matter of M-K,* a woman from Sierra Leone requested asylum in the United States on grounds of persecution based, in part, on an ongoing cycle of physical and verbal spousal abuse.[14] She sought legal protection on three occasions after being severely beaten but was told the police would not interfere, as it was a domestic matter. The abuse continued until she left her husband and fled her home country. Her husband threatened to kill her if she returned to Sierra Leone. Independent evidence produced on the situation of women in that country demonstrated that violence against women, especially wife-beating, is common. Disobedience or disrespect on the part of the wife is considered justification for punitive measures by a husband. The police were found to be unlikely to intervene in domestic disputes except in cases of severe injury or death; few cases of such violence went to court. Thus, the court made a finding of lack of national protection and made a finding of persecution. In defining "persecution," the judge referred to internationally recognized human rights and instruments, such as the Declaration on the Elimination of Violence Against Women, which specifically condemns battering as a serious violation of human rights.

The practice of female genital mutilation (FGM) is considered persecution by several international documents. In *Re: Khadra Hassan Farah,* the Immigration Board of Canada referred to the UN Convention on the Rights of the Child as a reason to extend protection to a claimant.[15] Immigration boards have noted the widespread nature of this "torturous custom" and note that "very little action has been taken by governments in the countries concerned to stop FGM." Courts have also granted asylum in situations where the applicant's home country has a serious problem of gender-related violence and where the courts consider the country's law enforcement and judicial system to be male-dominated. Repeated acts of violence that bring the acts within the meaning of "torture" and the availability of the critical issue of state protection or lack thereof is essential to the refugee claim. The claimant repeatedly sought the protection of the Bulgarian police. Courts will generally find a violation of more than CEDAW and will make reference to the Convention Against Cruel, Inhuman Treatment or Torture. The failure of the domestic justice system to provide protection for violence by private persons is deemed a violation of international humanitarian law.

The asylum law in the United States was also transformed to become gender-sensitive with the case of *In Re Kasinga.* This case was filed by a seventeen-year-old girl named Fauziya Kasinga, who sought asylum in the United States on grounds that she would be persecuted in her native country of Togo by members of her family and tribe by being forced to undergo FGM. In its decision, the U.S. Immigration and Naturalization Board of Appeals cautiously stated that FGM "under certain circumstances . . . may form the basis for asylum."[16] On June 13, 1996, the board agreed and granted Kasinga asylum. In its 11-1 decision, the board stated that Kasinga had established a well-founded fear of persecution and noted that "most African women can expect little governmental protection from FGM." Kasinga's plight drew the attention of powerful advocates like U.S. Rep. Patricia Schroeder and women's human rights groups like Equality Now, who publicized her case, mobilized support, and arranged for new legal representation. Kasinga had been in detention promptly after she sought asylum in the United States and remained there for sixteen months, enduring repeated strip searches as well as a tear-gassing during a June 1995 incident at the correctional facility where she was being held.[17] This infringement was the result of a prison incident, although endured by Kasinga while she was being held in custody with other common prisoners during her incarceration as an illegal alien. She was not treated as a human rights victim prior to her being granted asylum by U.S. immigration authorities.

The *Kasinga* case is an instance in which a government has granted a refugee asylum on grounds that the human rights of the victim were violated on the basis of gender-based violence. The court acknowledged that women were victims of persecution and violence solely because they belong to members of a gender group. Upon proof of the threat of imminent persecution as a cause of their belonging to that group, they qualified for protection under the U.S. Refugee Act, as the court recognized gender-based violence and the need for protection under international norms. The work of CEDAW and women's initiatives is a reason for granting women recognition as a group and for recognizing gender bias in crimes committed against women under international law.

## DO WOMEN HAVE GROUP RIGHTS?

Courts have argued in favor and against considering women as a group. Although recognizing that persecution may not be the sole defining characteristic of the group, courts have determined that may be a part of the definition of what constitutes a "group." Courts have not spoken in one voice but have considered women as a group in situations where they share a common, immutable characteristic.[18] The court in *Fatin v. INS* recognized that gender was a group and required the claimant to show that she would suffer, or that she has a well-founded fear of suffering, persecution solely based on her gender.[19] A scholar in the field of gender-related claims has stated as follows:

> Gender-based and gender-specific determinations of refugee status are a recent development. Claims of this nature are hampered by current interpretation of the "persecution" element of the [refugee convention] definition,

as well as by interpretation of the Convention grounds, which take account of the experience of men more than women. While it appears that there is greater scope in the "particular social group" category than race, religion, nationality or political opinion to accommodate gender-related claims, the drawback of this category is that its interpretation is to a large extent unpredictable.

Some decisionmakers have stressed that the shared experience of women who have suffered gender harms, such as violence against them, is insufficient to establish a social group, unless the fact of the earlier violation will make the group targets of future persecution. Women's claims to be part of a particular social group are also hampered by the fact that the suffering of applicants is frequently indistinguishable from the suffering experienced by the general population of women in the country of origin.[20]

## LIMITATIONS OF THE INTERNATIONAL LEGAL SYSTEM

The weakness in international law also limits the protection that this law provides to women. The process whereby the intentions of member states are transformed into practice is to ask the question as to why sovereign states must voluntarily comply with enforcing the law that they created for themselves and signed. Whether states are in compliance with international standards is addressed by the issue of whether states are willing and, more important, able to perform the duties and responsibilities under CEDAW. The challenges associated with meeting the requirements of the regime of women's rights are manyfold. The international legal system is constrained by the autonomy of states in accepting responsibility for the implementation of international law. Among other weaknesses is the law enforcement in the domestic state system.

The Vienna Convention on the Law of Treaties prohibits states from making a reservation that is incompatible with the object and purpose of a treaty.[21] States have limited their responsibility by way of reservations involving cultural and religious practices to refrain from abiding by essential parts of CEDAW. These states have used the system of reservations as a shield from aspects of CEDAW as adopted by the General Assembly.[22] Although more than 120 states have ratified CEDAW, approximately forty states have made some 105 reservations and declarations to CEDAW. The substantive reservations are wide-ranging and affect the integrity of CEDAW. Reservations range from reservations to reflect the exclusively male heritage in the exercise of royal power (Belgium, Luxembourg, Spain); to the exclusion of women from employment in the armed forces or access to combat duties (Germany, New Zealand, Thailand); to restriction of employment of women in night work or at jobs deemed hazardous to their health (Malta, the United Kingdom).

Finally, many Islamic countries reserved certain rights, insisting that equality be subordinate to the teachings of gender-subordinating religious law. Numerous countries wished to maintain restrictions on equality with respect to marriage, family, citizenship, and legal personality of women.[23] For example, one reservation reads as follows: "The Government of Bangladesh does not consider as binding upon itself the provisions of Article 2 (and other articles) as they conflict with Shari'a law based on Holy Quran and Sunna. Other states such as Egypt, Iraq and Libya have also made similar broad reservations."[24]

These reservations to treaty compliance are challenged by their critics in the UN CEDAW Committee as being possible violations of the Vienna Convention on Treaties. Reservations should not oppose the object and purpose of a treaty according to the Vienna Convention on Treaties. The CEDAW committee requested that the UN system as a whole "promote or undertake studies on the status of women under Islamic laws and customs." This request was met with hostility in the UN Economic and Social Council and the General Assembly. CEDAW was even asked to review its decision. Notwithstanding this decision, the Platform for Action of the Fourth World Conference on Women in Beijing established that any leeway given to religious particularities cannot deviate from international norms of women's human rights.[25] According to international scholars and the UN Commission on the Status of Women, cultural relativist arguments put forth by religious fundamentalists are resolved by the UN Charter, which makes clear that "the entitlement of human rights is not to be determined by any religious law and that race, sex and religious discrimination must be treated equally under the Charter."[26] The UN Human Rights Commission states that women's rights are to meet the general criteria of human rights and that women's rights under the Universal Declaration for Human Rights and the Political and Civil Conventions and the Social and Economic Rights Convention are unattainable without CEDAW.[27]


## DOMESTIC ENFORCEMENT OF INTERNATIONAL LAW

The CEDAW Committee has placed the burden on domestic legal institutions to enforce international women's human rights. Under CEDAW, an individual must first exhaust domestic remedies before coming forward in an international human rights court. National courts must remedy women's rights violations by their use of international women's human rights law. In the words of one member of the Human Rights Committee, the state is given "an opportunity to redress, by its own means within the framework of its domestic legal system, the wrongs alleged to have been suffered by the individual."[28] Each of the signatory states are to report on an annual basis to CEDAW's Committee on Women on the progress as laid out by CEDAW in their country. One shortcoming is that most states have not met their annual reporting requirements to the Committee.[29] Another weakness is that the time required to review the annual reports by the Committee on Women is a period of two weeks annually, which is too short for the purpose of reviewing all of the country reports on women.[30]

International law has indicated that states are to be held responsible for violations of discrimination performed by private individuals as well as for acts performed by public officials. Regrettably, the United Nations has concluded that women's rights, despite the rhetoric, have regressed in some instances, as the external social pressures on women brought on by physical displacement by wars, famines, and ecological disasters have made them more vulnerable to violence.[31] In practical terms, then, the legal changes brought about by women's rights have been implemented by women themselves. The result has been to change the focus of women from being "invisible" victims of persecution to being granted recognition as a group.

The Special Rapporteur on Women to the UN Commission on Human Rights has issued a series of reports on violence against women in different parts of the world, including South Africa, Brazil, and Haiti, among others. The Rapporteur's reports have outlined the extent of the problems facing women, which include rape and sexual violence, trafficking and forced prostitution, violence against migrant workers, violence against women, reproductive health, and child pornography.[32] The Rapporteur has urged member states to undergo criminal justice reform to create special cells for handling cases sensitive to the needs of women. The criminal justice system should show "due diligence" to prevent violence against women and work closely with health, social services, and education practitioners. Legal reform is necessary with the help of nongovernmental organizations to use UN model strategies to prevent violence against women in the home and in society.[33] The European Commission on Human Rights has stated that the state has a positive obligation to provide adequate protection for women against gender-based violence and harassment. In a significant use of the new law, eight Serbs were charged and convicted of crimes against humanity and grave breaches of international law for the gang rape, torture, and sexual enslavement of Muslim women in Foca. Additionally, the Statute of the International Tribunal for Rwanda represents another step forward by including rape, forced prostitution, and any form of indecent assault in article 4 of the statute. The Inter-American Commission on Human Rights on Haiti recognized that rape as a weapon of terror was used to "punish women for their militancy" and qualifies as torture.

## REPRODUCTIVE RIGHTS

The right to reproductive freedom is viewed as an "integral part of modern woman's struggle to assert her dignity and worth as a human being."[34] It is no wonder then that women's health and reproductive decisions have been a great source of controversy under domestic and international law. Women have the right to make decisions in regard to the reproductive process, an essential human right. The fundamentalist view of some state authorities is that the role of women is to bear men's children and to tend men's homes, as a family duty as well as a national duty. The impact of controls by the state over reproductive decisions is to reinforce this stereotypical role for women. According to a leading scholar, the cluster of human rights originating as reproductive interests can be broadly categorized as: reproductive security, reproductive health, reproductive equality, and reproductive decisionmaking.[35] Additionally, the health impact of human rights violations, such as rape and domestic violence, is considerable.

Occupations associated with reproductive process and feminine-gender qualities, such as nursing the young and caring for disabled and elderly persons, tend to have a low socioeconomic status. Homemaking, child care, and cottage agriculture tend not to be included in national estimates of economic output. In the context of modern reproductive rights, women continue to suffer both sex and gender discrimination. Women are considered incapable of prudent decisionmaking concerning abortion, access to which is governed by legislation that requires male or husband's authorization.[36] The authority of men in their homes is supported worldwide by governmental and social tolerance of violence directed against their wives.

Governments tend to view enforcement of women's rights as an issue of lower social and political priority or not one upon which an election would turn. Extensive public debate on social policy such as women's issues, hence, is frequently avoided, and the stereotypical cultural roles continue. The continued focus on motherhood is dysfunctional to women in that if the value of women arises solely through motherhood, then women acquire status only through pregnancy and childbirth. Where women possess additional and alternative values through which they contribute to society—economic, professional, cultural, artistic, and other capacities—then motherhood will be esteemed in balance with those other capacities. Societies and individual women will want more from women than their reproductive capacities and will balance reproductive roles against the benefits of women's additional capacities that contribute to social activities.[37] The health damage to women and the demographic consequences of excessive childbearing will be reduced where women are expected to contribute to their families and communities in ways other than motherhood. Women's education and employment status and health needs are related to the number of children they have. More educated and professionally qualified women tend to have fewer children. This has been shown to be true in developing and developed countries.

Population control policies may not take women's needs into account as to the most suitable methods of birth control and other contraceptive needs. Women are frequently not consulted as to the birth control method most suitable to them; instead they were to bear children according to their husbands' and wider families' expectations. Family planning services are inaccessible to women; frequently, lack of education may prevent women from utilizing these services most fully or making informed decisions as to their reproductive choices. The literacy rate among women is linked to the exercise of reproductive choices.

Men interpreted women's needs in lawmaking and law enforcement and within religious institutions. Religious leaders claimed to have the divine authority to interpret and decide whether women had reproductive rights. "The [Roman Catholic] Church, as a political institution, puts forward an agenda that rejects women's rights, reproductive rights, sexual rights, in spite of qualified lip-service to each."[38] Instead, law and legislation should be sensitized to women. The "woman question" contests common assumptions of laws' gender-neutrality. Almost all law at the domestic level emerges from male-defined value systems. Feminist legal methods question the impact of law on women's experience so as not to disadvantage them. Law should not be assumed to be gender-neutral; instead, law should be sensitive to the special circumstances and historical experiences of women.[39]

## FEMINISM WITHIN ISLAM

The feminist debate within Islamic societies is an interpretative answer to the challenge to the fundamentalist view of women's rights. Pakistan's feminists have tried to work within an Islamic framework and have incorporated women's rights in a secular alternative interpretation to Islam. According to feminists within Islamic societies, women's rights should not be perceived as simply one of achieving equality with men but to recognize that women have different experiences based on characteristics other than gender; to frame the issues around gender alone is to downgrade this diversity and to generalize the experiences of women. For example, gender-based oppression for upper-class women in Islamic countries is one of the few types of oppression they experience, whereas for other women it is one of many.

Gender issues in Islamic societies include violence against women, women's economic dependency, and male control over women's lives. Bread-and-butter issues have a larger impact on the lives of poor and working-class women, and they should not be subordinated to cultural issues such as Islamism.[40] The point made by the Islamic women's movement is not to reject Islam but to state clearly that the issue of women's rights is a secular issue of human rights.

The right to reproductive health is seen in conjunction with cultural relativist ideas. This debate has spanned the spectrum of women's rights as well as the more intense debate on the reproductive choices of women. The liberal view is clearly embodied in the language of CEDAW, linking reproductive rights to women attaining a penumbra of other rights. Women's equality is possible with the right to an abortion, the right to adequate health care, the right to an education, and the right to equality, as well as to the freedoms of a quality of life, liberty, and happiness. The women's right to choose is linked to overcoming the traditional stereotype of a woman's role as childbearer and her traditional tasks in childrearing and homemaking. To attain equality, women must have access to educational skills and training to work in higher-paying employment and have access to adequate health care and the right to change the equation on men. The visible role of women in society as serving men's need to have children is altered with the changes brought about by CEDAW.[41]

## OBSTACLES TO REGIME CHANGE FOR WOMEN

Changing cultural attitudes is difficult and progress is slowed and complicated by the weakness in a state's resolve to do so. As indicated by the reservations to CEDAW adopted by several states, they have explicitly indicated that they are unlikely to be able to meet these criteria, as their religious and cultural traditions are in contravention with international law. The lack of resolve to change attitudes is an indication that these states are unable to change domestic regimes and are captive to the very political attitudes toward women's equality required by international law. The state apparatus is likely to change only with domestic pressure groups by women and by changing the role of clerics and other fundamentalist political actors in defining the role of women in societies. To transform the debate is important in that it does not provide a ready rejection of international norms on women by Islamic countries or other countries of the South as merely another form of Western cultural imperialism. The fallacy of this debate is clear from the progress made in women's rights after the Bosnian policies of ethnic cleansing and persecution of the crime of rape under international law.

The United Nations has been at the forefront of new developments in international human rights initiatives to include women. For a century and more, women have sought to achieve political, economic, social, and legal equality; although on paper much progress has been made, much needs to be done. A vindication of women's equality in the United Nations fora is a necessary first step toward achieving equality.

The political struggles to control the UN agenda have given way to a new seriousness among women's groups to cooperate toward achieving consensus on women's rights. The United Nations has seen contentious debates on the position of women in society. Some states have viewed the universal standards on women's rights as an imposition of the liberal Western model upon their cultures. These nations have viewed it as a threat to their cultural and religious autonomy. The contentious issues of these debates have been overcome by new and important developments in post–Cold War politics. The end of the Cold War has allowed a more serious approach to women's issues and to the issues of gender equality. The new debates are centered upon achieving women's equality in the framework of new and developing social models for achieving the goals of the United Nations. Women's equality is essential to achieving a more just and peaceful society among nations. Women are making a substantial contribution to international cooperation on the environment, economic development, health, and social development. The United Nations has been a forum for improving women's status in their countries and consequently has been essential in helping to achieve women's rights.

The primary areas of progress made in women's international rights are in the enforcement of legal systems that made rape a crime under the statutes adopted by the international tribunals created for Yugoslavia and Rwanda, as well as the interpretation of asylum laws to grant women group rights against cultural persecution by states that do not enforce women's rights or grant them protection under international and domestic legal norms.

## DISCUSSION QUESTIONS

1. CEDAW has redefined women's rights with a view toward greater empowerment. What are the different ways by which this law can be used to further women's rights as a group?

2. Has the international community of nations focused on the correct reasons to deny women equal rights, that is, the religious aspect of interpreting women's social and cultural position in society? What are some of the other reasons women have not reached the goals set out in CEDAW?

3. The international system consists of sovereign states. How can women's rights be improved under the current system, where the primary responsibility for implementing the law lies with the individual nation-state?

4. The primary oversight organ in the United Nations to enforce CEDAW is the Committee on Women. What kinds of administrative reforms

would improve oversight? Should crimes against women be defined with greater specificity? Would the oversight actions by the Committee on Women include independent monitoring and greater accountability by states to the international system? Should a system oversee violations with new and reformed guidelines?

5. Should the international system use sanctions to enforce women's rights against states that use extreme measures to deny women basic rights as laid down by CEDAW? Can CEDAW address discrimination against women such as that imposed by the Taliban in Afganistan between 1995 and 2001; and how would states that engage in such discrimination be sanctioned?

## NOTES

1. Rebecca J. Cook, "Human Rights and Reproductive Self-Determination," *American University Law Review* 44 (1995): 1006.

2. The main premise of scholarship is that women's equality is customary international law that applies to all nation-states, even those who have not ratified the Women's Convention. See Comment, "Customary International Law and Women's Rights: The Equal Rights Amendment as a Fait Accompli," *Detroit College of Law Review* 1 (1987): 120–149; Courtney W. Howland, "The Challenge of Religious Fundamentalism to the Liberty and Equality Rights of Women: An Analysis Under the United Nations Charter," *Columbia Journal of Transnational Law* 35 (1997): 271–377.

3. M. Cherif Bassiouni and Marcia McCormick, "Sexual Violence: An Invisible Weapon of War in the Former Yugoslavia," Occasional Paper No. 1 (Chicago: De Paul University College of Law, International Human Rights Law Institute, 1996, pp. 32–33.

4. Ibid., p. 22.

5. Ibid., p. 23.

6. Ibid., p. 23.

7. *Final Report of the Commission of Experts Established Purusant to Security Council Resolution 780 (1992),* U.N. SCOR, Annex, at 3, 55, UN Doc. S/1994/674 (1994), cited in Linda A. Malone, "Beyond Bosnia and *In Re Kasinga:* A Feminist Perspective on Recent Developments in Protecting Women from Sexual Violence," *Boston University International Law Journal* 14 (1996): 319, 322.

8. Theodor Meron, Editorial Comment, "Rape as a Crime Under International Humanitarian Law," *American Journal of International Law* 87: 427; Krishna R. Patel, "Recognizing the Rape of Bosnian Women as Gender-Based Persecution," *Brooklyn Law Review* 60 (1994): 929–958.

9. Malone, "Beyond Bosnia," pp. 319, 326.

10. UNHCR Division of International Protection, "Gender-Related Persecution: An Analysis of Recent Trends," Special Issue of *International Journal of Refugee Law* (autumn 1997), p. 79.

11. Declaration on the Elimination of Violence Against Women (1993), Article 1.

12. Canadian and Australian Guidelines for Refugee Protection, cited in special issue of *International Journal of Refugee Law,* p. 84, n. 5.

13. Article 2 of the Declaration on the Elimination of Violence Against Women provides that: "Violence against women shall be understood to encompass, but not be limited to the following: (a) physical, sexual and psychological violence occurring in the family, including battering, sexual abuse of female children in the household, dowry-related violence, marital rape, female genital mutilation and other traditional practices harmful to women, non-spousal violence and violence related to exploitation; (b) physical, sexual and psychological violence occurring within the general community, including rape, sexual abuse, sexual harassment and intimidation at work, in educational institutions and elsewhere, trafficking in women and forced prostitution; (c) physical, sexual and psychological violence perpetrated or condoned by the State, wherever it occurs." Available online at http://www. unhchr.ch/huridocda/hur...mbol)A.RES.48.104.

14. *Matter of M-K,* Office of the Immigration Judge, Executive Office of Immigration Review, A72–374–558, August 9, 1995, cited in special issue of *International Journal of Refugee Law,* p. 89.

15. Canadian Immigration and Refugee Board, *Re: Khadra Hassan Farah,* July 13, 1994, cited in ibid., p. 98.

16. Robin M. Maher, "Female Genital Mutilation: The Struggle to Eradicate this Rite of Passage," *Human Rights* 23, no. 4 (fall 1996): 12–15.

17. Ibid.

18. The test of a group proposed is as follows in *Matter of Acosta,* 19 I. and N. Dec.211: (1) Groups defined by an innate or unchangeable characteristic; (2) groups whose members voluntarily associate for reasons so fundamental to their human dignity that they should not be forced to forsake their association; and (3) groups associated by a former voluntary status, unalterable due to its historical permanence.

19. *Fatin v. INS,* 12 F.3d 1233, cited in special issue of *International Journal of Refugee Law,* p. 110.

20. Jane Conners, "Legal Aspects of Women as a Particular Social Group," in ibid., pp. 114–128, esp. p. 127.

21. Article 19(c), *Vienna Convention on the Law of Treaties* (May 23, 1969), U.N. Doc.A/CONF.39/27.

22. Courtney W. Howland, "The Challenge of Religious Fundamentalism to the Liberty and Equality Rights of Women: An Analysis Under the United Nations Charter," *Columbia Journal of Transnational Law* 35 (1997): 217, 274.

23. Berta Esperanza Hernandez-Truyol, "Sex, Culture, and Rights: A Re/Conceptualization of Violence for the 21st Century," *Albany Law Review* 60 (1997): 612.

24. Anne F. Bayefsky, "General Approaches to the Domestic Application of Women's International Human Rights Law," in Rebecca Cook, *Human Rights of Women: National and International Perspectives* (Philadelphia: University of Pennsylvania Press, 1994).

25. Fourth World Conference on Women, Beijing, China, September 4–15, 1995, *Platform for Action and the Beijing Declaration.* New York: U.N. Department of Public Information, 1996). See also, "Further Promotion and Encouragement of Human Rights and Fundamental Freedoms, Including the Question of the Programme and Methods of Work of the Commission, Alternative Approaches and Ways and Means Within the United Nations System for Improving the Effective Enjoyment of Human Rights and Fundamental Freedoms," *Report of the Special Rapporteur on Violence Against Women: Its Causes and Consequences,* Ms. Radhika Coomaraswamy, Addendum. E/CN.4/1997/47/Add.4.

26. Howland, "The Challenge of Religious Fundamentalism," n. 18.

27. Beijing *Platform for Action,* n. 19.

28. Bayefsky, "General Approaches to the Domestic Application of Women's International Human Rights Law," in Cook, *Human Rights of Women.*

29. Ibid.

30. The time for reporting to the Committee was extended to accommodate this complaint.

31. Beijing *Platform for Action* and the Beijing Declaration, U.N. Department of Public Information, United Nations, New York, 1996.

32. "Further Promotion and Encouragement of Human Rights and Fundamental Freedoms, Including the Question of the Programme and Methods of Work of the Commission, Alternative Approaches and Ways and Means Within the United Nations System for Improving the Effective Enjoyment of Human Rights and Fundamental Freedoms," *Report of the Special Rapporteur on Violence Against Women, Its Causes and Consequences,* Ms. Radhika Coomaraswamy. E/CN.4/1997/47/Add.4.

33. *Strategies for Crime Prevention and Control, Particularly in Urban Areas and in the Context of Public Security, Elimination of Violence Against Women, Report of the Secretary-General, Addendum.* E/CN.15/1997/11/Add.1.

34. *Morgentaler v. The Queen,* I.S.C.R. 30, 172 (Can. 1988). Madam Justice Wilson of the Supreme Court of Canada explained: "Women's needs and aspirations are only now being translated into protected rights. The right to reproduce or not to reproduce which is in issue in this case is one such right and is properly perceived as an integral part of modern woman's struggle to assert *her* dignity and worth as a human being." Cited in Rebecca J. Cook, "Human Rights and Reproductive Self-Determination," *American University Law Review* 44 (1995): 975.

35. Rebecca J. Cook and Deborah Maine, "Spousal Veto over Family Planning Services," *American Journal of Public Health* 77 (1987): 39.

36. Ibid.

37. Mahmoud F. Fathalla, "Women's Health: An Overview," *International Journal of Gynecology and Obstetrics* 105 (1994); Carol Gilligan, *In a Different Voice: Psychological Theory and Women's Moral Development* (Cambridge: Harvard University Press, 1982), cited in Rebecca Cook, "Human Rights and Reproductive Self-Determination," *American University Law Review* 44 (1995): 984.

38. Frances Kissling, "The Challenge of Christianity," *American University Law Review* 44 (1994): 1345–1349. Kissling's explanation of the fundamentalist political agenda: "We need to understand that at the root of what we are dealing with and the reason that Catholicism and Islam got together in Cairo had nothing to do with family planning and had nothing to do with abortion. It had everything to do with that segment within both of those faith groups that shares a vision of women as inferior and a vision of men as in charge."

39. Ibid.

40. Fausia Gardezi, "Islam, Feminism, and the Women's Movement in Pakistan, 1981–91," in Kamla Bhasin et al., eds., *Against All Odds: Essays on Women, Religion and Development from India and Pakistan* (Delhi: Deep and Deep, 1996), pp. 51–57.

41. Rebecca J. Cook, "Human Rights and Reproductive Self-Determination," n. 31.

# 4

# State Ideology and Women in Rural China

## KELLEE S. TSAI

In old China, women were bound up by the shackles of power in politics, clan, husband and religion. They were kept at the bottom of society. Women were liberated after the birth of New China in 1949.
—Huang Qizao, Sichuan Province National People's Congress deputy, vice president, and first member of the secretariat of the All-China Women's Federation (1993)

The irony of Beijing hosting the United Nations (UN) Fourth World Conference on Women in 1995 was apparent to many observers, but not to the Chinese government and perhaps a few ideological holdovers in former socialist countries.[1] Revolutionary regimes inspired by Marxist theory during the first half of the twentieth century recognized the liberation of women as a key component of the transition to socialism.[2] Upon the communist political victory, women were granted full legal rights and mobilized to participate in production. Revolution seemed to have an empowering effect on women. Meanwhile, the authoritarian nature of the socialist state demonstrated command capacity to transform the structure of economic and social relations. Yet after several decades of communist governance, gender gaps in political and socioeconomic indicators remain salient—and women have arguably experienced disempowerment in the area of reproductive choice, one of the most fundamental measures of personal freedom for women.

By focusing on the position of women in post-1949 rural China, I seek to shed light on the persistence of gender inequalities in socialist countries despite their ideological commitment to the empowerment of women.[3] Analysis of this paradox raises two broader issues concerning the relationship between the state and women: (1) state capacity to implement its developmental strategy; and (2) the sources of gender biases. Accordingly, in

47

the first section my analysis proposes a synthesis of state-centered and women-in-development (WID) theories for explaining gender inequalities under socialism. Although a state's ideology and mode of production may have a substantial impact on the definition of gender, I argue that the endurance of gender inequalities suggests the centrality of patriarchy as a socially constructed system. In other words, the institutional dynamics of patriarchy may survive changes in particular political orientations or economic modes precisely because they are deeply embedded in the reform efforts themselves. In the bulk of this chapter, therefore, I take a policy-level perspective in examining the relative empowerment and disempowerment of women in rural China in both the Mao and post-Mao reform periods. In the third part I analyze how the state and the household have inhibited greater empowerment of women; the final section offers theoretical implications.

## THEORETICAL CONTEXT

Despite their efforts to conceptualize gendered distributional asymmetries, individually, neither standard political science nor WID frameworks can explain the persistence of gender inequalities in socialist countries. Conventional theories of the state may be employed to demonstrate the limits of state capacity for implementing policies beneficial to women, but they are not concerned with the sources of gender biases. WID theories in the liberal tradition generally focus on the effects of capitalist development on women.[4] Similarly, Marxist and neo-Marxist explanations of gender inequality point to the oppressive structures of capitalism.[5] Nonetheless, valuable concepts may be extracted from them for framing this analysis.

First, the state is a significant actor. In socialist countries, the Communist Party–dominated state formulates developmental policies that affect the structure of economic and social relations. However, the party-state's institutional capacity for policy implementation should not be assumed despite its apparent strength.[6] As more contemporary theorists of the state point out, state autonomy is neither a zero-sum function of power relative to society nor an isolated determinant of capacity.[7] To elucidate the state's relative effectiveness, the relationship between state and society may thus be analyzed as a series of linkages between policy elites, central and local authorities, local and village cadres, and cadres and households, which in turn are influenced by the interactions within each level.[8] It is also important to consider the role of informal actors and organizational structures relative to that of formal institutions and ideology in policy implementation. The operational tasks at this level are to examine the following: (1) state developmental policies relating to women; (2) the relationship between the state and societal institutions that directly involve women, particularly, and the household unit; and, as a result, (3) the relative impact of state policy on society in general and women in particular. Most state-society and WID theorists confine their debate to these considerations. They offer varying interpretations of the extent to which state policy reflects or shapes the interests of society and then evaluate the effectiveness of state action.

Acknowledging that the state has an impact on the household as a component of society provides a basis for explaining gender inequalities. To the extent that the household or family represents the most fundamental sphere of interaction between women and men and, hence, the most fundamental unit of society, it is relevant to bridge the gap between state policies and the household.[9] Furthermore, the liberal and Marxist feminist approaches offer insight on the specific consequences of economic development on the sexual division of labor and other gender-differentiated indicators.[10] They do not, however, explain the discrepancy between the relative success of socialist countries in transforming other social relations and their failure to eradicate biases against women. These theories generally assume capitalist development.[11] Still, these frameworks can be tested by the experience of socialist countries that have embarked on market-oriented reforms. With the decreased reliance on Marx-Engels ideology, are women becoming disempowered as Marxists would expect? Do they take on a different character? Or are women becoming empowered as a by-product of reform, thereby broadly confirming liberal hypotheses?[12] Given that the latter situation has yet to be evidenced, additional analysis is warranted.

In order to explicate the endurance of gender inequalities, it is necessary to go beyond fundamentally state-centered perspectives. State and economic policies alone cannot account for gender differentiation. An additional structural variable, as socialist feminists point out, is the institutionalization of patriarchal norms.[13] Although the state represents the most salient patriarchal institution within national boundaries, the definition of gender as a social construction implicates a broader range of sources in perpetuating biases. In other words, accepting that gender identities that inhibit women's empowerment are not innate, but learned through social and cultural interactions, means that the household plays an equally powerful if not greater role in this context.[14] Marx and Engels viewed the state and the household as the primary institutions that embody class antagonisms in society. The socialist feminist formulation of class and gender struggle derives from this argument. But recognizing the household as an oppressive institution and gender norms as a social construction does not require embracing the historical materialism of Marxist paradigms. Arguably, the class element of socialist feminist theory obscures its most important contribution: patriarchy as an institution. The reductionism of class analysis restricts its ability to delineate the expression of patriarchy in other terms that may be more appropriate for gender analysis. As Catharine MacKinnon, a feminist legal scholar, observes, "Method shapes each theory's vision of social reality. It identifies its central problem, group and process, and creates as a consequence its distinctive conception of politics as such."[15] The challenge for feminist theory, therefore, is "to demonstrate that feminism systematically converges upon a central explanation of sex inequality through an approach distinctive to its subject yet applicable to the whole of social life, including class."[16] A fundamental premise, then, is the recognition of patriarchy as a socially determined system that exists within and beyond state, economic, and societal structures. This assumption does not preclude materialist approaches. Rather, it adds depth to the analysis by identifying the sources of gender norms and exploring their interaction.

The persistence of gender inequalities in socialist countries may thus be seen as deriving from the relationship between the primary instruments of patriarchy: the state and the household. That is, gender norms are constructed and realized at both levels in a mutually reinforcing manner. Operationally, this entails examination of the state and the household as interactive rather than as parallel institutions in generating, perpetuating, and actualizing gender biases. This approach seeks to expand the definitional boundaries of state and society in mainstream discourse by focusing on the structural oppression of actors whose "interests" remain unarticulated by class, civil society, or the state.[17] The dynamics and consequences of patriarchy in post-1949 rural China are presented in the next section.

## THE STATE AND WOMEN IN POST-1949 RURAL CHINA

### Ideology and Postrevolutionary Strategy

The Russian experience in implementing a communist revolution in general, and the liberation of women as a component of the process, served as a model for the Chinese communists throughout the revolutionary period. Both the Bolsheviks and the Chinese Communist Party (CCP) mobilized the most oppressed groups in society—namely, peasants and women—to serve as the revolutionary base. Although women were not considered a distinct class, their oppression symbolized the dynamics of class struggle. Under V. I. Lenin, the Soviet Union enacted significant legislation to liberate women from "bourgeois feudalism" and empower them as participants in the continuing revolutionary process. Following victory in 1949, the CCP similarly launched a number of policies and programs to promote gender equality.[18]

First, the CCP legally stipulated the equality of women as full citizens in the 1949 constitution of the People's Republic of China (PRC). The 1950

Marriage Law legalized marriage, denounced patriarchal authority in the household, and granted both sexes equal rights to file for divorce.[19] The second and most prominent element of the strategy was integrating women into economic development. Women's employment was viewed as a prerequisite for emancipation from bourgeois structures as embodied in the patriarchal family.[20] Furthermore, at the core of the CCP's strategy for political consolidation was economic reconstruction and rural development. The full participation of women was not only an ideological imperative but also a pragmatic one. Third, the All-China Women's Federation (ACWF) was established by the CCP to mobilize women for economic development and social reform.[21] The First Congress of the ACWF in 1949 highlighted the following areas for the active participation of women: land reform, marriage law campaigns, political study, and agricultural development. The fourth objective—ideological redefinition of gender relations—quickly proved to be the area most resistant to the influence of mass campaigns. Although stories of revolutionary heroines and slogans proclaiming the equality of women were well known, traditional Confucian beliefs about gender roles retained a stronghold, particularly in rural China.

The above strategy for achieving gender equality was pursued broadly throughout Mao's tenure, though official policy on women has varied with the direction of general political and economic priorities. In addition, initiatives that would appear to empower women encountered obstacles in implementation; and as suggested by WID theorists, broader developmental efforts have yielded mixed results for the overall position of women. As discussed next, state policies that have had direct impact on the household include the following: (1) land reform and marriage laws; (2) collectivization and communization; and (3) post-Mao reform, including the household responsibility system and family planning policies.

## Early Mao: Land Reform and Marriage Laws

Women's participation was considered integral to the success of the land reform and marriage law campaigns during the early 1950s.[22] The CCP actively recruited rural female cadres and encouraged the proliferation of women's organizations. Both campaigns intended to destroy feudalistic institutions and practices, which included, respectively, the traditional extended family and the most blatant abuses against women (footbinding, polygamy, concubinage, child brides, and dowry payments).

Land reform succeeded in eliminating the extended family's material basis and, hence, its potential for posing as a political threat to the regime. Small plots were redistributed to each family member regardless of age or sex, and land reform provisions stipulated that property would be equally divided in the case of divorce. Nonetheless, land reform did not empower women, as any land allotted to women was effectively controlled by their husbands. Patriarchal familial relationships in the Confucian tradition seemed to remain intact.[23]

At the same time, the new marriage laws generated much controversy. During the first five years, more than 500,000 women filed for divorces annually.[24] Male peasants threatened female cadres attempting to enforce the divorce provisions, and mothers-in-law sought to preserve their status over daughters-in-law in the traditional, extended family structure. Some women even committed suicide to protest the refusal of their husbands and male cadres to comply with the new law. In 1953, the National Committee for Thorough Implementation reported that more than 75,000 deaths or suicides annually could be attributed to marriage differences and unsuccessful implementation.[25] The difficulties encountered in enforcement revealed not only the depth of tradition but also the institutional deficiencies in rural China for their acceptance.[26] The traditional family system served important functions for which the party-state did not offer alternatives. Families ensured the provision of old-age security, child care, and medical facilities.

The early reforms also focused on collectivization and communization. After only two years of agricultural production based on small, family-owned plots, the CCP's Central Committee decided that accelerated agricultural growth was necessary to fuel industrialization. The resulting nationwide collectivization drive from 1955 to 1956 aimed to abolish private landownership. Ninety percent of rural society was restructured into cooperative farms (or collectives), where members received compensation according to the socialist principle of "each according to his labor." Legislation relating to collectivization contained provisions emphasizing the importance of female employment in rural cooperatives.[27] In addition, propaganda went beyond encouragement of women's economic participation and explicitly linked their empowerment to the structural implications of collectivization. Shortly after CCP approval of the shift to collectivization, *People's Daily* quoted Engels's contention that the emancipation of women requires participation in social labor and "to achieve this, individual families are no longer required to be units of the social economy."[28] The establishment of cooperatives effectively separated production from the household and provided women with a wider range of employment opportunities.

However, the employment of women in rural cooperatives posed a strain on their provision of domestic services. To a limited degree, older women were mobilized to handle child care and other household responsibilities. But domestic services were not fully collectivized.[29] Continued responsibility for housework and official employment meant that women were not able to earn as many workpoints as their male counterparts. The resulting dual burden was not only recognized but justified by *People's*

*Daily:* "Participation in agricultural production is the inherent right and duty of rural women. Giving birth to children and raising them, as well as preoccupation with household chores are also the obligations of rural women. These things set women apart from men."[30] In rural China, as in other rural societies, the dual burden itself was certainly not a new phenomenon for peasant women. But the specific socialist ideology of each according to his labor drew attention to the gender gap in wages; and the state ultimately sanctioned traditional norms regarding the sexual division of labor in the household.

By 1958, Mao declared that China had completed the transition to socialism and was prepared to make a "great leap forward" in the transition from socialism to communism. The people's commune was identified as a new form of social organization to complete the revolution. Communization proceeded rapidly: within one year, more than 90 percent of peasant households—briefly organized in cooperatives—were amalgamated into communes. At the same time, peasants, including more than 300 million women, were mobilized into production brigades. The demand for full-time female labor in the agricultural sector led to the creation of communal dining and nurseries, which were primarily staffed by older women. One source estimates that by 1959 there were nearly 5 million nurseries and 3.6 million public dining rooms in rural areas.[31]

Despite increased communization of domestic services, women continued to earn approximately one-half to one-third fewer workpoints than men did. The gender gap in compensation was excused as reflecting the amount of physical energy expended. Hence, activities performed by men were considered "heavy," whereas women's work was "light."[32] Incomplete empowerment of women was justified by their limited physical power relative to men. As illustrated in Table 4.1, however, the "lighter" work was not necessarily less physically demanding.

**Table 4.1   Division of Labor on Communes, 1956 and 1977**

| | 1956<br>Rice, Corn, Sweet Potatoes, Wheat | 1977<br>Double Rice Cropping, Winter Wheat |
|---|---|---|
| Men | Heavy work (plowing, carrying heavy loads); irrigation, fostering well-grown seedlings; tilling rape fields; subsidiary occupations. | Plowing with water buffalo; carrying water; driving tractors; rural industries. |
| Women | Lighter work; preparing ash compost; harvesting rape; growing early crops. | Sowing seed; transplanting rice seedlings; harvesting; carrying manure to the fields; raising pigs. |

*Sources:* Foreign Languages Press, *The Upsurge of Socialism in the Countryside* (Beijing: FPL), p. 289; Elisabeth Croll, "Jiang Village: A Household Survey," *China Quarterly* 72 (1977): 805.

Furthermore, in regions where nonagricultural employment opportunities were available, women performed a wider range of agricultural tasks as men pursued other forms of work.[33] A government document in 1958 indicated that women would be expected to compensate for the shortage of labor in agriculture caused by male employment in newer industries:

> Women should shoulder agricultural production. Men's labor power is needed to open mines, expand machine building industry, power plants, cement plants. Generally speaking, these departments of industry employ mainly men laborers and provide only a few types of work that can be undertaken by women workers. Thus, up to a certain stage in the development of socialist construction, agricultural production will have to be undertaken mainly by women.[34]

As such, the percentage of peasant women engaged in nondomestic production increased rapidly—from 50 percent to nearly 90 percent during the first decade of socialist rule.[35] Nonetheless, large-scale employment in agricultural production did not indicate equality. It increased the demands on rural women without commensurate wage compensation. Although the policy of "equal pay for equal work" was actively promoted, as shown above, the household and agricultural tasks performed by women were valued less than those performed by men. In villages where women performed the same work alongside men, or replaced the work of men, male peasants protested and prevented the equal allocation of workpoints.[36] They demanded greater compensation as a structural requirement: as heads of households, they needed to contribute more than women to the family budget.[37] The relative decrease in the sexual division of labor in agriculture did not restructure the sexual division of authority or labor in the patriarchal household. Furthermore, by the 1960s the financial cost of maintaining the communal facilities was considered too high when the services could be performed within the household by women for "free."[38]

As in other socialist countries, the incorporation of women into the public production was not matched by comparable levels of political participation.[39] This asymmetry was not a calculated outcome of state policy. Numerous campaigns encouraged women to join decisionmaking bodies, particularly during the 1970s. Special education courses were established to train female party cadres and educate women in the Thought of Mao Tsetung; and women's guidance teams were formed in each brigade, down to the smallest village unit.[40] Although there was incremental growth in the political participation of women, they were better represented among production cadres than in higher levels of the party-state apparatus. For example, between 1965 and 1973 the percentage of women in the Central Committee increased from 8 percent to 13 percent,[41] whereas women generally accounted for 20–30 percent of rural cadres during the same period, with slight provincial variations.[42] But ultimately the dual burden of women's work played a key role in limiting their incentive to participate in political activity. This was particularly evident during the Cultural Revolution, when political study sessions were held each evening.[43] Most women were simply too busy with farmwork, housework, and two hours of Mao Thought to contemplate additional political responsibilities.

### Post-Mao Reform:
### Household Responsibility System and Family Planning Policy

Following Mao's death in 1976, the rural sector was targeted as one of the Four Modernizations in the developmental strategy promoted by the Hua Guofeng–Deng Xiaoping coalition. By the early 1980s, the reforms had effectively transformed the political economic structure of rural China, with contradictory implications for the relationships between the party-state and villages, rural cadres and the household, and women and men. On the one hand, central bureaucracies relinquished their control over the agricultural sector. Under the household responsibility system (HRS), communal arrangements were replaced by the household as the primary unit of production to increase incentives for output.[44] On the other hand, the state asserted control over the reproductive process to ensure sustainable growth. Both of these developments have directly affected the nature of gender relations within and beyond the peasant household and had a disempowering effect on women.

The HRS decentralized rural production by transferring decisionmaking power over the allocation of land and labor resources to the household. Whereas production teams formerly determined the distribution of agricultural tasks and the means to fulfill output quotas, now the head of the household possesses that authority. In rural areas with fewer men and more female-headed households, women have significantly higher rates of labor force participation than in areas with more male-headed households.[45] This is consistent with the observation that decommunization has increased the dual burden and reduced the visibility of women's work.[46] Instead of working in the fields with the rest of the production team, marriage-age women are more likely to engage in domestic work and cultivate household plots while men seek employment in rural industry.[47]

Furthermore, just as official statements during the Great Leap Forward advocated a greater role for women in agricultural production to increase the pool of manpower for industrialization, the post-Mao regime has encouraged women's activity in domestic sideline production. Unlike small-scale commodity production, domestic sidelines "serve the public interest by using only spare household time and labor," that is, the work of women.[48] Domestic sideline production includes household production of food, handicraft goods, plastic or silk flowers, embroidery, and knitting. More important, they represent income-generating opportunities for women. Initially, the products were primarily sold in local peasant markets, but it quickly became apparent that the quality and aggregate volume of output would be suitable for exports as well.[49] The government has thus instituted many incentives for domestic sideline production, which has increased the portion of peasant household incomes generated from such work. In some areas, nearly 80 percent of peasant women are involved in weaving, embroidery, and other handicraft activities alongside farmwork.[50] Of particular interest, a 1987 survey of the 34 million specialized rural households in Sichuan province found that female-headed households had a higher annual income than male-headed households: 882 yuan as compared to 712 yuan.[51]

With the increased economic contribution of women to household income through domestic sideline production, liberal and Marxist feminists would expect corresponding increases in decisionmaking authority as one indicator of relative empowerment. A 1990 survey conducted by the ACWF revealed that 53 percent of the women respondents believed that household decisionmaking was jointly shared with their husbands.[52] A 1991 survey administered by the Chinese Academy of Social Sciences found that women and men shared economic decisionmaking in 81 percent of the surveyed rural households and 76 percent of the surveyed urban households.[53] My own 1996–1997 survey of microentrepreneurs found that decisionmaking over household income was made jointly by husband and wife among 50.3 percent of the respondents.[54] But these surveys do not constitute a sound basis for comparison over time because they employed different methodologies. An analytical attempt at deducing the impact of the household responsibility system and increased household income on women's relative "bargaining power" predicts adverse effects.[55] That is, women's control over household "entitlements" is expected to decline as they engage in productive activities in the private, domestic sphere. Elisabeth Croll similarly expresses skepticism about the degree to which women's increased income will affect intrahousehold relations of exchange.[56] It is less disputable, however, that community welfare services such as child care and primary health care have returned to the realm of individual households— adding to the responsibilities of women.

Although rural reform has increased the autonomy of the household in economic production, the One-Family, One-Child policy launched in 1979 has turned reproduction into an area of direct state intervention.[57] The new regime under Deng made the neo-Malthusian observation that the economic gains from reform were barely sufficient to accommodate a population of 1 billion, given the natural population growth rate of 1.26 percent, much less provide a basis for advanced industrial development. The One-Family,

One-Child campaigns have therefore targeted women to limit their child-bearing as a "patriotic duty."[58]

The family planning policy is implemented by local units of the Women's Federation, barefoot doctors, and health workers who are mainly women. Each family is visited individually by members of the local family planning committee. After the first child, women are awarded a one-child certificate that entitles them to a number of privileges. Standard regulations concerning the type of birth control method employed require IUDs after one child, sterilization after the second one, and abortion for unapproved pregnancies.

The policy rests on a coercive system of sanctions and rewards. Economic sanctions include: payment of an "excess child levy" as compensation to the state for the cost of another child to the country;[59] reduction in the family's grain ration (or higher prices) for producing a "surplus" child; limitations on additional land for private plots and the right to collective grain in times of flood and drought; and ineligibility for promotion for four years, demotion, or reduction in wages.[60]

Moreover, the offending couple has to bear all expenses for medical care and education of excess children, and "extra" children have the lowest priority in admission to kindergarten, school, and medical institutions. In contrast, one-child families are entitled to many privileges, including monthly or annual cash subsidies for health or welfare until the child reaches fourteen years of age, as well as additional private plots from the commune. Single children are entitled to free education, health services, and priority in admission to nurseries, schools, and hospitals. Parents receive an additional subsidy to their old-age pension.[61]

The most serious consequence of the family planning drive has been the rise in abortions and female infanticide. The Ministry of Public Health reported that during the five-year period ending in 1984 there were 53 million abortions (equivalent to the population of France).[62] The current figure estimates that one in three pregnancies are terminated by abortions. In response to international criticism of China's population control tactics, the State Family Planning Commission has repeatedly stated that forced abortions are illegal, but it also acknowledges that they occur at the grassroots level because family planning cadres are under pressure to conform with population growth quotas.[63] Although official statistics are not available to specify the prevalence of female infanticide, the sex ratio of reported births reveals significant differences in the number of males and females.[64] As shown in Table 4.2, the "official" number of male births per 100 female births has increased since the family planning campaigns were instituted, and the average sex ratio has reached 1.20 (120 males to 100 females).[65]

The distorted sex ratios are attributed to abortions (ultrasounds are used to identify the gender of the fetus); female infanticide through drowning,

Table 4.2  Male Births per 100 Female Births and Percentage of Unaccounted
Female Births, 1978–2000

| Year | Male Births per 100 Female Births | Percentage of Unaccounted Females Births[a] |
|---|---|---|
| 1978 | 105.9 | 0.2 |
| 1980 | 107.4 | 1.3 |
| 1982 | 107.2 | 1.1 |
| 1984 | 108.5 | 2.4 |
| 1986 | 111.4 | 5.3 |
| 1988 | 112.3 | 6.2 |
| 1990 | 113.8 | 7.7 |
| 1992 | 118.5 | 12.4 |
| 1994 | 116.3 | 10.2 |
| 1996 | 120.0 | 13.7 |
| 1998 | 120.0 | 13.7 |
| 2000 | 120.0 | 13.7 |

*Sources:* S. Johanson and O. Nygren, "The Missing Girls of China: A New Demographic Trend," *Population and Development Review* 17, no. 1 (March 1991): 39; Yi Zeng, Ping Tu, Baochang Gu, Yi Xu, Bohua Li, and Yongping Li, "Causes and Implications of the Recent Increase in the Reported Sex Ratio at Birth in China," *Population and Development Review* 19, no. 2 (June 1993): 283–302; and PRC State Statistical Bureau, *Zhongguo renkou tongji nianjian* (China Population Statistics Yearbook), various years.

*Note:* a. Calculated by author based on the natural sex ratio of 1.055 (105.5 males per 100 females).

poisoning, or desertion; as well as underregistration of female infants, as the PRC birth registration system excludes infants who die within three days of birth.

A less publicized aspect of the family planning policy is its impact on mothers. Delia Davin points out that "women were traditionally held to be responsible for the sex of their infants and, despite attempts at scientific education, this notion persists."[66] The limited number of opportunities to conceive a son thus increases the pressure on women. There are reports that women who bear girls, or are suspected to be pregnant with girls, have been abused by their husbands and in-laws and even murdered.[67] However, short of suicide, the emotional and psychological effects of the policy on mothers and their unwanted daughters has yet to be acknowledged.

From its inception, the family planning policy has faced particular resistance in the rural areas, as it contradicts the economic and cultural incentives of the peasant household to have more than one child.[68] First, under the HRS, peasant incomes rely on the number of workers in the family. Second, a growing proportion of peasant households sell their production on the free market and therefore possess the economic means to finance unauthorized births. Third, for similar motivations, rural women cadres—the key link in enforcing family planning—are finding it more rewarding to cultivate their private plots and increase their earnings than to antagonize neighboring peasant families.[69] Fourth, peasant families choose to keep bearing children until they have at least one son. Due to Confucian, patrilineal practices, sons are assigned more economic value. They remain with the family after marriage and are expected to care for their parents in old age, whereas daughters leave the family and incur dowry expenses upon marriage. Although the policy has been more relaxed in rural areas since 1984—by permitting peasant families to have more than one child if the first-born is a daughter—resistance continues. Couples with one son or two daughters often bear more children, and "village leaders conspire with relatives and friends to conceal 'excess' births from higher authorities."[70] At the same time, the coercive presence of the state in regulating reproduction remains apparent, as evidenced by the increasing distortion in sex ratios shown above.

Although rural households have responded to pressure under the One-Family, One-Child policy by aborting, underreporting, or abandoning their female offspring, economic reform has revived the commoditization of women and children. There has been a resurgence of abduction and trafficking of peasant women, particularly those between the ages of sixteen and twenty-five.[71] They are generally sold into marriage in destitute mountain villages where families cannot afford betrothal gifts and banquets, or kidnapped by gangs and sold into prostitution in urban areas such as the coastal cities and special economic zones where there are fewer women.[72] If the gap in sex ratios continues to expand, or even if they level off at 120 males to 100 females, within one generation the demand for women will probably exacerbate such practices.

## IMPACT AND ANALYSIS

### The Impact of the State on Women

The socialist state has clearly played a significant role in defining gender roles in the economy and society in general. On the basis of standard socioeconomic indicators, the gender gap has decreased substantially under communist rule.[73] Even political representation has improved. The percentage of women deputies in the National People's Congress (NPC) increased from 11.9 percent during the First NPC in 1954 to 21.8 percent during the Ninth NPC in 1998, and the proportion of women members of the Chinese People's Political Consultative Conference grew from 7 percent to 15.5 percent during the same period. This is credited to the decline in female illiteracy from more than 90 percent in 1949 to 23 percent in 1997—and an increase in women with higher education: at year-end 1998, women constituted

38.3 percent of all students in postsecondary institutions. On balance, however, striking gender inequalities remain. Women constitute 70 percent of the 220 million illiterates in China.[74] And political participation at the highest levels is minimal: only one of the five State Councillors is a woman, and only two of the twenty-nine ministers in the State Council are women. No women currently sit on the fourteen-member Politburo, and the Central Committee is only 6.3 percent women.

Despite periodic exaggeration to the contrary, the central government acknowledges that the PRC still faces obstacles before gender equality as envisioned in the socialist ideal can be achieved.[75] Since the United Nations named Beijing as the site of the 1995 Fourth World Conference on Women, apparent efforts to comply with international standards for improving the condition of women have increased.[76] In 1992, the Fifth Session of the Seventh NPC passed the Law on the Protection of Women's Rights and Interests of the PRC, which was drafted with the assistance of Women's Federation branches throughout the country. The 1992 law stipulates the protection of women's rights in the areas of political representation, education, employment, property rights, personal protection, and marriage.[77] And on the eve of the conference itself, Beijing announced a five-year plan—the Program for the Development of Chinese Women (1995–2000)—to improve the status of Chinese women by increasing their access to top government positions, protection from kidnapping, and elimination of female infanticide.[78] However, if the results of the first two decades of socialist rule are any indication, gender equality cannot simply be legislated from above.

The state's limited success in empowering women resonates in part with the paradoxical effects of state policy in other areas. The mass mobilization strategy for agricultural development, for example, relied on cultivating strong provincial-local and cadre-village linkages. These ties have evolved into local clientelistic networks that circumscribe the central government's relative power over rural society, and reform has reinforced this decentralization.[79] Similarly, much of the continuing gender inequality may be traced to the combination of direct state intervention into the household and the contradictions embedded in state policy. But it is important to distinguish between the sources of contradictions in general developmental policies and those that target gender issues. The socialist state placed higher priority on class struggle over gender struggle during the revolutionary phase, as well as modernization over women's empowerment during the postrevolutionary and reform periods. Therefore, the emergence and reinforcement of structural anomalies that inhibit gender equality also reflects the fact that it has not been a central concern. This is apparent in each of the policies that have altered the economic organization of rural society.

For comparative purposes, two policies that exemplify this dynamic are discussed from the Maoist and reform periods, respectively.

First, communization of domestic services was only partially implemented during the collective period and then abandoned. Although the sexual division of labor was maintained—that is, the communal halls were staffed primarily by older women—it represented public recognition of their value-added labor. In addition, communization enabled working-age women to increase their contribution to agricultural output and participate in political activities. It is worth considering the potential long-term impact of domestic service communization if the state had pursued it as rigorously as collectivization.[80] In terms of agricultural output, the communal form of production was an undeniable failure. Peasants lacked the incentive to maximize their efforts due to ceilings on compensation (grain and workpoints) and unrealistic quotas imposed from above.[81] Communal domestic facilities were also deemed to be too expensive. But the methodology for calculating their cost is not clear.[82] If economic value were assigned to the "domestic" services rendered, the dual burden might have been alleviated. Perhaps male peasants would be fighting for workpoint-earning opportunities. The state sanctioned the sexual division of labor in the household and excluded household labor from each according to his labor.

Second, rural reform transferred the collective's authority over production to the household. A regressive consequence of this reform is the strengthening of patriarchal relations in the household. In other words, with increased decisionmaking power, the household continues to define gender in traditional terms and values their roles asymmetrically. Moreover, the concentration of economic authority in the family reinforces the material basis of patrilineal culture. The communal structure had weakened practices of village exogamy whereby women are only temporary members of their natal village and upon marriage join their husbands' villages as outsiders. This disempowering tradition limits the incentives for developing women's nondomestic production skills, as they are viewed as short-term assets.[83] The payment of bride prices represents the transfer of control over a woman's economic productivity from her parents to her husband's family, with no establishment of independent rights to property in either household by the individual woman.[84]

Both decommunization of domestic services and the HRS call into question the state's official commitment to liberating women through mass employment. Rural women were ideologically mobilized to participate in social production, only to be relegated to the sphere of the privatized household and informal sector.[85] The state's actual path of development has not only reinforced traditional biases against women but also obstructed the ability of women to influence their own fates through political participation.

## The Patriarchal State and Household

In the broadest terms, the impediments to women's empowerment and gender equality in China may be attributed to political and economic inconsistencies and feudalistic tradition. But that diagnosis does not identify its etiology. The relationship is not conceptualized fully. It is not clear whether Chinese tradition fuels counterintuitive policies or the other way around and, indeed, whether one exists without the other. Moreover, the interaction between policy and culture requires specification. As proposed previously, the underlying structure that fuels the endurance of gender inequalities may be traced to patriarchy. The primary institutional expressions of patriarchy are the state and the household. Both embody a male-dominated hierarchy that exercises its authority over women through maintaining the sexual division of labor in productive and reproductive relations. In China, patriarchy has demonstrated resilience to changes in economic structure because the processes of gender-norm construction and actualization at the state and household levels are ultimately mutually reinforcing. The patriarchal family defines and values the productive roles within the household in gender-differentiated terms and reproduces members (assuming noncompliance with the one-child policy) in its likeness. The patriarchal state provides incentives for specific relations of production, including the terms of reproduction, and produces a web of party officials and cadres who reproduce the demands of dominant ideology. As in the process of human reproduction, gender is defined, produced, and reproduced by both men and women. But the analogy is misleading. Gender norms are not biologically determined but rather socially constructed and institutionalized through power relations between and within the state and the household.

This is not meant to imply that the state and the household are monolithic agents in an overdetermined system of patriarchy. Although male domination persists, socialist ideology raised the consciousness of women to the existence of their subordinate social valuation. Women did not receive as many workpoints as men for comparable labor in the agricultural commune. Women were encouraged to contribute more to farmwork so that men could pursue more important forms of production. Women were recruited for political activities but then expected to fulfill their domestic responsibilities and serve the patriarchal interests of the state. In each case there were women who attempted to challenge the privileged status of men. But then there were also women enlisted by the party-state to reorient the terms of equality under socialism. In an ironic recognition of the intersubjective synergy between the patriarchal state and household, *Women of China*'s editors wrote the following in response to the resistance of rural women cadres to housework:

Family and state are interdependent and interrelated. For this reason, in China home work and social labor are mutually geared together, and home work is just a part of social labor and plays an important part in socialist construction. . . . If a woman can integrate what little she can do into the great cause of socialist construction and if she has the ideal of working for the happiness of future generations, she would be a noble person, a woman of benefit to the masses, a woman of communist morality.[86]

Even though the articulated interests of women were never a priority, their productive capacity was recognized and molded according to the prevailing patriarchal requirements. The succession of intra-elite power struggles and consequent policy shifts have all produced ideological reverberations that affect gender norms and their institutional reproduction.[87]

## CONCLUSION:
## THEORETICAL IMPLICATIONS

Conceptually, reform marked the Chinese state's shift from a Marxist feminist approach to a liberal feminist approach toward women. Although the preferred economic systems differ, both frameworks rest on the premise that sexual division of labor will dissipate with the integration of women into the waged labor force and supporting legislation. Under both socialism and market-oriented reform, however, the participation of women in economic production has not eradicated gender inequalities in rural China. To be sure, women have experienced relative economic "empowerment" (as have rural households in general), particularly during the first two decades of reform, but constraints exist on the state's ability to command equality.[88] Moreover, the state's developmental priorities have generated contradictions that commodify women while limiting their reproductive freedom. Although the theories are ideal types, China's experience suggests the presence of a deeper obstacle to women's empowerment than state policies or mode of production, namely, institutionalized patriarchy.

Socialist feminists would expect reform to fortify patriarchy due to its capitalist orientation. A patriarchal sexual division of labor facilitates capital accumulation because women are responsible for domestic and subsistence-level production.[89] As predicted, post-Mao reform has strengthened patriarchal relations. The peasant household has regained control over the sexual division of labor in domestic and nondomestic production. The state exercises patriarchal authority over the productive as well as reproductive capacity of women. But it is ahistorical to associate the institutionalization of patriarchal norms solely with capitalist development. Patriarchy predated socialism, endured under socialism, and reconfigured itself under reform.

The socialist state's failure to empower women in a more comprehensive manner reflects the inadequacy of Marx-Engels ideology as a model for feminism.[90] The "first class antagonism" may be between men and women, but the socialist solution is fundamentally class-based, and women are not a distinct class. If they were, then capitalism would only be one manifestation of patriarchy instead of the justification for patriarchy. The prescription would be broader yet focused on the interests of women. Ultimately, the particular expressions of patriarchy have changed alongside changes in the relations of production, but the foundation of a male-dominated hierarchy has been preserved.

This analysis has attempted to highlight the interdependence of the primary patriarchal institutions in society—the state and the household—in limiting women's empowerment and perpetuating gender inequalities. Further research is required to elucidate the prospects for institutional change, that is, social reconstruction or transformation of patriarchal norms. For example, patriarchy may be bounded by its contradictory effects. Within the next generation the demographic trend of distorted sex ratios and over-indulged single children (sons) will have significant repercussions on political, social, and economic relations. Meanwhile, a growing proportion of rural women are engaged in profitable domestic sideline activities while their male counterparts work in urban areas.[91] These women entrepreneurs represent a new stratum in rural China, and their relative autonomy has already inspired Women's Federation[92] and, to a lesser degree, nongovernmental initiatives to increase their access to credit, information, training, and markets.[93] Such efforts undermine patriarchal authority and have proven to be empowering means for legitimizing women's work in the informal sector.[94]

A basic challenge facing women-in-development theorists is how to conceptualize the adaptability of patriarchy to different political and economic structures. In other words, additional research should build toward a theory of patriarchy. To avoid the determinism of Marxist and cultural frameworks, a comparative approach may yield more progressive insights than country-specific studies. This analysis, for example, starts out by questioning the endurance of gender inequalities under socialist rule and concludes that patriarchy is not so much a function of political economic orientation as it is a system itself. The inquiry is driven by apparent gaps in theory, namely, the inability of either state-centered or WID theories alone to explain the persistence of gender inequalities in socialist countries. I have thus examined some of the concrete sources and manifestations of patriarchy in post-1949 rural China to demonstrate its potential for being more than yet another black-box concept. Without additional empirical corroboration, however, alternative interpretations could also be drawn. The starting point is recognizing that patriarchy remains at the same time embedded in societal institutions and constructed by their interaction, versatile yet intransigent. The adaptability of patriarchy represents the main challenge for women's empowerment in China.

## DISCUSSION QUESTIONS

1. To what extent did the Chinese communists truly "liberate" women? Refer specifically to the economic, social, and political spheres in answering this question.

2. Do you think that the Chinese Communist Party could be considered a "feminist" organization? If not, why not? If so, what branch of feminism (liberal, Marxist, socialist) best describes the party's ideology?

3. In what ways did the introduction of the household responsibility system change gender relations in the countryside?

4. Given the large gap between the ideology of gender equality and the practice of gendered policies, does ideology matter? Why or why not?

5. Given the embeddedness of patriarchal norms in China, can you think of policy or other options for enhancing women's empowerment?

## NOTES

1. In this chapter, "communist" refers to the political structures, that is, party and state, dominated by the Communist Party; "socialist" refers to the orientation of the regime in practice since socialism is the stage prior to communism in Marxist historical materialism.

2. In 1846 Marx and Engels wrote, "The first division of labor is that between man and woman for child breeding." Engels later added that the "first class antagonism which appears in history coincides with the development of the antagonism between man and woman in monogamous marriage." Robert C. Tucker, ed., *The Marx-Engels Reader*, 2nd ed. (New York: W. W. Norton, 1978), p. 739. The first quotation is from Marx and Engels, *German Ideology* (1846); Engels developed the argument more fully in *The Origin of the Family, Private Property and the State* (1884; New York: International Publishers, 1972).

3. An earlier version of this chapter was published as "Women and the State in Post-1949 Rural China," *Journal of International Affairs* 49, no. 2 (winter 1996): 493–524. Columbia University provided financial support during the writing of the original article, and the revisions were undertaken under the auspices of the Harvard Academy for International and Area Studies, Emory University, and Johns Hopkins University. The opening quote (Huang Qizao is a woman) is from "Comments On: The Law on the Protection of Women's Rights and Interests," *Zhongguo Funü* (Women of China), in *Women's International Network News* (WIN) 19, no. 1 (winter 1993): 53.

4. The classic articulation of liberal WID theory is Ester Boserup, *Woman's Role in Economic Development* (New York: St. Martin's, 1970), pp. 15–80. Boserup contends that the introduction of technology has created and exacerbated gender differences in agricultural production.

5. Marxist and dependency WID theorists view global capitalism as the structural source of women's exploitation. Examples of this perspective include: June Nash and Maria Patricia Fernandez-Kelly, eds., *Women, Men, and the International Division of Labor* (Albany: State University of New York Press, 1983); and Heleieth Saffioti, *Women in Class Society* (New York: Monthly Review, 1978). They further develop Marx and Engels's association of male domination with the emergence of private property and argue that gender inequalities are maintained to serve the interests of world capitalist elites.

6. During the Cold War, it was popular to depict Marxist-Leninist regimes as monolithic entities, typically led by personal dictatorship, which penetrated every aspect of social and economic life. The extensive structure of the party-state apparatus and its tyrannical means of social control was equated with command capacity.

7. Peter B. Evans, Dietrich Rueschemeyer, and Theda Skocpol, eds., *Bringing the State Back In* (New York: Cambridge University Press, 1985), esp. chapter 11, "On the Road Toward a More Adequate Understanding of the State," pp. 347–365.

8. Vivienne Shue describes this as a "weblike" pattern of relations, as distinguished from the more rigid "honeycomb," that is, cellularized structure of the Marxist-Leninist state. Vivienne Shue, *The Reach of the State* (Stanford: Stanford University Press, 1988), pp. 125–152.

9. For insightful critiques of the use of the household as a unit of analysis in neoclassical developmental economics, see, for example, Partha Dasgupta, *An Inquiry into Well-Being and Destitution* (Oxford: Clarendon, 1995), pp. 135–268, 305–370; Naila Kabeer, *Reversed Realities* (New York: Verso, 1994), pp. 95–135; and Caroline Moser, *Gender Planning and Development* (New York: Routledge, 1993), pp. 15–36. Cf. Daisy Dwyer and Judith Bruce, eds., *A Home Divided: Women and Income in the Third World* (Stanford: Stanford University Press, 1988).

10. Boserup and other liberal feminists note that development reinforces the "dual burden" of women's work, that is, waged labor and continued provision of unpaid household services, which also increases gender wage differentials. Overall, however, liberal feminists do not question the economic rationale behind development; instead, they advocate the integration of women into the development process by increasing their access to credit, technology, and training. Examples include: Marguerite Berger and Mayra Buvinic, *Women's Ventures: Assistance to the Informal Sector in Latin America* (West Hartford, Conn.: Kumarian, 1989); Barbara Rogers, *The Domestication of Women: Discrimination in Developing Societies* (New York: St. Martin's, 1979); and Kate Young, *Planning Development with Women* (Hong Kong: Macmillan, 1993). Rogers's book has been particularly influential in identifying the sources of discrimination against women in development planning.

11. A notable exception is Barbara Wolfe Jancar, *Women Under Communism* (Baltimore: Johns Hopkins University Press, 1978). She posits a "multi-staged evolution of equality" as a function of regime type (highly authoritarian versus pluralistic) and stage of modernization (early versus late), but offers a fundamentally liberal modernization conclusion: in pluralistic modernized societies, "sex-role differentiation gradually disappears" (pp. 206–213).

12. For what is considered the origin of liberal feminist theory, see John Stuart Mill, *On the Subjection of Women* (Greenwich, Conn.: Fawcett, 1970), pp. 91–93. Essentially, legal recognition of women's equality is expected to ameliorate inequality in the household. A more recent discussion is Gay Young, "Gender Inequality and Industrial Development: The Household Connection," *Journal of Comparative Family Studies* 24, no. 1 (spring 1993): 1–20, esp. 8–13. The relationship between modernization and peasant family relationships in Europe is analyzed in

Louise A. Tilly and Joan W. Scott, *Women, Work, and Family* (New York: Holt, Rinehart, and Winston, 1978). At the early stages of industrialization, they note that peasant families attempt to retain traditional roles but then gradually change with increased exposure to new experiences.

13. Socialist feminists extend the Marxist position by highlighting the patriarchal norms embedded in capitalism. Gita Sen and Maria Mies have pioneered the global aspect of this approach. See Gita Sen and Caren Grown, *Development, Crises, and Alternative Visions* (New York: Monthly Review, 1985); and Maria Mies, *Patriarchy and Accumulation on a World Scale* (London: Zed Books, 1986). Other important contributions include: Lourdes Benería, ed., *Women and Development: The Sexual Division of Labor in Rural Societies* (New York: Praeger, 1982); Annette Kuhn and AnnMarie Wolpe, eds., *Feminism and Materialism: Women and Modes of Production* (London: Routledge and Kegan Paul, 1978); and Jane L. Parpart, ed., *Women and Development in Africa: Comparative Perspectives* (Lanham, Md.: University Press of America, 1989).

14. Socialist feminists draw this notion from the work of feminist anthropologists. In particular, see Nancy Chodorow, "Family Structure and Feminine Personality," and Michelle Rosaldo, "Women, Culture and Society," both in Michelle Rosaldo and Louise Lamphere, eds., *Women, Culture, and Society* (Stanford: Stanford University Press, 1974), pp. 44–66, 14–42.

15. Catharine A. MacKinnon, "Feminism, Marxism, Method, and the State: An Agenda for Theory," *Signs* 7, no. 3 (spring 1982): 527.

16. Ibid., p. 328. MacKinnon proposes consciousness-raising as the feminist method. See Catharine A. MacKinnon, *Toward a Feminist Theory of the State* (Cambridge: Harvard University Press, 1989).

17. Although most definitions of "civil society" exclude the household, note that some would include the "intimate sphere" of the family. For example, see Jean Cohen and Andrew Arato's Habermasian formulation, *Civil Society and Political Theory* (Cambridge: MIT Press, 1992).

18. For discussions of women in revolutionary China, see Phyllis Andors, *The Unfinished Liberation of Chinese Women* (Bloomington: Indiana University Press, 1983), pp. 12–28; Elisabeth Croll, *Chinese Women Since Mao* (Armonk: M. E. Sharpe, 1983), pp. 1–22; Delia Davin, *Women-Work, Women, and the Party in Revolutionary China* (Oxford: Clarendon, 1976); Christina Gilmartin, *Engendering the Chinese Revolution: Radical Women, Communist Politics, and Mass Movement in the 1920s* (Berkeley: University of California Press, 1995); Kay Ann Johnson, *Women, the Family, and Peasant Revolution in China* (Chicago: University of Chicago Press, 1983); Marion J. Levy, *The Family Revolution in China* (New York: Octagon, 1971); Judith Stacey, *Patriarchy and Socialist Revolution in China* (Berkeley: University of California Press, 1983); and Roxane Witke and Margery Wolf, eds., *Women in Chinese Society* (Stanford: Stanford University Press, 1975).

19. Mao recognized the oppression of women as a function of other oppressive systems of authority in Chinese society: "political authority, clan authority, theocratic authority, and authority of the husband represent the whole ideology and institution of feudalism and patriarchy, and are the four great cords that have bound the Chinese people and in particular the peasants." Socialist transition would destroy these authority systems. See "Investigation into the Peasant Movement in Hunan," in *Selected Works of Mao Zedong*, vol. 1, pp. 46–47, cited in Andors, *The Unfinished Liberation of Chinese Women*, p. 22.

20. Mao echoed Engels's contention that women must participate in public production to achieve gender equality. Engels wrote, "The emancipation of women will

be possible when women can take part in production on a large social scale, and do-mestic work no longer claims anything but an insignificant amount of her time." Engels, *The Origin,* p. 46.

21. As an organization for developing and implementing party policies relating to women, the ACWF and its local branches never represented the articulated inter-ests of women in society. Rather, its mandates were and continue to be defined from the center as a function of broader goals.

22. Mass campaigns to implement the new marriage law usually followed the land reform campaigns in the countryside.

23. In the ideal patrilineal society, Confucian mores require women to obey their husbands and sons, expect women to remain pure and virtuous, and forbid widows from remarrying.

24. Marimus Johan Meijer, *Marriage Law and Policy in the Chinese People's Republic* (Hong Kong: Hong Kong University Press, 1971), pp. 112–114.

25. Andors, *The Unfinished Liberation of Chinese Women,* p. 35.

26. In traditional Chinese society, men were entitled to file for divorce based on the following Seven Conditions: failure to bear sons, adultery, lack of respect for parents-in-law, excessive gossiping, stealing, jealousy, or disease. A woman had no right to divorce and was expected to comply with the demands of her husband and his family. In practice, divorce was rare and considered scandalous. See Ta Chen, *Zhongguo Funü Shenghuo Shi* (History of the Livelihood of Chinese Women) (Shanghai: Commercial Press, 1937).

27. The directives, however, did not mention the participation of urban women. Andors, *The Unfinished Liberation of Chinese Women,* p. 40.

28. Editorial, "Mobilize Women to Join the Cooperativization Movement," *Renmin Ribao* (*RMRB,* or *People's Daily*) (November 5, 1955), pp. 14–17. Collec-tivization was formally launched in October 1955.

29. In 1955 ACWF chair Liu Shaoqi led a brief campaign in urban areas that glorified housework as the proper domain of women. Davin, *Women-Work,* p. 66.

30. Editorial, "Safeguard the Health of Women and Children in Rural Areas," *RMRB* (May 16, 1956).

31. Such a broad attempt at collectivizing domestic services has not occurred in other socialist countries. Croll, *Chinese Women Since Mao,* p. 25.

32. Davin, *Women-Work,* pp. 145–146.

33. Elisabeth Croll, "The Sexual Division of Labor in Rural China," in Lour-des Benería, ed., *Women and Development: The Sexual Division of Labor in Rural Societies* (New York: Praeger, 1982), pp. 228–229.

34. *New China News Analysis* (*NCNA*), January 1, 1959, cited in ibid., p. 230.

35. *People's Daily,* March 16, 1950; *NCNA,* September 22, 1959, and July 31, 1958. The Great Leap represented the peak demand for women's work in agricul-ture. Furthermore, the reliability of these "official" statistics is questionable. They probably reflect the percentage of women engaged in part-time and full-time pro-duction.

36. In villages with strong women's federations, women were able to call mass meetings of the commune to discuss the problem. Although parity in workpoints was not achieved, the average wages for women's labor were raised by one or two points, for example, from 4.5 to 6.5, *RMRB,* April 9, 1960. See also Andors, *The Unfinished Liberation of Chinese Women,* pp. 57–60.

37. For example, see Isabel Crook and David Crook, *The First Years of Yangyi Commune* (London: Routledge and Kegan Paul, 1966), pp. 126–129; cited in Croll, "The Sexual Division of Labor," p. 234.

38. See William L. Parish and Martin K. Whyte, *Village and Family in Contemporary China* (Chicago: University of Chicago Press, 1978), p. 202.

39. An insightful collection of articles is Sharon L. Wolchik and Alfred G. Meyer, *Women, State, and Party in Eastern Europe* (Durham, N.C.: Duke University Press, 1985).

40. Jancar, *Women Under Communism,* p. 108.

41. *Beijing Review* (April 30, 1969), pp. 41–48.

42. *RMRB*, March 6, 1972; *Beijing Review* (July 19–25, 1993).

43. During the Cultural Revolution, local women's federations continued to play an active role in mobilizing women in rural areas. However, women's issues were relatively peripheral to official ideology until the Anti–Lin Biao and Confucius Campaign in 1973. *Zhongguo Funü* (Women of China) limited its discussion to general development issues; and the ACWF was even disbanded for seven years (1966–1973) during a political struggle to purge it of "revisionist" elements. See Elisabeth Croll, "The Movement to Criticize Confucius and Lin Piao: A Comment on the Women of China" *Signs* 2, no. 3 (spring 1977): 721–726; and Fu Wen, "Doctrine of Confucius and Mencius the Shackle That Keeps Women in Bondage," *Beijing Review* (March 8, 1974), pp. 16–18.

44. A variety of responsibility systems exist, ranging from those that "contract" specific production tasks to small work teams or individual laborers, to those in which output or land is contracted to households. The dominance of the latter form has undermined the collective structure.

45. For an empirical study, see Richard E. Barrett, William P. Bridges, Moshe Semyonov, and Xiaoyuan Gao, "Female Labor Force Participation in Urban and Rural China," *Rural Sociology* 56, no. 1 (spring 1991): 1–21. The government claims that nearly one-third of the specialized households are headed by women and that 42 percent of the 85 million rural workforce in township enterprises are women. Committee on Elimination of Discrimination Against Women, *The Status of Women in China,* 11th sess. (Vienna, Austria, CEDAW, January 23, 1993), p. 26; and *WIN News* (autumn 1992): 56. Surveys conducted in the 1920s and 1930s indicate that only 1–8 percent of all rural households were headed by women. See Ta Chen and Penwen Sun, "Population," in *Chinese Economic Yearbook,* 2nd ed. (Shanghai: Commercial Press, 1935), pp. 8–12, cited in Parish and Whyte, *Village and Family in Contemporary China,* p. 135, n. 9. Based on a small sample ($n = 131$) in the Guangdong province, Parish and Whyte estimate that in 1973 15 percent of rural households were headed by women.

46. Croll, *Chinese Women Since Mao,* p. 28.

47. This is consistent with Boserup's findings. See Feng Xiaoshuang, "The Costs and Benefits of Rural-Urban Migration—A Report on an Inquiry Conducted Among Rural Women Employed in the Service, Retail, and Other Trades in Beijing," *Social Sciences in China* 18, no. 4 (winter 1997): 52–65, trans. Huang Shiqi, orig. published in *Zhejiang Xuekan* (Zhejiang Academic Studies) 6 (1996); and Meng Xianfan, "'Men in Nonagricultural Occupations and Women on the Land' and the Development of Women," *Social Sciences in China* 17, no. 1 (spring 1997): 78–82, trans. Xiao Xiaomao, orig. in *Shehui kexue zhanxian* (Social Sciences) 1 (1995). Note, however, that male out-migration and the broader sexual division of labor in the rural economy have also enabled women to express agency in organizing their economic activities. See Ellen R. Judd, *Gender and Power in Rural North China* (Stanford: Stanford University Press, 1994); Kellee S. Tsai, "Banquet Banking: Gender and Rotating Savings and Credit Associations in South China," *China Quarterly* 161 (March 2000): 142–170; and Kate Xiao Zhou, *How the Farmers Changed*

*China: Power of the People* (Boulder: Westview, 1996), pp. 206–230. Zhou also discusses rural women migrants at pp. 218–222. For an argument that substantial gender differences do not exist in migratory patterns, see Delia Davin, "Gender and Migration in China," in Flemming Christiansen and Zhang Junzuo, eds., *Village Inc.: Chinese Rural Society in the 1990s* (Surrey, U.K.: Curzon, 1998), pp. 230–240.

48. Croll, *Chinese Women Since Mao,* pp. 31–32. Cf. Tamara Jacka, *Women's Work in Rural China: Change and Continuity in an Era of Reform* (New York: Cambridge University Press, 1997), esp. pp. 120–161.

49. For sample success stories, see Huang Wei, "Rural Women and Reform," *Beijing Review* (December 6, 1992), pp. 21–22; "Rural Women Come Into Their Own," *Beijing Review* (March 9, 1987), pp. 24–26; "Rural Women Gain Economic Status," *Beijing Review* (October 15, 1984), pp. 9–10; Xuan Fenghua and Chen Yao, "Jiangxi Women Contribute to Rural Economy," *NCNA*, August 13, 1990, p. 1; "Status of Rural Women Improves with Reforms," *NCNA*, November 6, 1987, in Foreign Broadcast Information Service, FBIS-CHI-87–215, p. 20. In an empirical study, Marshall Johnson, William L. Parish, and Elizabeth Lin conclude that foreign market exposure had a positive effect on women's wage-earning opportunities before 1949 and does not adversely affect their position in the post-Mao era. "Chinese Women, Rural Society, and External Markets," *Economic Development and Cultural Change* 35, no. 2 (January 1987): 257–278. Dependency theorists would disagree.

50. Croll, *Chinese Women Since Mao;* Jacka, *Women's Work in Rural China.*

51. "Status of Rural Women Improves With Reforms," *NCNA,* November 6, 1987, in FBIS-CHI-87–215, p. 20.

52. Wu Naito, "Changes in Chinese Women's Social Status," *Beijing Review* 34, no. 52 (December 31, 1991–January 5, 1992), pp. 22–23.

53. Zhongguo shehui kexueyuan renkou yanjiusuo (Institute of Population Studies, Chinese Academy of Social Sciences), *Dangdai zhongguo funu diwei chouyan diaocha ziliao* (Sampling Survey Data of Women's Status in Contemporary China) (Beijing: International Academic Publishers, 1994), p. 278. A summary analysis of this survey and one conducted by the All-China Women's Federation in 1990 is Jean K.M. Hung, "The Family Status of Chinese Women in the 1990s," in Lo Chi Kin, Suzanne Pepper, and Tsai Kai Yuen, eds., *China Review 1995* (Sha Tin, New Territories, Hong Kong: Chinese University Press, 1995), 12.2–12.24.

54. Kellee S. Tsai, *Banking Behind the State: Private Entrepreneurs and the Political Economy of Informal Finance in China, 1978–1998,* Ph.D. diss., Columbia University, New York, 1999.

55. Nahid Aslanbeigui and Gale Summerfield, "Impact of the Responsibility System on Women in Rural China: An Application of Sen's Theory of Entitlements," *World Development* 17, no. 3 (1989): 343–350. They employ Amartya Sen's theory of entitlements to illustrate that a woman's controllable income may differ from her contribution to production inside and outside the household.

56. Croll, *Chinese Women Since Mao,* p. 36. In their prereform study, Parish and Whyte found that although Hakka women never bound their feet, were traditionally more active in agriculture, and play a prominent role in cultivating income-generating private plots, they are less likely than women in non-Hakka villages to manage family finances; Parish and Whyte, *Village and Family in Contemporary China,* pp. 26, 207, 238.

57. Previous initiatives to limit population growth occurred in 1953, 1962, and 1971. Judith Banister, "Population Policy and Trends in China, 1978–83," *China Quarterly* 100 (December 1984): 717–722; Tyrene White, "Implementing the 'One-Child-per-Couple' Population Program in Rural China: National Goals and Local

Politics," in David M. Lampton, ed., *Policy Implementation in Post-Mao China* (Berkeley: University of California Press, 1987), pp. 284–317.

58. Since China accounts for 22 percent of the world's population with only 7.3 percent of its land, and only 15 percent of the land is arable, Deng's diagnosis in 1979 was not unreasonable. But the identified solution was too narrow in focus since the regime failed to address the fact that due to environmental mismanagement, an additional third of China's farmland would become unarable over the next generation. See Vaclav Smil, *The Bad Earth: Environmental Degradation in China* (Armonk, N.Y.: M. E. Sharpe, 1983).

59. Total family income is reduced by 5–10 percent over a period of ten to sixteen years after birth. For the third or fourth child, the levy can be as high as 15–20 percent of the couple's income.

60. Andors, *The Unfinished Liberation of Chinese Women*, p. 52; Croll, *Chinese Women Since Mao*, p. 90.

61. Croll, *Chinese Women Since Mao*, p. 89.

62. Jeff Somer, "China Denies Reports of Forced Abortions," *Newsday*, April 4, 1985, p. 15; Sheryl WuDunn, "China, with Ever More to Feed, Pushes Anew for Small Families," *New York Times*, June 16, 1991, p. A1.

63. See, for example, "Official Says State Opposes Forced Abortion," *NCNA*, October 29, 1998, reported in FBIS-TEN-98–302.

64. Jack Anderson and Dale Van Atta, "Infanticide Continues in Rural China," *Washington Post*, October 24, 1991, p. B23. Nicholas Kristof, "A Mystery from China's Census: Where Have Young Girls Gone?" *New York Times*, June 17, 1991, p. A1; "The Lost Girls," *Economist* 328 (September 18, 1993), p. 38. For a dissenting view based on a study of the minorities' fertility patterns, see Barbara A. Anderson and Brian D. Silver, "Ethnic Differences in Fertility and Sex Ratios at Birth in China: Evidence from Xinjiang," *Population Studies* 49, no. 2 (July 1995): 221–226. One source estimates that sex ratios may be as high as 130 or 140 males to 100 females in rural areas. Anna Maria Gillis, "Sex Selection and Demographics," *BioScience* 45, no. 6 (June 1995): 384–385.

65. Sex ratios from the 1953, 1964, and 1982 censuses are 107.0, 106.2, and 107.1. Zeng Yi et al., "Causes and Implications of the Recent Increase in the Reported Sex Ratio at Birth in China," *Population and Development Review* 19, no. 3 (June 1993): 283–302.

66. Delia Davin, "Gender and Population in the People's Republic of China," in Haleh Afshar, *Women, State, and Ideology: Studies from Africa and Asia* (London: Macmillan, 1987), pp. 111–129. An example of a man who abused his wife after she bore a daughter but reformed his ways after learning that he contributed to the sex of the child, is Wu Jinbo, "Wo cuo guai le ta" (I Mistakenly Blame Her), *Zhongguo Funü* (Women of China), October 10, 1982, p. 42, cited in Emily Honig and Gail Hershatter, *Personal Voices: Chinese Women in the 1980s* (Stanford: Stanford University Press, 1988), pp. 204–205. Davin, "Gender and Population in the People's Republic of China," p. 118; Honig and Hershatter, p. 294; and Margery Wolf, *Revolution Postponed: Women in Contemporary China* (Stanford: Stanford University Press, 1985), p. 258.

67. Davin, "Gender and Population in the People's Republic of China," p. 118; Honig and Hershatter, *Personal Voices*, p. 294; and Wolf, *Revolution Postponed*, p. 258.

68. Although overall national birthrates have declined, they have actually increased in rural areas. For example, in 1981 more than 90 percent of the 20.7 million births were from rural areas; and birthrates are generally 50 percent higher in rural than in urban areas. John P. Burns and Stanley Rosen, eds., *Policy Conflicts*

*in Post-Mao China* (Armonk, N.Y.: M. E. Sharpe, 1984), p. 337 and n. 1. See also Tan Keijian, "Inaccurate Population and Family Planning Statistics," *Renkou yu jingji* (Population and Economy), no. 109 (July 25, 1998): 28–31; Jie Zhenming, "Why Do People Emphasize Male Children Over Female?" *Renkou yu jingji* (Population and Economy), no. 109 (July 25, 1998): 56–61; and Zhou, *How the Farmers Changed China,* pp. 176–205.

69. In attempting to enforce the family planning policy, some rural women's cadres face threats of abuse or assault. Su Suining, "There Are Many Causes of Strained Relations Between Cadres and Masses in the Rural Areas," *Nongmin Ribao*, September 26, 1988, p. 1, cited in White, "Implementing the 'One-Child-per-Couple' Population Program," p. 61.

70. White, "Implementing the 'One-Child-per-Couple' Population Program," p. 63. One case study of Hebei finds that if the daughter-only stipulation for second births were lifted, only 20 percent of the couples would actually have another child. Jiali Li, "China's One-Child Policy: A Case Study of Hebei Province, 1979–88," *Population and Development Review* 21, no. 3 (September 1995): 563–585.

71. Along with the family planning policy, this issue has attracted much attention in the Western press. For example, see Louise Branson, "Sales of Women and Children Recurring in Chinese Provinces," *San Francisco Chronicle,* August 21, 1989, p. A14. The New China News Agency reports that girls under the age of eighteen account for 60 percent of the abductions. In addition, the number of officially reported cases of abduction and selling of women and children has declined from more than 20,000 cases in 1992 to 6,000 in 1997. "Ministry Official on Women, Children Abductions," *NCNA*, November 13, 1998, reported in FBIS-CHI-98–317.

72. Most of the kidnapping victims are from the poorer parts of Yunnan, Sichuan, Guizhou, Hunan, Hebei, and Guangxi and sold in Zhejiang, Jiangxi, and Shanxi provinces and Inner Mongolia.

73. Information Office of the State Council of the People's Republic of China, "Fifty Years of Progress in China's Human Rights," Beijing, June 2000, section 4 ("Protection of the Rights of Women and Children").

74. Farhana Haque Rahman, *The Status of Rural Women in China* (Beijing: International Fund for Agricultural Development, 1994), p. 62. The ACWF holds programs in the countryside to reduce female illiteracy and increase technical knowledge. See Huang Wei, "Rural Women and Reform," *Beijing Review* 35, no. 48 (November 30–December 6, 1992): 21–22; and Zhang Zhaowen, "Eliminating Female Illiteracy in China," *Beijing Review* (August 13–19, 1990), p. 33.

75. Huang Qizao, Sichuan province NPC deputy, vice president, and first member of the Secretariat of the ACWF, notes, "China is still in its initial stage of socialism . . . and still has a long way to go before realizing the goal of sexual equality, the securement of women's rights and interests and giving full play to women's role in society." *WIN News* (winter 1993): 53.

76. For example, as a signator of CEDAW, the PRC is required to submit comprehensive status reports every four years. In 1992 China finally submitted a report, which was five years late. Furthermore, in September 1990, the ACWF and the State Statistical Bureau jointly surveyed more than 40,000 men and women in twenty-one provinces, autonomous regions, and municipalities to determine social attitudes toward women. This was the first national survey of its type. Since then, several provincial-level surveys have also been undertaken.

77. Lisa Stearns, "The New Chinese Women's Law," *Women's News Digest* (Hong Kong: Association for the Advancement of Feminism, 1993); and "The Law

on the Protection of Women's Rights and Interests," *Zhongguo Funü* (Women of China) in *WIN News* (winter 1993).

78. The program is summarized in UNDP Beijing, *Gender and Development in China* (Beijing: UNDP, 1998), pp. 7–10.

79. Many China scholars have made this observation. For example, see Cheng Li and David Bachman, "Localism, Elitism, and Immobilism: Elite Formation and Social Change in Post-Mao China," *World Politics* 42, no. 1 (October 1989): 64–94; Lampton, *Policy Implementation in Post-Mao China;* Andrew J. Nathan, "China's Path From Communism," *Journal of Democracy* 4, no. 2 (April 1993): 30–42; Jean Oi, "Fiscal Reform and the Economic Foundations of Local State Corporatism in China," *World Politics* 45, no. 1 (October 1992): 99–126; Elizabeth J. Perry and Christine Wong, eds., *The Political Economy of Reform in Post-Mao China* (Cambridge: Harvard Contemporary China Series, 1985), no. 2, part 1.

80. Laurel Kendall has pointed out to me that attempts in other contexts (such as the Israeli kibbutz system and utopian communities) have generally been resisted. Nonetheless, I am still inclined to pose the hypothetical scenario with perhaps the overly optimistic implication that the full application of Mao-style mass mobilizational tactics might have yielded different results. For example, during the Cultural Revolution, the party-state did succeed in inverting the traditional social hierarchy whereby intellectuals and bureaucrats were relegated to the lowest tier.

81. Jean Oi, *State and Peasant in Contemporary China: The Political Economy of Village Government* (Berkeley: University of California Press, 1989).

82. Benería discusses the significance of accounting for "use-value" as well as "exchange-value" production in the economy. Conventional labor force concepts only measure production for exchange instead of production that involves the satisfaction of basic human needs. In statistics, "active labor" should include all workers engaged in use-value as well as exchange-value production, which includes all activities such as household production and all types of subsistence production. See Lourdes Benería, "Accounting for Women's Work," in Benería, ed., *Women and Development: The Sexual Division of Labor in Rural Societies* (New York: Praeger, 1982), pp. 119–147. Boserup was one of the first WID theorists to point out that statistics on production and income usually omit "the subsistence activities which are largely women's work," p. 165. Cf. Dasgupta, *An Inquiry.*

83. Gates traces the commoditization of women back to the Song Dynasty (A.D. 960–1279). Under the petty capitalist mode of production, the patriarchal family became the primary unit of production, and the male head of the household sold female kin into marriage, adoption, slavery, or prostitution. Gates argues that commodization emerged with the new class of neo-Confucian bureaucrats who emphasized patrilineal family production over that of individual labor. Hill Gates, *China's Motor: A Thousand Years of Petty Capitalism* (Ithaca: Cornell University Press, 1996).

84. Low divorce rates in rural China have been attributed to the endurance of arranged marriages and the payment of bride prices. One study reveals that men are reluctant to initiate divorce because they fear the loss of their bride price "investment." See Cailian Liao and Tim B. Heaton, "Divorce Trends and Differentials in China," *Journal of Comparative Family Studies* 23, no. 3 (autumn 1992): 413–429.

85. Some claim, however, that rural women are not better off than their urban counterparts who are being laid off by state-owned enterprises. See Kate Xiao Zhou, "Women Divided," *Harvard International Review* 20, no. 1 (winter 1997/1998): 24–28.

86. *Zhongguo Funü* (Women of China), February 1, 1958, in Andors, *Women-Work*, p. 46.

87. Jean Lock argues that political ideology in post-1949 China has succeeded in eliminating disparities in gender-role expectations. But she relies solely on official documents and literary references to support her position. See "The Effect of Ideology in Gender Role Definition: China as a Case Study," *Journal of Asian and African Studies* 24, nos. 3–4 (1989): 228–238. For an analysis of PRC legislation that institutionalizes discrimination against women, see Ann D. Jordan, "Women's Rights in the PRC: Patriarchal Wine Poured from a Socialist Bottle," *Journal of Chinese Law* 8 (spring 1994): 47–104.

88. Note, however, that legislative efforts to protect the rights and interests of women and children continue. See Ronald C. Keith, "Legislating Women's and Children's 'Rights and Interests' in the PRC," *China Quarterly* 149 (March 1997): 29–55.

89. They reason that costs are suppressed for the "reproduction of labor power" and for marketable consumer commodities. Mies, *Patriarchy and Accumulation on a World Scale,* p. 184. From an economic perspective, however, it is debatable whether the long-term interests of capitalist development are served by excluding domestic services from marketization. Although it is beyond the scope of this chapter to explore the issue in detail, a capitalist case could be made for the industrialization of domestic services that is apparent to a certain degree in advanced industrialized countries.

90. For feminist critiques of Marx-Engels theory, see Heidi I. Harmann, "The Unhappy Marriage of Marxism and Feminism: Towards a More Progressive Union," in Lydia Sargent, ed., *Women and Revolution* (Boston: South End, 1981); Allison M. Jaggar, "Problems for the Marxist Conception of Human Nature," in Jaggar, ed., *Feminist Politics and Human Nature* (Sussex: Harvester Press, 1983), pp. 69–82; and MacKinnon, *Toward a Feminist Theory of the State,* pp. 13–36.

91. As of 1995, the Ministry of Labor estimated that women constituted 80 percent of the active agricultural labor force. UNDP Beijing, *China Human Development Report 1997* (Beijing: UNDP, 1998), p. 49.

92. The changing role of the ACWF is discussed in Jude Howell, "The Struggle for Survival: Prospects for the Women's Federation in Post-Mao China," *World Development* 24, no. 1 (January 1996): 129–144.

93. For a guide to internationally supported gender and development activities, see UNDP Beijing, *Gender and Development in China: A Compendium of Gender and Development Projects Supported by International Donors* (Beijing: UNDP, 1998). The Ford Foundation in Beijing has also compiled a list of Chinese NGOs run by women; see Ford Foundation, *Interim Directory of Chinese Women's Organizations* (Beijing: Ford Foundation, August 1995).

94. At the grassroots level, rural credit programs noted for their reach and impact on women include Grameen Bank in Bangladesh, Kupedes in Indonesia, and Self-Employed Women's Association Bank in India. Such indigenous NGOs have enabled poor, often illiterate female entrepreneurs to expand their businesses beyond subsistence levels. Numerous Grameen Bank replications and related microfinance projects are under way in China. They are summarized in Asia Pacific Development Research Center, *China Development Briefing,* no. 3 (October 1996, Hong Kong).

# 5

# The State, Development, and Empowerment in India

## REKHA DATTA

In this chapter I argue that state policies can provide an enabling environment for empowerment when successfully integrated with international and grassroots initiatives. My focus will be on national policies, which combine economic and political aspects of development, leading to empowerment of women.[1] This is a case study of India, one of the most enigmatic of developing countries in South Asia. I seek to establish the importance and effectiveness of state policies that seek gender transformation and contribute to the process of empowerment. My goal in this chapter is to analyze the data that is available now to make an assessment of whether the government has undertaken gender transformative policies and what their impact has been. In other words, I analyze whether such policies have generated greater economic activity, health care opportunities, literacy, and decisionmaking ability for women—essential aspects of the process of gender empowerment.

## EMPOWERMENT AND DEVELOPMENT: AN INTERRELATED PHENOMENON

The notion of gender empowerment is closely related to that of gender and development. Although it is customary to consider the economic and political aspects of development, since roughly 1990 there has been a shift toward a more comprehensive definition of development, culminating in the notion of human development. According to the *United Nations Human Development Report* of 1993,

> Human Development is a process of enlarging people's choices. In principle, these choices can be infinite and change over time. But at all levels

of development, the three essential areas are for people to lead a long and healthy life, to acquire knowledge, and [to] have access to resource needs for a decent standard of living. If these choices are not available, many other opportunities remain inaccessible.[2]

First introduced in the *Human Development Report* of 1990, the Human Development Index (HDI) is a composite index that measures human development. It measures longevity by life expectancy, knowledge by examining adult literacy and mean years of schooling, and standard of living by purchasing power based on real gross domestic product per capita adjusted for the cost of living.

To be sure, this broader definition of development, which includes various aspects of human development and the security among people that comes from it, is particularly valuable in the rapidly changing international climate. One of the major aims of HDI is to determine the nature of development that evolves from various policies and whether or not human beings feel secure in their work, health, and education. The underlying aim is to empower human beings, create opportunities for them to participate in interstate cooperation, and create a global climate more conducive to a people-centered world order.

Coupled with this is the initiative of women in development (WID). Since the 1970s WID literature has demonstrated how development actually weakened the status of women in many traditional societies.[3] Therefore, over recent decades, researchers, policy analysts, governments, and international organizations have emphasized the need to examine and reassess how development affects women in developing societies.[4] The United Nations (UN) declared 1975 as the Year of the Woman and the decade 1976–1985 as the UN Decade for Women: Equality, Development, Peace. The International Conference for Women addressed similar issues once again in Beijing in September 1995 and at the Beijing +5 Conference in 2000 in New York. With comprehensive data available recently from the United Nations, it is possible to compare experiences of men and women, and of women across countries, spanning decades of development.[5]

All of this culminates in a realization that development concerns ought to focus on people's needs.[6] Development priorities, therefore, need to emphasize a comprehensive outlook. Within the purview of this expanded notion of development priorities, it is crucial that we assess how development policies affect the status of women and whether they empower or disempower them.

## From Development to Empowerment

Embedded in the notion of empowerment is power. Power is situational and relational. The fundamental notion of power implies a relational context—

that is, individual or group.[7] In social relations, power has to be considered in gendered terms. Increased power of women will be reflected in their increased decisionmaking authority in family and community affairs. Empowerment thus becomes instrumental in changing the relationship of women vis-à-vis men in society. This notion of empowerment follows from the WID literature. According to this view, women become "empowered" to participate in the development process.[8] This does not clearly answer the question "Who empowers women?"—it implies structural changes in the labor market and in the decisionmaking process, which lead to women's empowerment.

Noted researcher and development expert Caroline Moser argues that empowerment can only occur through a bottom-up mobilization. Success of programs to empower women depends on participation by women. Nongovernmental organizations (NGOs) can make gender planning successful because they can reach the grassroots, where real people are.[9] Another researcher, Naila Kabeer, supports this view. According to Kabeer,

> Because there are risks and costs incurred in any process of change, such change must be believed in, initiated, and directed by those whose interests it is meant to serve. Empowerment cannot be given, it must be self-generated. All that a gender-transformation policy can hope to do is to provide women with the enabling resources which will allow them to take greater control of their own lives, to determine what kinds of gender relations they would want to live within, and to devise strategies and alliances to help them get there.[10]

This approach recognizes that gender-transformative policies provide women with the necessary resources, which they can use to empower themselves. Therefore, it becomes necessary to examine whether national governments are providing women those resources.

In this chapter I argue that empowerment can be effective as a complex, composite whole—integrating grassroots activism, national policies, and international efforts. As such, the role of women's groups, NGOs, and movement politics needs to be examined alongside the role that the state and international agencies play in generating empowerment. Empowerment occurs at several levels, and these dimensions must be incorporated in any comprehensive analysis of women's empowerment.[11] Thus, while recognizing that policies alone do not lead to empowerment it is necessary to examine whether national policies have set the groundwork leading to empowerment.

## The State, Development, and Women's Empowerment

One of the fundamental aspects of empowerment is equality. If we consider the relational aspect of power, it is the absence of equality among men and women that creates disempowerment of women. Marx's idea of income distribution leading to inequality in capitalist societies was based on an assessment of the "ability" and "needs" of each.[12] Social theorists have recently expanded this and related notions of inequality by including "capabilities" and "functionings." According to Amartya Sen, "Functionings represent parts of the state of a person—in particular the various things that he or she manages to do or be in leading a life. The capability of a person reflects that alternative combinations of functionings the person can achieve, and from which he or she can choose one collection."[13]

Accordingly, gender as a social construct assigns different degrees of freedom and equality to women in most societies. Such differences rest on many attributes, including nutrition, education, mortality, wealth, and so on.[14] In this chapter I therefore seek to include equality in the process of development. More specifically, I focus on the question of whether women in India have become empowered as a result of government policies in the following basic areas: women and the economy; women and education; health and environment; and leadership and decisionmaking. These are also attributes that enable both the rise in capabilities and functionings of women amid challenges of "functionings" as manifest in economic capacity and health, and "capabilities" that accrue from greater power in these areas reinforced by literacy and decisionmaking abilities. It is not easy to separate these categories, as empowerment often occurs as a composite of these basic factors in the development process.

There are several ways to examine the role of states with regard to human development and gender equality. One can look at specific policies that states make, which affect the status of women. Such policies are in areas such as: family planning, property ownership, women's education, and the like. These issues, allowing for specific policy evaluation, may be gender neutral, that is, they may not give a true picture of whether women have become empowered as a result of development.

Alternatively, one can look specifically at how development policies have affected women. Often, development policies (i.e., policies including structural adjustment, welfare and health care reform, etc.) determine whether or not states are mindful of the effect they have on the status of women. This is the thrust of my analysis in this chapter. Instead of looking exclusively at policies, I will also explore policy ramifications in broad areas that reflect development and how women fare in that scenario.

India is full of contrasts. It is a country that has lagged far behind in growth rates for the most part of its independent history since 1947. India ranks 134th among 173 countries on the HDI.[15] It prides itself as a stable democracy in the developing world but has often ignored the legitimate claims of women. In 1986, for example, under Rajiv Gandhi, one of India's most liberal prime ministers, a law prohibiting divorced Muslim women from demanding alimony came into effect. This measure was undertaken and sided with by the government to appease rising discontent among fundamentalists with the government. Other than protests from women's groups and activists, this measure did not see much widespread opposition. In this case, political and electoral considerations became more important than the implications of the policy on Muslim women and their status in society. The consideration was that if Gandhi alienated the fundamentalists, his party would lose Muslim votes. Such policies surely jeopardize women's empowerment and other government efforts aimed at ensuring gender equality.

## WOMEN, THE STATE, AND DEVELOPMENT IN INDIA: HISTORICAL OVERVIEW

The status of women in India is intertwined with socioeconomic and political hierarchies. Since the Vedic times, women have received different status depending on class and caste hierarchies.[16] There are varying accounts about the status of women in the early and later Vedic period; most studies indicate that there was a gradual decline in the sociopolitical and economic status of women.

Subsequently, the colonial government during British rule was not keen in creating an infrastructure per se but contributed to several social legislations that positively affected the status of women. Two such examples: Widow remarriage was permitted in 1854, and *sati,* the practice of burning wives along with their deceased husbands, was banned in 1859. Even though the British government was instrumental in passing these laws, it alone, by no means, initiated the reforms. Several indigenous leaders and social reformers, Vidyasagar and Raja Ram Mohun Roy, for example, spearheaded the reforms. Women played an important part in the struggle for national liberation, even though they were not at the forefront of the struggle in large numbers. Mahatma Gandhi was the first national leader who included and gave women a prominent role in the freedom movement. Gandhi believed that a nation advances as much as its women do.[17]

This belief was translated into the new constitution of independent India, which took effect in 1950. Article 15(3), by emphasizing that the state can make special provision for women and children, created the basis for affirmative action to improve the status of women. Education and women's reproductive health concerns were addressed by subsequent plans, but the gains were not obvious. In 1971, the Committee on the Status of Women was appointed to evaluate the status of women. In 1975, in conjunction with the international Year of the Woman, the Status of Women Committee issued a report on the status of women in independent India.

This report highlighted that even though in absolute numbers there were more educated women in India than in the past, women were not adequately represented in the economic sector and in public life. Between 1911 and 1971, women's employment in the organized sector fell from 34.4 percent to 17.3 percent.[18] (According to the Employment Review of 1972–1973, the growth rate in women employees was 9.5 percent as compared to 5.6 percent the previous year.) Furthermore, there was a "visible link between female poverty and the depressing demographic trends of the declining female-male sex ratio, lower life expectancy, higher infant and maternal mortality, declining work participation, and rising rates of illiteracy and immigration among women."[19] Subsequent policy evaluations demonstrated that a major problem remained the difficulty of reaching poor women. In 1985, the government introduced the Department of Women and Child Development within the Ministry of Human Resources Development. The department was to oversee the implementation of programs geared toward welfare of women. Since 1992, a monitoring body, the National Commission on Women, has been entrusted with promoting and guaranteeing women's rights.[20]

Thus, the government of India was willing to take the necessary policy initiatives in order to empower women. What it lacked at that point was the awareness that the roots of women's inequality were widespread and complex, permeating areas of work, cultural beliefs, education, health, and environment. Consequently, structural changes within the policy framework were not sufficient in bringing empowerment to women; a much more entrenched approach was needed.

## Women and the Economy:
## Wages, Employment, and Empowerment

For a long time, women's work or contribution in the economy was either largely ignored or dismissed, for traditionally women worked in the informal sector and within the household. Women were not considered to be economically active. What is "economic activity"? Is housework an economic activity? There are many ambiguities in the concepts of economic activity—work, job, employment, and so on. Women who participate in household agricultural farms may consider their farmwork as part of housework. Recently, international organizations such as the United Nations as well as economists have begun to stress the importance of work that contributes to production or has the potential to earn an income or profit as well as production for household consumption.[21] This constitutes the "economically active" population.[22]

Since 1980, women have been entering the labor force in larger numbers. In India, in 1985, the total number of economically active persons was about 315 million. Out of this total, 223 million were men and 91 million were women. In 1989–1991, 38 percent of the total population was in the labor force, and in 1990, women constituted 26 percent of the total labor force.[23] Recent data from the World Bank show a decline in women's participation in the labor force between 1980 and 1999.[24] Surprisingly, however, whereas in most countries women's economic activity rate has increased, rates in India have steadily declined. In 1950, there was 30.45 percent female economic activity rate; by 1991, that figure declined to 22.70 percent. During this same period, the figures in China rose from 47 percent to almost 54 percent. Female economic activity rates have increased during this period in most other Asian and Latin American countries, even in Sri Lanka and Cuba. Comparable declines, as in India, are prevalent in African countries such as Kenya, Nigeria, Senegal, Zaire, and others.[25]

The predominant explanation for this discrepancy is mechanization and modernization in the agricultural sector. As factories and mills replaced traditional modes of agricultural production, more and more women lost jobs in the agricultural sector.[26] This is not a new phenomenon.[27] Since the 1970s, this has been the case in most traditional societies and was the focus of Ester Boserup's pathbreaking analysis of women and economic development in 1970.

The impact of such policies notwithstanding, in other areas the government has taken some important steps to alleviate the working conditions of women. Since 1948, the government of India has initiated several laws to regulate the working hours of women in mines, factories, plantations, and elsewhere. Examples of such policies and regulations include the Factories Act of 1948, the Mines Act of 1952, and the Equal Remuneration Act of 1976 (requiring equal pay for equal work and preventing discrimination against women). Although it is necessary to look at government directives and policies that seek to redress the situation, policies alone will not suffice to ensure better working conditions for women or to reinstate displaced female workers.

As already discussed, there is a marked discrepancy in the benefits that men and women are receiving as a result of the development process. This discrepancy is rooted in the question of what kinds of work women do. In India, for example, we find that women are predominantly employed in agriculture and in low-paying, low-profile jobs. The situation is not unique to India. It is a global trend, particularly in developing countries. There are deep cultural and social attitudes that assign low status to women's jobs. According to the World Bank, one way that "public policy can affect household processes and reduce women's dependency is to alter the economic environment. In a sense, this means that market forces should be allowed to influence the boundaries of culturally acceptable women's activity."[28] Although this attitude permeates the fabric of most countries, the inequality is even more prominent in the access to education that men and women have in different societies.

## WOMEN, EDUCATION, AND EMPOWERMENT

Education and training are crucial to women's access to technical, adminis-trative, and managerial positions. Several findings suggest that without ad-equate education and training women have been adversely affected by tech-nological development.[29] Recent findings suggest that more women were literate in 1990 than in 1970. In 1970, forty-three women per 100 men were literate; in 1990, that number rose to fifty-five.[30] These numbers, though, ought to be evaluated against the background of a continuing gap between male and female literacy rates in the upper and postsecondary levels.[31] Such comparisons are valuable because they present a picture of the de-clining enrollment of female students in upper levels of education and in technical and postsecondary levels. This means that women will have low-paying, low-skill jobs.

In India, the regional variation in literacy rates is also significant. Ac-cording to a government report, despite an increase in female enrollment in primary schools, there is gross disparity from region to region. There is a discrepancy between northern and southern India. In one district in the northern state of Uttar Pradesh, the enrollment is only 14 percent. In the southern state of Kerala, in contrast, the enrollment is 65 percent. In fact, Kerala is the only state with enrollment rates over 50 percent.[32] Studies have found that there is a direct link between lack of education and the growth in population rates. In the north, most women still have five or more children, have early marriage, and are subordinate to men. In contrast, in the south, the status of women is higher, there is more gender equality, and the birthrates have fallen significantly.

> The state of Kerala, for instance, is not economically advanced, and its women have the same access to family planning services as do others elsewhere in the country. Yet Kerala, where women have long enjoyed high status and where literacy among them approaches 90 percent, has completed the "demographic transition" to replacement-level birth rate, while most of the rest of India is experiencing the higher birth rates that Kerala experienced 25 years ago.[33]

The link between education and population control is therefore strik-ing. With more education, women learn the value of family planning. Women of Kerala have as much access to birth control as do women from other parts of India. Without adequate literacy, however, women from states with low literacy levels are unable to grasp its significance in the context of a burgeoning population. Educated women participate in reproductive decisionmaking and are taken seriously by their spouses. The government's efforts at educating women in family planning and birth control and distribution of contraceptives will therefore be more meaningful in a situation where women have the basic education to understand and appreciate its value.

Furthermore, education is directly related to the status of women in general. Once the literacy rates rise, people, especially men, perceive women differently. A woman with education enjoys higher status than one without. This helps in areas where men have traditionally perceived the primary role of women as mothers and wives. Education liberates women from their traditional roles.

## HEALTH AND THE ENVIRONMENT: BROADENING EMPOWERMENT STRATEGIES

Health, housing conditions, and the environment affect a woman's overall ability to live, give birth, and raise healthy children—all essential to empowering women. International organizations such as the United Nations and the United Nations Children's Fund are directing serious attention to the importance of women's health and well-being as an agenda item for policy directives aimed at development. Development analyses in the past scarcely examined women's health issues as a vital part of development. Today, there is a shifting concern. It is crucial that we consider the health of women in the general health and security of the population. Proper nourishment, immunization against deadly diseases, sanitary living conditions— all constitute essential aspects of the development process and contribute to empowering women.

As in most other countries—developed and developing alike—in India maternal mortality rates, infant mortality rates, and fertility rates are areas of concern in the overall health of women and the population at large. Fertility rates declined from 5.7 percent to 4.3 percent between 1970 and 1990. This is still fairly high, especially when we consider comparable data from China to reflect a decline from 6 percent in 1970 to 2.4 percent in 1990. China's strict one-child policy may be behind this decline. Such a policy, merits and demerits aside, would not work in India. History has shown that the democratic process in India would challenge such state policies. In the early to mid-1970s, when Indira Gandhi's government tried to implement forced sterilization programs, there was widespread protest and discontent, eventually resulting in the Gandhi government being voted out of office.

Given this situation, as well as the need for slower population growth, it is necessary to enhance the role of education as an important policy imperative. As already discussed, and as the data show, in states where women are more literate the population growth rates are lower. Moreover, studies show that women in states with higher literacy rates enjoy higher status. This distinction is marked among southern states in India, where literacy levels and rates are higher than in northern India. In states such as Kerala, with a high literacy rate (almost 90 percent among women), life expectancy at birth also remains higher than states such as Uttar Pradesh, where literacy rates are below the national average.

In addition, traditional cultural beliefs, such as the preference for a male child, need to be addressed. The sex ratio demonstrates a clear cultural preference for boys. In 1981, there were 933 females per 1,000 males; by 1991, that number had declined to 927.[34] According to one estimate, "Of 8,000 abortions in Bombay after parents learned the sex of the fetus through amniocentesis, only one would have been a boy."[35] It will take more than government policy alone to rid the society of such prejudice in favor of the male child. Perhaps when the benefits of education permeate the social fabric there will be a change in this scenario.

It is notable that recent efforts toward sustainable development have brought environmental concerns to the forefront. As already discussed, only recently have researchers and international organizations begun to consider women's work within the household as economically productive. Furthermore, the literature, especially feminist scholarship, has highlighted that women are constantly facing challenges to environmental deterioration. "Women who manage rural households experience soil erosion, deforestation, and contaminated water supplies directly, because these events impinge on their ability to provide for their families. . . . Farming families, for example, experience soil degradation in the form of productivity declines."[36] Other perspectives contend that women, who are more intricately related to the "earth,"[37] often find ways of expressing the need to refurbish and replenish environmental deterioration "naturally." Noted environmentalist and ecofeminist critic Vandana Shiva argues that Indian women are capable of re-creating a relationship with the feminine "nature."[38] This is also witnessed in many rural settings where women have found innovative ways of guarding against environmental degradation and have organized themselves indigenously to protect the environment. Examples include the Chipko movement in the early 1970s, when the "tree-huggers" in northern India—literally by hugging trees—prevented a sporting goods company from cutting down trees.

To be sure, such approaches and movements, even though strong, sometime fail to assess the deeper complexities in the situation and the role that women have to play. Within the Chipko movement, for example, some women supported one faction that was in favor of limited logging along with development needs for the region.[39] Other cases and situations indicate that

Indian women's status and work atmospheres may be hazardous without them being aware of it. According to one estimate, while cooking, women were inhaling carcinogens and benzopyrene that would have been equivalent to smoking twenty packs of cigarettes a day.[40] In such situations, there is a need for governmental intervention. Women have to make compromises with environmental threats because of economic needs of survival (possibly explaining why some women in the Chipko movement supported limited logging). Or they are unaware and helpless in situations where they are being exposed to lethal fumes while doing household chores. In either case, the government's role becomes crucial in addressing environmental issues that stand in the way of empowering women to lead healthy lives. Availability of cooking gas, proper maintenance, and affordability are the major aspects that government intervention could ensure.

On the other end of the spectrum is the need for government to ensure that development efforts reach out to areas, both rural and urban. In some regions of India, for example, women still have to spend close to eight hours a week drawing and carrying water. Although the situation is worse in some African countries, comparable data show that women spend 2.5 hours in Nepal and Bangladesh and about an hour a week in Indonesia. Part of the reason this situation persists is that women do not have a strong say in the development priorities that are often drawn up by state and local authorities.[41] Because women continue to be the primary source of labor for household chores and raising children, development efforts that ignore conditions affecting women ought to be reassessed. Notions of sustainable development, therefore, ought to include the well-being and upliftment of women and men in the development process.

## LEADERSHIP, DECISIONMAKING, AND EMPOWERMENT

So far, I have discussed the need for the government to play a more proactive role in making gender transformative policies and in ensuring that the fruits of development reach all women. Coupled with grassroots participation and activism, this can go a long way toward empowering women. An essential aspect of this process is women's participation in decisionmaking, both within the community and in formal administration at the local, regional, and national levels. The global disparity in gender representation in public life is alarming. In 1990, women headed only 3.8 percent of the UN member states. In ninety-three of the 159 member states as of 1990, women held no ministerial positions.[42] Even though India has had a woman head of government, overall women's participation in government is still dismal. In 1975, women occupied only 4.3 percent of the parliamentary seats. In 1987, that number reached 8.3 percent.[43] As of 1997, women held a little more than 7 percent of the seats in both houses of parliament. This was lower than the global standards of 12 percent in the lower house and 9.8 percent in the upper house.[44] As of 2000, women held 8.9 percent of the parliamentary seats in India. It is difficult to assess where India falls in this criterion, as there is wide variation globally: in Sweden, women hold 42.7 percent of the parliamentary seats; in China, 21.8 percent; in the United States, 12.5 percent; and in Pakistan, 2 percent.[45]

It is true that numbers alone will not indicate that states will adopt more gender-sensitive policies. But if more women hold leadership positions in local, state, and national governments, the perception of women as decisionmakers will change favorably. In Pakistan, for example, under Prime Minister Benazir Bhutto, there was a social acceptance to women providing leadership in public policy. A similar situation is witnessed in Sri Lanka and Turkey.

There are several other reasons why there are prospects for more women's participation in India. Political participation by women is not rare in Indian history, dating back to ancient times. In modern India, many prominent women were at the forefront in the struggle for Indian independence. Even though India's female former prime minister, Indira Gandhi, cannot be credited with ushering in a wave of gender-sensitive policies, her contribution to raising the self-esteem of millions of poor women, as well as policies toward poverty alleviation, were significant.[46]

Moreover, recent efforts by the government to address the issue of women's participation in the political process contribute to the empowerment process directly. This includes the passage of the Seventy-third Constitutional Amendment Act in 1992, introducing a phased self-government system for the villages. This is called the Panchayat Raj Institution system. The new amendment calls for a reservation of one-third of the seats in the *panchayat* (local village government unit) for women, including reservation for scheduled castes and tribes.[47] By making it easier for women to be a part of the formal administrative system, the government is playing a proactive role in the empowerment process. Representation in local self-government will eventually lead to a gendered perspective on issues and policies. Another step toward affirmative action by the government to include more women in the policy process is the proposed legislation to reserve 33 percent of parliamentary seats for women. This bill, originally introduced in 1996, has yet to pass.[48]

Political participation is not restricted to formal administrative positions alone. In the past few decades, women have organized and agitated against inequality in the workplace, social and cultural practices such as bride burning and dowry, and domestic violence, and for the right to better health and education. "They use legal means, direct confrontation, press and media campaigns, popular education, and street theater to wage war against various aspects of male domination."[49] This is an essential aspect of political empowerment. And these movements "may be the best vehicles for bringing women into the mainstream of Indian political life. For women to be able to press a political agenda, to engage in public life, they must first be empowered privately: they must have some control over their own lives. To the extent their personal autonomy is limited by social, cultural, and religious structures that confine women . . . these structures must be defied."[50]

Thus, there is tremendous potential for grassroots movements combining with state and national policies to result in empowerment. There are numerous cases of activism where women have had to take the initiative in areas such as land redistribution. Even though land redistribution seeks to benefit male peasants, if women do not receive land titles, it may eventually widen the gender gap in landownership.[51] Similarly, women have shown great strength in uniting forces, as in the Chipko movement. Other examples include the leadership provided by the Self-Employed Women's Association, the All India Women's Conference, the Working Women's Forum, Maitree (an umbrella organization coordinating the activities of various agencies working to support women in cases of domestic violence and other abuses of women's rights in Calcutta), and other organizations.[52]

## CONCLUSION

This discussion has shown that the Indian government, as in most other states, advocates equality irrespective of gender, race, ethnicity, religion, and so on. The constitution of India enshrines these principles. Central and local governments are also directed against discrimination on the basis of sex in their hiring processes. Yet there is gross disparity in gender representation in public offices and in administrative and entrepreneurial positions. This is not to suggest that empowerment has not occurred at all. Some of the empowerment has occurred as a result of activism by women's groups and trade unions.

India is an enormous country with a tremendous degree of regional variations in socioeconomic and cultural processes. Thus, some of the national aggregates discussed here may not truly capture the vicissitudes of the complexity and differential trends that are otherwise manifest. For instance, the notion of governance is changing the face of villages in India and including more and more women in the bargaining process. To make such efforts more meaningful at the national level, the government has to be at the forefront, providing the resources for the transformation to happen. There are fundamental aspects such as education, in which the government's efforts can lead to an "enabling" process, which would then generate empowerment. As the case of Kerala has shown, education enables women to exercise more power and decisionmaking authority within the family structure. With more strict enforcement of literacy programs, perhaps the rest of India can also feel the "trickle up" effect of this southern state.

Given the complexities of life in India, the challenge is to integrate women from all levels and walks of life in the process of empowerment. Even if there are no widespread changes in the status of women right away, even small gains should be noteworthy. Education may be the key in such an empowerment process. There is a need to incorporate the educated women into the mainstream workforce. One study notes that "the vast majority of educated middle class [women are] still confined to domestic activities."[53] Women constitute the central force in this unit. Successful integration of rural, urban, literate, and illiterate women in a common goal of empowerment as an ongoing process is crucial in this endeavor.

Furthermore, developing countries such as India need to find indigenous mechanisms and indicators of gender relations and status and not always follow the parameters set by the experiences of industrialized countries. Gender relations have traditionally been studied through the lens of advances made by women in developed and industrialized countries.[54] As the case of India suggests, India's problems are unique. Therefore, the strategies needed to empower women in India have to be indigenous. Likewise, there is need to distinguish between the status of rural versus urban women, as a number of factors that are pertinent to rural women may not be relevant to urban women. There are differences, for example, in rural and urban household types and authority structures as well as production relations and patterns.[55]

All this shows that empowerment in India will have to incorporate all the levels—international, national, and subnational. The government alone has not and cannot generate empowerment. Gender-sensitive policies need to be reinforced by other agencies. In order for policies to have any net effect on empowering women, there has to be a concerted effort involving the government, NGOs, women's groups, men, and the overall cultural perception of the need to empower women.

## DISCUSSION QUESTIONS

1. Women's economic activity, despite decades of development, seems to have declined even though women work harder than before. Why do you think this has happened? What are some of the ways in which women can be more empowered in the area of economic activity?

2. What would be the cornerstone of empowerment of women in India as far as state policies go, that is, which policies would lead to empowerment and which ones would lead to disempowerment? Compare with instances from other countries.

3. Do you agree that education leads to empowerment of women? Compare the situation in India with that of China and a developed country such as the United States to argue your case.

4. Suggest possible ways in which state policies can be combined with other agencies like international organizations and grassroots activism to attain better results in the empowerment process.

5. If you were advising the government of India about empowerment of women and someone suggested that the government cannot empower women, that women have to do it themselves, how would you respond?

6. For further information on these issues, see Table 5.1.

**Table 5.1 Summary Gender Profile of India**

| | India | | | | South Asia | | Low Income Countries | |
|---|---|---|---|---|---|---|---|---|
| | 1980 | 1985 | 1990 | 1999 | 1980 | 1999 | 1980 | 1999 |
| GNP per capita (U.S.$) | 270 | 290 | 390 | 440 | 270 | 440 | 380 | 410 |
| Population | | | | | | | | |
| Total (millions) | 687.3 | 765.1 | 849.5 | 997.5 | 902.6 | 1,329.3 | 1,612.9 | 2,417.1 |
| Female population (% of total) | 48.2 | 48.3 | 48.3 | 48.4 | 48.2 | 48.5 | 49.3 | 49.4 |
| Life expectancy at birth (years) | | | | | | | | |
| Male | 55 | 57 | 59 | 62 | 54 | 62 | 53 | 58 |
| Female | 54 | 57 | 60 | 64 | 54 | 63 | 54 | 60 |
| Adult illiteracy rate (% of people aged 15+) | | | | | | | | |
| Male | 45 | 42 | 38 | 32 | 48 | 34 | 43 | 29 |
| Female | 74 | 69 | 64 | 56 | 75 | 58 | 65 | 48 |
| Labor Force Participation | | | | | | | | |
| Total labor force (millions) | 300 | 329 | 361 | 441 | 389 | 588 | 709 | 1,090 |
| Female labor force (% of total) | 34 | 32 | 31 | 32 | 34 | 33 | 38 | 38 |
| Youth illiteracy rate (% of people aged 15–24) | | | | | | | | |
| Male | 33 | 30 | 27 | 21 | 36 | 23 | 30 | 19 |
| Female | 58 | 52 | 46 | 36 | 62 | 41 | 51 | 31 |
| Health and Nutrition | | | | | | | | |
| Total fertility rate (births per woman) | 5.0 | 4.4 | 3.8 | 3.1 | 5.3 | 3.4 | 5.3 | 3.7 |
| Contraceptive prevalence (% of women aged 15–49) | — | 35 | — | 52 | 7 | 53 | 4 | 46 |
| Birth attended by skilled health staff (% of total) | — | 30 | 44 | — | — | — | — | — |

*Source:* Genderstats, *A Database of Gender Statistics* (The World Bank), available at http://genderstats.worldbank.org/menu.asp (accessed June 15, 2001).

## NOTES

1. United Nations, *1999 World Survey on the Role of Women in Development* (New York: United Nations, 1999), p. x.

2. United Nations, *Human Development Report* (New York: United Nations, 1993), p. 105.

3. Ester Boserup, *Women's Role in Economic Development* (New York: St. Martin's, 1970); Bina Agarwal, "Neither Sustenance nor Sustainability: Agricultural Strategies, Ecological Degradation, and Indian Women," in Agarwal, ed., *Structures of Patriarchy: The State, the Community and the Household* (London: Zed Books, 1988); Gita Sen, "Women Workers and the Green Revolution," in Lourdes Benerìa, ed., *Women and Development: The Sexual Division of Labor in Rural Societies* (Westport, Conn.: Praeger, 1985).

4. For the purposes of this study, developing societies will constitute essentially third world countries as well as countries such as China, which are considered developing.

5. United Nations, *Women's Indicators and Statistics Database* (*WISTAT*) (New York: United Nations, 1994). It compiles international statistics on the situation of women for 212 countries covering 1970–1993.

6. Ibid., p. 7.

7. For example, see Robert Dahl, *Who Governs? Democracy and Power in an American City* (New Haven: Yale University Press, 1961); N. W. Polsby, *Community Power and Political Theory* (New Haven: Yale University Press, 1963). Both have defined power in similar ways.

8. Jo Rowlands, "A Word of the Times, but What Does It Mean? Empowerment in the Discourse and Practice of Development," in Haleh Afshar, ed., *Women and Empowerment: Illustrations from the Third World* (New York: St.Martin's, 1998), pp. 11–34.

9. See, for example, the work of noted gender planner Caroline Moser, *Gender Planning and Development: Theory, Practice, and Training* (New York: Routledge, 1993), p. 191.

10. Naila Kabeer, *Reversed Realities: Gender Hierarchies in Development Thought* (New York: Verso, 1994) p. 97.

11. See Afshar, "Introduction," in *Women and Empowerment.*

12. Karl Marx, *Critique of the Gotha Program* (New York: International Publishers, 1938).

13. Amartya Sen, in Martha Nussbaum and Amartya Sen, *The Quality of Life* (New York: Oxford University Press, 1993), p. 31.

14. Amartya Sen, *Inequality Reexamined* (New York: Russell Sage Foundation, 1992), chap. 8.

15. This rank is according to the *Human Development Report* of 1993. To give a few relevant examples: Japan ranks number 1; the United States, 6; China, 101; Sri Lanka, 86; Pakistan, 132.

16. R. C. Majumdar, H. C. Raychaudhuri, and Kalikinkar Datta, *An Advanced History of India* (Madras: Macmillan, 1994), p. 43.

17. See quote in Tara Ali Baig, *India's Woman Power* (New Delhi: S.Chand, 1976), p. 3.

18. *Status of Women Committee Report* (1975), cited in ibid., p. 28.

19. Neera Kuckreja Sohoni, "Women in India," in Nelly P. Stromquist, ed., *Women in the Third World: An Encyclopedia of Contemporary Issues* (New York: Garland, 1998), p. 576.

20. Ibid., p. 577.

21. United Nations, *The World's Women: Trends and Statistics, 1970–1990* (New York: United Nations, 1991), p. 94.

22. Ibid., p. 85. This definition corresponds with United Nations and ILO recommendation.

23. *Human Development Report* (1993), p. 169.

24. Data from World Bank website, available online at http://genderstats. worldbank.org/SummaryGender.asp?WhichRpt=country&Ctry=IND.India.

25. United Nations, *1994 World Survey,* p. 52.

26. Ibid., p. 60.

27. Boserup, *Women's Role in Economic Development.*

28. Cited by Sohoni, "Women in India," p. 579.

29. Boserup, *Women's Role in Economic Development.*

30. *Human Development Report* (1993), p. 153.

31. *WISTAT* (1994).

32. Cited in Myron Weiner, *The Child and the State in India* (Princeton, N.J.: Princeton University Press, 1991), p. 93.

33. From an excerpt of a report entitled "The 'Second India' Revisited," coordinated by Dr. Robert Repetto; see *New York Times,* September 6, 1994.

34. Sohoni, "Women in India," p. 577.

35. United Nations, *The World's Women* (1991), p. 1.

36. Jane L. Collins, "Women and the Environment: Social Reproduction and Sustainable Development," in Rita S. Gallin and Anne Ferguson, eds., *Women and International Development Annual,* vol. 2 (Boulder: Westview, 1991). The quote is from p. 35.

37. Ibid.

38. Ibid., p. 46.

39. Ibid.

40. United Nations, *The World's Women* (1991), p. 75.

41. Ibid.

42. United Nations, *The World's Women* (1991), p. 31.

43. Ibid., p. 41.

44. See Sohoni, "Women in India," p. 580.

45. Compiled by UNIFEM, *Progress of the World's Women Report,* available online at www.unifem.undp.org/progressww/index/html; based on Inter-Parliamentray Union website, www.ipu.org (page numbers not available).

46. R. Datta, "Gender, Leadership, and Development: A Profile of Indira Gandhi," in *A Leadership Journal: Women in Leadership* 3, no. 2 (spring 1999): 63–70.

47. For fuller discussion of the amendment and its prospects, see Devaki Jain, *Panchayat Raj: Women Changing Governance,* available online at www.undp.org/ undp/gender/resource/mono5/html (September 1996).

48. Nilanjana Bhaduri Jha, "Women's Reservation Bill: Set Aside Yet Again," *Times of India,* April 2001, p. 1.

49. Raka Ray, *Fields of Protest: Women's Movements in India* (Minneapolis: University of Minnesota Press, 1999), p. 19.

50. Leslie J. Calman, *Toward Empowerment: Women and Movement Politics in India* (Boulder: Westview, 1992), p. 167.

51. Amrita Basu, *Two Faces of Protest: Contrasting Modes of Activism in India* (Berkeley: University of California Press, 1992).

52. See Elisabeth Bumiller, *May You Be the Mother of a Hundred Sons: A Journey Among the Women of India* (New York: Random House, 1990).

53. Joanna Riddle and Rama Joshi, *Daughters of Independence* (New Brunswick, N.J.: Rutgers University Press, 1986), p. 72.

54. Lourdes Benerìa and Gita Sen, "Accumulation, Reproduction, and Women's Role in Economic Development," in *Signs: Journal of Women in Culture and Society* 7, no. 2 (1981): 279–298.

55. Lynne Brydon and Sylvia Chant, *Women in the Third World* (New Brunswick, N.J.: Rutgers University Press, 1989).

# 6

# Structural Adjustment and the Empowerment (or Disempowerment) of Women in Niger and Senegal

## Lucy Creevey

In this chapter I explore the status of women in Niger and Senegal (West Africa), particularly among those who are in the most vulnerable sector: the poor engaged in the informal sector.[1] The question that informs the whole is whether or not Nigérian[2] and Senegalese women are being *dis*empowered in the aftermath of structural adjustment programs (SAPs),[3] as many contend.[4] Women in Niger and Senegal, like women in other African countries, face the changes imposed by SAPs without any strong, concomitant government policy to protect them given their greater vulnerability. Much of the writing on the subject has been to expose the injustices to women perpetrated by the adoption of these World Bank–inspired (i.e., *–required*) policies. SAPs, however, are only one factor (or group of related factors) in a larger and ever-changing context in which women operate. The situation has never been static for African women. Their roles—as well as their power and authority in the family and community—have varied in the different circumstances that their societies have faced over time. In some instances they have gained, then lost (as circumstances changed), then regained or altered in some way their position. The problem is to understand exactly what is going on at any point in time for groups of women differentiated by ethnicity, religion, location, and family status.

Niger and Senegal share a common past as former colonies of France and members of the French West African Federation (AOF; Fédération de l'Afrique Occidentale). Both countries became independent in 1960, and currently rank in the World Bank list of low-income countries. Both countries underwent devaluation of their common currency in 1994 as part of the process of structural adjustment. But Niger is a landlocked country bordering the Sahara Desert and has had minimal contact with Europe, whereas

Senegal, although also in a Sahelian climatic zone, is on the coast and was the capital of the AOF and a transit center for Europeans arriving on the continent. Both have adopted French as their national language and are Muslim countries, but differences between the two are striking in regard to the size, extent, and type of informal and formal economic sectors and the role of women in them. Women in both countries have had to react to the effects of structural adjustment but in differing social, political, and economic contexts.

Certain basic economic differences between the two cases strongly influence the outcomes observed. For one thing, Niger is far more rural, with a substantially poorer population, but both countries are very poor (see Table 6.1).

Comparing the positions of women is less easily accomplished because there is no agreed-upon measures. Tables 6.2 and 6.3 give some indicators that are often cited. Rate of fertility is one such measure, as is share of the labor force (meaning the reported wage-paid workers) and education.

Table 6.3 gives more detail on the status of women. Where Table 6.2 indicates (surprisingly) that women in Niger are a larger share of the labor force than in Senegal, this is nullified by the fact that subsistence agriculture remains much more important in Niger and that there is little industry. Thus, more than 80 percent of the population still depends on agriculture

**Table 6.1  Comparison of National Context: Niger and Senegal**

| Country | Population (millions) | % Urban | GNP per capita, U.S.$ 1992/1995 | Average Annual Growth, 1990–1995 | Life Expectancy | Poverty (% living on less than $1 per day) | External Debt (millions $), 1992/1995 |
|---------|------|------|---------|------|----|------|------------|
| Niger | 9.0 | 23 | 280/220 | .5% | 46 | 61.5 | 1,711/1,633 |
| Senegal | 8.5 | 42 | 780/600 | 1.9% | 50 | 54.0 | 3,607/3,845 |

*Sources:* World Bank, *World Development Report, 1994* (New York: Oxford University Press, 1994), pp. 162–163, 200–201; and World Bank, *World Development Report, 1997* (New York: Oxford University Press, 1997), pp. 214, 234.

**Table 6.2  Comparison of Education, Share of Labor Force, and Fertility**

| Country | % of Females in Primary School, 1980/1993 | % of Females in Secondary School, 1980/1993 | Female Share of Labor Force, 1992 | Fertility Rate, 1990–1995 |
|---------|------|------|----|-----|
| Niger | 18/21 | 3/4 | 46 | 7.4 |
| Senegal | 37/50 | 7/11 | 39 | 5.9 |

*Source:* World Bank, *World Development Report, 1994* (New York: Oxford University Press, 1994), pp. 218–219, 212–213.

**Table 6.3  Percentage of Women in the Labor Force: Niger and Senegal**

| Country | Agriculture, 1980 | Industry, 1990 | Service Section, 1990 | % of Women Who Are Unpaid Family Workers | % of Women Who Are Employers, Own Acc't Workers | % of Women Who Are Illiterate, 1995 |
|---|---|---|---|---|---|---|
| Niger | 93/91 | 3/4 | 8 | 24 | 17 | 93 |
| Senegal | 81/76 | 6/7 | 10 | — | — | 77 |

*Sources:* United Nations, *The World's Women, 1995: Trends and Statistics* (New York: United Nations, 1995), pp. 142–144; and World Bank, *World Development Report, 1997* (New York: Oxford University Press, 1997), pp. 220, 226.

that is still primarily traditional in organization and in which women play a significant role (60–90 percent of food production and processing was done traditionally by women in West Africa).[5] Table 6.3 reports women's share of the modern economic sector. Here the lack of inclusion of women in Niger is shown. Illiteracy rate differences are linked to the ascending access of women in the two cases to education and modern jobs but are still extraordinarily high in both countries.

Where the modern wage sector is growing slowly and women are relatively disadvantaged in their access to education and to wage-paid jobs, their source of income is the informal sector. This has been variously defined as irregular, usually low-paying employment in a variety of production, processing, and marketing activities, distinguished from the formal sector in that enterprises are not registered with the government and do not abide by labor laws. The informal sector begins to decline in importance as the formal sector grows; that is, a smaller proportion of the population depends on it for their livelihood. But its current role in the developing world remains very significant. Indeed, in the two cases considered here, the size of the informal sector is under dispute, but almost all observers suggest that it is very important for the economic survival of the population. In 1995, it was estimated that 90 percent of all paid employment in Senegal was in the informal sector; in Niger, the estimate ranged from 20 percent to 66 percent of all employment, with the latter figure appearing more realistic to this author based on in-country observation. Thus, although a 1991 study of the informal sector in Niger found only 6.5 percent of the firms sampled to be either owned or managed by women or have one or more permanent female employees, in actuality the contribution of women to the sector is much higher. Out of 130,000 microenterprises cited in the 1988 census, 37,890, or 29 percent, were owned by women.[6]

Meaningful comparisons of differences in the national context in which poor women live and work must, however, go beyond statistics to try and capture the more ephemeral social expectations and attitudes toward women in each society. Where women are viewed as relatively equal and move freely in public and in the workplace, where they have traditionally had control of the income they produce, and where they expect to produce income, they are more easily able to work outside the home or family farm when that becomes an economic necessity. Being relatively experienced overall, then, puts them in quite a different situation from one in which women have been expected to stay in the house and not work, at least not in a way so they will have any contact with strangers outside their home. Indeed, the women who have the freedom to work and move about as they choose also have much more control over their own lives generally and play a larger role in the decisions made by their community.

The two cases here are quite different in this regard. In contrast to Senegal, Niger is an anomaly: Nigérian women have a level of importance (stemming in part from their essential economic roles), but many of them do not have the social and political freedom that most women have in Senegal. Indeed, according to the United Nations (UN), in 1995, Niger had one of the worst situations for women in the world. According to the UN Development Programme, using the Gender-related Development Index (GDI) (which not only measures the indicators used in the Human Development Index[7] but also penalizes the country in its ranking for inequality between men and women in the indicators), Niger has the lowest GDI of any country, ranking 174 out of 174.[8] In the Gender Empowerment Measure (GEM), which looks at the relative capacity of men and women to actively participate in economic and political life, Niger is again the lowest-ranking country. Table 6.4 illustrates the relative "empowerment" of men and women in Niger according to this source.

Yet Nigérian women are active, not only in subsistence agriculture but also in the informal sector. Prior to the SAP reforms, in 1976, observers documented women's multiple activities in commerce, production, and service. In 1995, post-SAP, this author found an even more varied set of female roles in the same three sectors. For example, women are engaged making pottery, baskets, jewels, cosmetics, clothes, and dying cloth. They

**Table 6.4  Gender Empowerment Index: Niger, 1995**

| Seats in Parliament (% women) | Administrators and Managers (% women) | Professional and Technical Workers (% women) | Earned Income Share (% to women) |
|---|---|---|---|
| 3.6 | 8.3 | 0.1 | 37 |

*Source:* United Nations, *The World's Women, 1995: Trends and Statistics* (New York: United Nations, 1995), pp. 142–144.

sell all manner of raw and processed food products, including peanuts, peanut oil, fruits, nuts, vegetables (including truck garden products), rice, millet, meat, fish, cakes, and breads. They act as praise singers, midwives, hairdressers, cooks for small roadside restaurants, and even moneylenders. They also engage themselves as seasonal workers.

The role a woman in Niger actually plays in informal sector activities differs depending on several important factors, including (among others) ethnic group, religion, geographic location, age, family status, education, and the growth of the formal economic sector in the given zone. Although there are no statistically reliable surveys to confirm this, reports suggest that the Hausa tradition and culture—far more than the cultures of the other Nigérian ethnic groups—supported and encouraged commercial activities among men as well as women. In towns the number of women in the markets increases no matter what the predominant ethnic group. Urban women are forced into or attracted to income-generating activities to provide food for their families because they have less access to wild fruit and plants for food and to land for their own cultivation, and also because they are directly and indirectly (through radio, television, etc.) exposed to women who are active in trade. Nonetheless, there appears to be a residual ethnic difference even in urban areas, which would suggest that Hausa women have a greater probability of entering into production and commerce than other women. Thus, women's involvement in the informal sector appears greatest in the geographic locations in and around Niamey (the largest town) and core Hausa areas such as Zinder and Maradi.

Inconsistently, religion as a factor that might affect women's business activities is much more powerful and negative among the Hausa as opposed to other women. Islam as a religion accepts the custom of women keeping separate accounts for the money they earn and even supports women carrying out income-generating activities. But the most conservative Hausa Muslim groups in Niger are linked to northern Nigeria, and, among them, women's freedom of action is severely restricted by religious beliefs. Women are secluded (*kublé*) in a compound from the day of their marriage until they are no longer of childbearing age. For the majority, this means they continue to be involved in production and marketing but have to carry on any business outside the compound through their unmarried daughters or sons or other relatives. The strong family and religious ties to Nigeria are the basis of successful trade for many of the women, which they could not have used were they to somehow reject the web of religious and cultural traditions by which they were bound. But this form of Islam still must be considered a deterrent for women to themselves participate fully in market activities and is probably a major reason why these women do not rival women to the south in the volume and profitability of their production and trade.

Not all Hausa women in Niger are *kublé,* although it is still a sign of status in and around the main commercial city, Maradi, where most (but not all) marriage-age Hausa women are secluded. Seclusion operates increasingly strongly as a factor as one moves south from Maradi toward Nigeria and diminishes moving to the east or moving out of the Hausa region to the west. Age and marital status are clearly intervening variables relating the strict religious prohibitions to individual women. For this reason, it is most often old women, women who are divorced or never married, or widowed women and young girl children who are to be seen in the markets of Maradi, whereas in Zinder, to the east, and Niamey, to the west, many more girls and young women can be seen.

Education (including formal schooling as well as business training) challenges or modifies both the ethnic and the religious factors shaping women's business roles. Women who have gone to school are significantly more likely to reject being secluded, and men with formal education are equally less likely to demand this observance. In Niger today, however, some 72 percent of the population is illiterate. Women, moreover, are much less likely to receive education than men. Only 21 percent of school-age girls were in primary school in Niger in 1995, and only 4 percent were in secondary school. Even this accomplishment is threatened by the current SAPs and decentralization policies. Currently women have great difficulty in finding entry into the few wage-paying jobs that exist. The informal sector is overwhelmingly the largest employer of women in Niger and the chief source of cash income. Because most women are in trade and are petty traders, and most deal primarily with women, their financial and economic network is by and large separate from the network on which men depend.

Senegal is an interesting contrast to Niger. Also Muslim and also suffering from an economy experiencing little growth and staggering under the combined impacts of government downsizing (with a resultant loss of services) and devaluation (with a sharp rise in prices for all imports and even some domestic commodities), the country, nonetheless, exhibits a different climate for women's work. Although most women are Muslim and profess allegiance to a Muslim brotherhood, few are *kublé.*[9] Women work openly in markets and other workplaces. In the largest ethnic groups (the Wolof and the Serer) women have played and continue to play a major role in traditional agriculture and have today begun to move into informal-sector activities, where they occupy a more central place than in Niger. Nonetheless, Senegal is not noted for the equality that women experience vis-à-vis men. The GDI and the GEM rank Senegal 153rd out of 174 countries.[10] (See Table 6.5, which illustrates how Senegal compared to Niger in 1995 in terms of political participation.)

In Senegal, women participate in the formal wage economy and in the informal sector but, predictably, not on an equal basis with men. Nonetheless,

Table 6.5 Gender Empowerment Index: Comparison of Niger and Senegal, 1995

| Country | Seats in Parliament (% women) | Women at the Ministerial Level (% women) | Professional and Technical Workers (% women) |
|---|---|---|---|
| Niger | 6 | 5 | 0.1 |
| Senegal | 12 | 7 | — |

Source: UNDP, Human Development Report, 1996 (New York: Oxford University Press, 1996), p. 143.

the situation has changed markedly in recent years.[11] In a study published in 1988, women were 26 percent of the "employed," that is, those who receive wages. However, the survey done in 1991–1992 found that women were already 46 percent of this group. Furthermore, they had moved from being 23 percent of the "unemployed" (those seeking wage-paying jobs) to being 46 percent of this group. Thirty percent of Senegalese women still are listed as "homemakers" but these women usually work in the fields to produce crops for sale and for family consumption, so they are also economically active, although not so listed in statistical tables.[12] Yet women are 49 percent of those listed as "independent," or those who are either in the informal sector or in agriculture working for themselves. And 58 percent of women in Senegal earn their primary economic livelihood as independents. Independents, both in agricultural zones and in urban areas, are often those who have established small enterprises.

Senegalese women's small enterprises often produce traditional (artisanal) products such as dried fish, breads, vegetable oils, sour milk, and butter. Women are also traders in a variety of items such as cloth, cosmetics, and food, and they provide a variety of services such as laundering. There are some major women traders in the agrobusiness sector and in commerce generally. Notable are some large-scale female traders in textiles and producers, as well as traders of fish. But overall, studies on informal-sector establishments show that Senegalese women are disproportionately located in the smaller, less well established, and less profitable firms.[13] Thus, the ability of Senegalese women to respond to the changing structure of costs and opportunities caused by structural adjustment and, particularly, to use financial services to do so is lower than that of men overall.

Since 1982, the government of Senegal has made a special effort to target women directly because of their weaker position in the economy through its Plan of National Action for Women, including programs in education, training, health, nutrition, employment, and income-generation at a cost of CFA 8 billion (Communauté Financière Africaine franc). One core element of the Plan of National Action was incentives for the formation of women's groups and associations, hierarchically organized from the smallest at the village base through to the regional and the national associations of women's groups. These groups were eligible to receive government-sponsored credit for income-producing activities, which was seen as a key to their eventual economic success. The result since then has been a proliferation of registered women's groups. However, significant improvement in the relative economic position of women has not yet resulted from this initiative.

Despite strong encouragement by the government, few formal loans have been available to women in any sector of activity. Given women's relatively weaker position vis-à-vis men in the formal and informal sectors of the Senegalese economy, their lesser access to credit is not surprising. Three main factors militate against their being able to get a loan from a formal bank or other lending institution: lesser education than men, lesser access to collateral, and perceived lower profit potential because of the nature of their businesses. Under the region's banking structure, collateral is likely to be either buildings or land, and in Senegal few people and fewer women are registered as property owners. When ownership is recorded, it is generally done in the name of the male head of household, thereby excluding women who may have contributed to or even paid for the dwelling.[14]

In urban areas, especially Dakar, women are increasingly likely to acquire property in their own name, but even today few women nationwide enjoy this privilege. Instead, women tend to save in the form of gold jewelry or other assets such as sheep. These assets are usually not accepted by banks and lending institutions as securities. Women have more access to credit (and savings) for income-generating activities in the semiformal institutions set up throughout Senegal, often with money provided by foreign donors (at least initially). These may be cooperatives set up to allow members to save and to receive credit, financial institutions that offer credit services only, or multifaceted projects that offer credit as one of their services. Conditions for membership or for borrowing differ depending on the institution. Certain generalizations can be made, however. For one thing, the size of loans in rural areas is much smaller than in urban centers, and women get only a minority of these loans in both rural and urban environments. But taking the all-female loans programs together and assuming one-quarter of the other groups' membership is female, there are as many as 20,000 women who have access to credit for their economic activities, a hundred times or more than those who will have access to a formal bank loan.[15]

No such statistics are available for Niger, but research in 1995 indicated that the commercial banks made few loans to informal-sector businesses in part because the interest-rate ceiling was too low (16.5 percent in 1995). These loans went to the larger traders and producers, few of whom were women. Six donor-funded nongovernmental organizations (NGOs) provided the major part of financial services to this sector.[16] General information on all the programs taken together suggests that significantly fewer

Nigérian than Senegalese women got formal loans or loans from an NGO. Women in Senegal, then, are more likely to be in business in the informal sector than their Nigérian counterparts, and they have greater opportunity to acquire credit to open or expand their businesses. Many more nonprofit institutions exist with programs to support their work in Senegal, and the overall economic atmosphere is more supportive because traditions forbidding their work outside the home are fewer and because subsistence agriculture is less central to the economy and has been more rapidly replaced by an increasing agrocommercial sector and a growing production/industrial sector.

## EMPOWERMENT OR DISEMPOWERMENT OF NIGÉRIAN AND SENEGALESE WOMEN

The final question remains as to what the empowering or *dis*empowering impacts of structural adjustment have been on women. In the first place, certain of the statistics cited above do suggest a disempowering impact. Writers critical of structural adjustment have frequently pointed out that one result is that women are forced to seek paid employment to compensate and maintain the level of the family economy. They also point out that simultaneously more women than men become unemployed (seeking but not finding wage-paying jobs) because women are laid off first and hired last when there is a downsizing in the workforce.[17] These trends are easily observable in Senegal, as the tables above indicate. Women are a sharply increased proportion of the labor force *as well as* of the unemployed. Indeed, women's unemployment percentage has grown at an even higher rate than the percentage of those employed, consistent with the impact suggested by other critical observers.

So few women have jobs in the modern wage sector in Niger that the same trend is more difficult to observe, such that this impact can be examined only within the context of other socioeconomic aspects. One obvious area to explore is education, where Hausa women reported to this author of substantially lost ground. A study on the impact of the SAP in the Ivory Coast shows that Ivoirien girls had decreased access to schools relative to boys after structural adjustment.[18] In Niger, in 1995, the overall economic situation appeared to be worse. Schoolteachers were government employees. When this study was conducted, they had not been paid for many months and were on strike. Public schools were closed. Among the families interviewed, some of the wealthier were seeking to send their sons to Niamey, where a private school might be found, or increasing their participation in the traditional Quranic (religious) schools. Girls were not being given the same option, at least not among the Hausa. Hausa families had valued education for girls, which made them better household managers and traders even when they were expected to be cloistered after marriage. Thus, early marriages, in which the girl was fifteen or younger, had become less common. Now that schooling was not available, that situation was reversing. Families interviewed in the 1995 study were reverting to marrying their daughters at the traditional early ages.[19]

Closer examination, however, shows a complicated pattern. Girls' loss of access to schooling relative to boys in both countries is hard to demonstrate statistically with available figures; in fact, the percentage of boys *decreased* in both countries between 1987 and 1993 while that of girls rose marginally. In both cases, the upward trajectory of the percentage of children in school was flattening because of fewer schools owing to government cutbacks, but the proportion of girls in schools relative to boys increased in the late 1980s and early 1990s, the SAP period. Clearly the lack of schooling impacted boys at least as much as girls. One may hypothesize that poorer families now had to send their boys to work and that only a small minority could afford to send them to a private school. The claim by Hausa women that they had reverted to marrying their daughters earlier may still be true, as these statistics refer to the whole country; the largest amount of extant schools are in the cities, particularly Niamey, and not the primarily Hausa areas. However, in the absence of a full survey of these areas, there is no data to back up this contention. Few girls are able to attend primary school, and the SAP has not improved that situation. However, there is no concrete evidence that the SAP worsened the situation in Niger and Senegal (see Table 6.6).

Two factors further complicate the situation and make it difficult to conclude here that SAPs were, are, and will be barriers to be overcome by women in either of these countries or that SAPs operated solely as disempowering influences. One of these factors has to do with traditional economic, social, and political linkages (discussed below). The second involves a debate on what exactly "empowerment" means. Use of the word is widely spread in the literature on women in developing countries, with the

Table 6.6 Percentage of Females and Males (F/M) in Primary School: Comparison of Niger and Senegal

| Country | 1970 | 1980 | 1987 | 1990 | 1993 |
|---|---|---|---|---|---|
| Senegal | 32/50 | 37/56 | 49/71 | 49/67 | 50/67 |
| Niger | 10/18 | 18/33 | 20/38 | 21/37 | 21/35 |

*Sources:* UNDP, *World Development Report, 1990*, p. 240; *World Development Report, 1996*, p. 200; *World Development Report, 1997*, p. 226 (New York: Oxford University Press, various years).

common meaning of enabling women to achieve for themselves better incomes and a higher overall quality of life.[20] At issue are, first, what constitutes better quality of life, and, second, what it is that will permit women to obtain this state of being once defined. In an earlier study done by this writer, the issue of quality of life presented a real problem in the analysis. UN sponsors of that research considered that their projects, which were being analyzed, should be judged in terms of better quality of life. Results from the studies, however, showed that in most cases women now worked harder and for longer hours. They had less time for their families and less time to rest. Related to this was a measure of empowerment, where these projects were supposed to make women more independent—that is, more able to make their own decisions about their work, income, and family matters. Results showed, however, that in successful projects in Africa, women *lost* independence as men became involved in their work decisions in ways they had not formally been before.[21]

The question was whether these projects should then be judged as failing along these dimensions, although the project organizers as well as participants had seen the projects as successes. A closer look suggested that the problem was in the measures, not in the projects. It is true that the women now worked harder and longer in areas where they already had worked twelve-hour days before the projects ever began. But the women themselves felt that their lives were better because they felt they now had an ability to gain an income, which was helping their families. They felt empowered because of this and they felt their control over their lives was greater. Asked if they wanted to work less, their response was "no"—they wanted to work even more if it would produce more income. The same kind of definition problem existed with "empowerment" as such. The African women interviewed in this 1992 study said they were more respected in family councils and other decisions because of their increased income. Their loss in independence came because their work was being taken more seriously by their husbands and other family members because their income was so much more important than it had been previously to their families. They felt empowered as a result.

What, then, are we observing in Niger and Senegal after the SAPs? On the one hand, the process, which is most clearly documented in Senegal, is what has been called elsewhere a "proletarianization" of women: financial exigency draws the women out of the subsistence economy (organized around household and home plot activities) to struggle to find cash incomes in wage-paying jobs and small businesses of their own.[22] The context is one of greater hardship for the women and their families. Immediate results of structural adjustment are at least in part to blame for this. But SAPs, of course, were not totally at fault. In both Senegal and Niger, the economies were stagnant, the modern wage sector was growing very slowly, and, previous to the

1994 devaluation, the terms of trade were increasingly unfavorable for private entrepreneurs dealing outside the national borders. When the SAPs were introduced, women had already begun to feel the pinch and were already moving toward both formal wage-paying jobs and, more regularly, toward the informal sector.[23] What the SAPs did was to give a sharper push to the existing process.

In the immediate aftermath of devaluation in a survey in February 1994, Senegalese women entrepreneurs were more likely than men to recount hardships in business owing to the cost of supplies, spare parts and fuel, energy (electricity), and food for their families, especially in outlying suburban or rural areas.[24] But in the space of one year, both men and women had begun to be more optimistic and see signs that their financial positions were improving (although women were slower to perceive this owing to their weaker financial position). In other words, the economic context had already begun to readjust to take the new parameters into account. It was harder for women, but they too were adapting, and at the top end they were beginning to benefit from the changes at least by the spring of 1995.

In terms of the empowerment issue, then, women were struggling to overcome greater odds, but as they succeeded it is arguable that they were being empowered because they were taking charge of their own situations and, where successful, were perhaps more able to control their own lives and families. Insofar as this is true, they were being empowered, not disempowered, by the process of being drawn out of the routine of bare survival in the traditional subsistence system. But for those who did not succeed, the process could hardly be described as empowering. The levels of poverty some women endured, and to which some succumbed and died, were intolerable and inhumane even in the sample of women interviewed in the 1995 study. However, the appropriate conclusion seems to be that some women, among the poor in Niger and Senegal in urban and rural areas and in the major ethnic groups, were able to overcome economic difficulties imposed by the SAPs; some were able to profit from the new economic environment (at least after a year or two had passed since devaluation); and some, sadly, were overwhelmed and drowned by the additional hardship. There was no single empowering or disempowering impact even for the poor.

The situation was worse in Niger than Senegal because the economy had been far weaker and the existing supports to women fewer. The breakdown of all government services (which culminated in the overthrow of the government in January 1996) was far more extreme in Niger. But even in Niger, the net result was not a uniform disempowerment of poor women. There were those who told of moving into processing and selling peanut oil again and beginning to get larger returns on their labors. Others were beginning to trade the newly competitive Nigérian products in Nigeria.

Slowly, but perceptibly, some of the smaller, poorer producers and traders were beginning to reap benefits. For those women who did, the process was empowering.

The second factor related to empowerment in Senegal and Niger is the web of financial interrelationships established over time upon which women in these countries depend. Businesses rely on networks of relationships that stretch from wealthy traders and producers to the smallest vendors in the markets. Thus, if there is a gain by larger producers or traders at the top because SAPs opened markets to them, they can and do on-lend larger amounts through suppliers' credit to smaller producers, who themselves continue the on-lending to the bottom of the chain. This is the infamous "trickle down" in its purest form without the intervention of formal private banks or government institutions. Because the whole notion of trickle down has been so thoroughly discredited by those working on the theory of development since the 1960s (myself included), this has to be closely examined to see if there really is merit in the idea that this system permits the advantages of the SAPs to eventually reach the poorest traders in the market. What follows here is an effort to examine women in the agrobusiness sector in Niger and Senegal to see what has happened to them since the SAPs were adopted and how this network affects that position.

Taking Niger first, work in the agrobusiness sector is divided by gender just as society is; however, this does not mean that women cannot begin to take on the same business activities as men. Women are rapidly beginning to enter all sectors of production and trade, including many that traditionally were done only by men. The 1995 research found, for example, a woman raising cattle and selling hides, formerly a male activity. Other traders were operating on a large scale, dealing in *niébé* (black-eyed peas) and onions (although the largest number were in some facet of the peanut trade). Women grew the crops, sold them, and also produced food products from the crops. Women did some or all of the chain, from growth as a crop to final processed product or by-product. Women traded in a variety of nonagricultural items as well, including even electrical equipment and building supplies, as well as the more traditional cloth, utensils, jewelry, and the like. The difference from male traders was that women had a number of constraints that the men did not. Furthermore, women at the lower levels, especially when they are starting out, tended to deal within a women's network only. Their traditional form of savings was through a *tontine* (mutual savings association) open only to women members. Their traditional form of credit was suppliers' credit offered primarily to other women traders. They also tended to sell to other women generally.

As women's businesses grow and diversify in Niger, they may begin to trade in the national and international markets, competing with male traders on relatively equal terms. At this level, they will get loans from banks and will be selling primarily to government agencies and national and international businesses. But very few women make it so far in their business. Women in Niger—in contrast to the coastal countries to the south—were rarely large-scale producers or merchants in 1995. Most women traders were at best medium-scale traders on a standard applied to traders generally. Probably fewer than ten Nigériennes would really have qualified as major traders in the international market.

To put all this in context, the web of financial relationships on which business is based in the informal sector in both countries must be considered. In Senegal, women relied on their own informal savings and credit organizations (*tontines*), established for a fixed period in which each member would give a set amount weekly or biweekly and then each take turns in using the amount gathered. A large-scale survey of credit and savings in Senegal published in 1991 found that loans from *tontines* are used for productive purposes such as commerce, which contradicts some earlier case studies.[25] In this 1991 study, which looked only at women already involved in business activities, all respondents belonged to *tontines* and all used their savings through the *tontines* for their business activities, although some mentioned groups to which they had belonged in the past and their money, which they had used for domestic needs. Thus, although *tontines* are a widespread institution covering many purposes other than directly productive activities, they are an essential source of fund mobilization and credit to women in agrobusiness.

In Niger, use of *tontines* by women is widespread as well. A study in 1993 found 50 percent of women in rural areas and 70 percent in urban areas saved through *tontines*.[26] A 1986 study on rural finance in Niger indicated a very similar structure to that described for Senegal.[27] *Tontines* in Niger are more widely used by women than men and are usually single-sex providers, although mixed ones exist.[28] The *tontines* may add new members, change the amount members contribute, and even institute a second cycle of saving-borrowing. They are also flexible in that a member may take the money ahead of her/his turn in case of emergency (with the agreement of the group). No interest is paid on *tontine* loans, and *tontine* savings are not invested. As in Senegal, *tontine* records and money are kept by *la mere de la tontine*, who may also act as the person to whom villagers come to place their savings independent of their contributions to the *tontine* fund.[29]

Like men, women in Senegal and Niger obtain money to start and grow small business activities primarily from their own savings, or from loans or gifts from relatives. Loans from relatives are often extended without any interest charge. Loans for productive activities from other individuals may or may not have a charge for the use of money (although most women will state that there is no interest involved because interest is contrary to Muslim law). One example of how such a charge is made is a woman producer of peanut oil in Kaffrine, Senegal, who obtains her peanuts from a large merchant in town. She pays slightly more per kilo for her peanuts than do other women who buy with cash; she repays in cash once her oil is made and sold. When peanuts are scarce, this merchant sells first to those who can pay directly, so her need for credit may mean she cannot always get the peanuts she needs. In another example, a woman trader in onions and rice offers loans to other smaller-scale women traders, which she makes in-kind. She calculates her repayment in terms of the value of the bags of rice and sets the value lower than in fact she will sell the rice for, once she is repaid in bags of rice. The difference is her charge for the loan.

The system of loans is very extensive and well-established within each of the fields of agrobusiness activity and sometimes crosses between activities. It is based on personal knowledge and trust. The wealthier woman trading at a slightly higher scale will loan to smaller-scale producers and traders, often in-kind but sometimes in cash. The latter woman will make credit available to those who buy from her. At the very bottom level, where items are being purchased singly or in small amounts for individual family consumption, credit is less likely because the credit is generally suppliers' credit made to those who will sell the product and repay with their earnings.

In a society where work is still most often organized by gender, it is not surprising that women tend to borrow from other women and loan to them within a women's financial network. This is not completely exclusive of linkages with men's networks, however. Women will buy (and borrow) from male large-scale producers and merchants and may on-lend to men as well within their field of activity. Individual men reported occasionally participating in women's *tontines* or saving in women's associations to which they do not belong. However, most commonly, women interviewed described working with, and lending to, other women. Because the system is based on personal acquaintance and/or relationships and trust, anyone who is seen as outside the network will not be able to participate in the lending system.

The chief form of savings for women in the informal sector is still individual savings held in the form of commodities such as grain, cattle and sheep, gold jewelry, and, more rarely, cash, either in a box at home (74 percent in rural areas) or through the services of a moneykeeper (20 percent).[30] However, many, perhaps most, women also save through participation in *tontines*, mutual aide societies/solidarity groups, or religious-based associations (*dahiras*). Most of these solidarity groups (60 percent) have both a savings and a credit function. The principal purpose of both individual and solidarity group savings is to finance the means of production (e.g., needed agricultural inputs and tools). In urban areas, however, the savings are primarily needed for commercial activities Improving the home or other noneconomic purposes (utensils, health, social needs) are secondary reasons for savings, contrary to the assumption about women's groups cited above.

Structural adjustment had been strongly felt in the rural areas of Niger by the spring of 1995. Countless women recounted that they were no longer able to go to Nigeria to buy the cloth, cosmetics, corn, sorghum, dried fish, and other items that they used to buy there to distribute in Niger. The devaluation of the CFA franc relative to the Nigerian currency had caught them unaware, and many found their savings (kept by moneykeepers or heads of *tontines*) worth very little compared to the predevaluation situation. Many were struggling to find ways of adapting to the changed market situation. Some were succeeding. Peanuts grown in Niger and peanut oil produced in Niger were now relatively cheaper than Nigerian products. Large-scale producers were already shifting to sell these commodities (and many other crop and animal products), whereas before they had purchased them outside the country. Smaller producers were making and selling peanut oil and found a larger market now than before. Women who had purchased dried fish in Nigeria were now going to outlying areas to purchase the same product in Niger. The markets in Maradi and Zinder were bustling with trucks from Niger, Nigeria, and the Ivory Coast picking up the commodities for trade in the south.

The overall picture was skewed, however. Women at the lower end were having a much more difficult time. Having less resources, they were more burdened with the debt resulting from devaluation, and they found it difficult to buy the new stock that they needed to begin operating in the new market climate. In numerous interviews, women traders discussed their businesses over their lifetimes, and, for almost all, the high point had been in the 1970s (1980s for the younger ones). The 1990s found them with few, if any, employees and smaller inventories, having to sell properties they had owned and unsure of how they could go forward.

In Senegal, the situation was parallel but less stark. There were a larger number of women in commerce on a larger scale in peanuts, rice, market crops, and fish as well as cloth, prepared foods, cosmetics, jewelry, and other items. Women were more evident in trading than in Niger, and large sections of women traders, some of whom traded on a very large scale, were to be found in all the major markets, including those in the more conservative north. Women at the lower end, however, were more numerous even in Senegal, and they, like their Nigérian counterparts, were suffering from SAP-induced market conditions in 1995.

In both Senegal and Niger, where women still rely on informal savings and credit schemes and depend on the traditional network of loans, it is not surprising that what emerged in the 1995 rural financial study was a picture of interdependency in which there was a trickling down of benefits. Merchants with larger stocks could on-loan greater amounts. Handling larger amounts produced larger profits down the chain. Producers and merchants also could and did assist others down the chain to change the commodities they handled adapt to the new market conditions. In this manner, the benefits that were already being perceived at the top by larger dealers were beginning to reach the bottom. One interesting anecdote illustrates the process. A 1993 report, which studied loans provided by an NGO-funded program (CARE BRK), disclosed that women were using their loans not for the stated purpose for which the money had been granted—to buy new or different stock or produce new or better products—but to on-loan the money to smaller vendors and producers in their chains of dependent business relationships. At first, CARE officials were angered and thought to discontinue loans to those women who admitted this practice. Later, however, they acknowledged that this was indeed a way of reaching the smaller, poorer, less accessible producers and vendors and they ceased penalizing for on-lending.[31]

But the system, although to some degree distributing benefits, is far from perfect, and the benefits are not equally shared. One example is the Harratin women who smoke and dry fish in Saint Louis and have been from time immemorial considered outsiders because of their Maure origins (and low caste). They suffer directly from being unable to participate in the supplier credit system, although they help each other as much as they can. They were excluded from the major fish dealers' financial chain and were in dire poverty, with only themselves to rely on. Their situation had worsened as staple foods and utilities had become more expensive owing to devaluation. Their efforts to compensate had not borne fruit in 1995. In the markets of Niger, women at the lowest level of trading had also not yet been able to benefit. Many had not yet found ways to change their stocks and also found the market weaker for those items that they could still sell because everyone around them had suffered from devaluation. Some medium-scale traders had been reduced to petty vendors, hanging on to their subsistence. A few, however, had begun to benefit. The increase in the market for peanuts, peanut oil, and other peanut products was noted among some of the poorer vendors in Niger. In Senegal, an increasing demand for fish, onions, peanut oil, as well as market garden crops had allowed some previously small, poor vendors to move toward gaining their own means of transportation and opening wider and more lucrative markets to their produce despite the rise in the price of spare parts and gasoline for vehicles.

## CONCLUSION

In sum, by 1995, some of the benefits of an open market for trade and a relative price advantage for domestically produced products had started to become discernible even among poorer women producers and traders in both Niger and Senegal. Thus, the SAPs appeared to have had an initial negativ effect on poor women of all ethnic groups and in all locations, which was moderating as time went by. Some women, depending on what they produced or what they traded, would find greater difficulties than others in adjusting. All of the poor women found the process difficult, but they were less disadvantaged by the loss of government programs than one might have supposed. The informal financial network was the basis of their business, not government social welfare programs, and this continued to operate as effectively as it had before. As ordinary people began to recover their purchasing power, the poorer producers and vendors began to regain their earlier position. Some were even able to develop much more successful businesses in the aftermath. The informal network was not undermined by the SAPs and continued to provide a safety net as well as a basis for possible business development for the poor at the bottom of the chain.

SAPs had a negative impact on the poor; this discussion is not meant to whitewash this fact. The emphasis on capitalism and private entrepreneurship is all well and good, but no one can honestly say this is an emphasis on equity and justice. Government programs that tried to promote equality in hiring and access to all resources were few and weak in Senegal and Niger, but they were better than nothing. In their absence, the weaker will have a harder time and suffer more than the strong and wealthy unless the recently added SAPs are given teeth, thus far absent in Senegal and Niger.[32] Women, by virtue of their preexisting position in society, had fewer resources for their struggle to adjust. Some succeeded, probably empowered in the process. Some did not, left as they had been—hanging on to survival—or specifically disempowered, even to the point of losing everything they had ever owned. It is a mistake, however, to assign a blanket impact for the SAPs where none existed. This approach blinds us to the best policies that might be introduced to help those who have the greater difficulty in taking advantage of the new economic conditions. Such approaches need to be creative and look to the existent traditional linkages and to family and community networks and build on them. But what these might be is a subject for another discussion.

## DISCUSSION QUESTIONS

1. What is the nature of women's informal financial networks and why are they important?

2. What are the reasons for the greater effect of SAPs on poor women than poor men in Niger and Senegal?

3. How and why is religion used to disempower women in Niger?

4. Why is the informal sector so important to women in the process of modernization?

## NOTES

1. Research for this paper was conducted while participating in a study sponsored by USAID. The latter study focused on rural financial networks throughout sub-Saharan Africa. Findings from that study are published in Lucy E. Creevey, Olaf Kula, Juneas Lekgetha, Catherine Neill, Eric Nelson, and Roland Pearson, *Rural Financial Institutions, Economic Policy Reform Programs, and Agribusiness in Sub-Saharan Africa,* Gemini Project (DHR-5448-Q-81-9081-00) (Washington, D.C.: USAID, September 1995).

2. The adjective used here is "Nigérian," with an accent to distinguish these women in the country of Niger from the women living in the much larger nation of Nigeria to the south.

3. Structural adjustment policies were adopted in an effort to reduce government debt in poor countries and make national exports more competitive. Policies primarily included opening markets, withdrawing government from investment in or ownership of banks, businesses, industries, and so on, and drastically reducing the size of government bureaucracy, encouraging private entrepreneurship by ending many government regulations of same, and devaluing the overpriced currencies.

4. The arguments are particularly well laid out in Pamela Sparr, "Feminist Critiques of Structural Adjustment," in Sparr, ed., *Mortgaging Women's Lives: Feminist Critiques of Structural Adjustment* (London: Zed Books, 1994), pp. 13–39. See also Diane Elson, "From Survival Strategies to Transformation Strategies: Women's Needs and Structural Adjustment," in Lourdes Benería and Shelley Feldman, eds., *Unequal Burden: Economic Crisis, Persistent Poverty* (Boulder: Westview, 1992).

5. Lucy Creevey, ed., *Women Farmers in Africa: Rural Development in Mali and the Sahel* (Syracuse: Syracuse University Press, 1984).

6. The USAID study can be found in Richard Vengroff, "Monitoring Action in the Private Sector (MAPS): Report on the Formal and Informal Sector Surveys in Senegal and Niger" (Dakar, Senegal: USAID, 1990). Other information comes from Pierre-Olivier Colleye, "Niger," in Leila Webster and Peter Fidler, eds., *The Informal Sector and Micro Finance Institutions in West Africa: Preliminary Version* (Washington, D.C.: World Bank, Private Sector Development Department, September 1995), pp. 11, 144.

7. The HDI is an index based on three indicators: longevity, educational attainment, and standard of living (measured by real GDP per capita, or PPP). See UNDP, *Human Development Report 1996* (New York: Oxford University Press, 1996), p. 106.

8. Ibid., p. 140.

9. Some marabouts' wives are cloistered, but this is uncommon even among pious Muslims of a very conservative persuasion in Senegal. See Barbara Callaway and Lucy Creevey, *The Heritage of Islam: Women, Religion, and Politics in West Africa* (Boulder: Lynne Rienner Publishers, 1994).

10. UNDP, *Human Development Report 1996*, pp. 140, 143.

11. Statistics on women's employment in Senegal are based on three studies: the National Census of 1988, a survey entitled *l'Enquete sur les Priorités* carried out by the Statistics Division of the government of Senegal (DPS) between 1991 and January 1992, and a survey entitled *l'Enquete l'Emploi, Sous-emploi, Chomage en Milieu Urbain,* also carried out by DPS in 1991. See government of Senegal, *Situation Economique Edition 1993* (Dakar: DPS, August 1994), pp. 43–84.

12. Ministére de l'Economie, des Finances et du Plan, *Dimensions Sociales de l'Adjustement: Enquête sure les Priorités: Resultats Préliminaires Dakar,* Direction de la Prévision de la Statistique, February 1993, pp. 22, 56.

13. Callaway and Creevey, *The Heritage of Islam,* pp. 132–137.

14. Ibid., chap. 5.

15. These data are drawn from tables prepared by the Banc Central des Etats de l'Afrique de l'Ouest and the Ministère des Femmes du Sénégal, "Femmes et Crédits" (1992), p. 61. See also Maurice Samaan and Yolanda Takesian, "Final Evaluation: Small-Scale Enterprise Component, Community Enterprise, and Development Project" (Dakar: USAID, December 1993), pp. 8–9.

16. Creevey, *Rural Financial Institutions,* p. 150.

17. Sparr, "Feminist Critiques of Structural Adjustment," pp. 21–22.

18. Winifred Weekes-Vagliani, "Structural Adjustment and Gender in Côte d'Ivoire," in Haleh Afshar and Carolyne Dennis, eds., *Women and Adjustment Policies in the Third World* (New York: St. Martin's, 1992), reprinted in the OECD Development Centre Reprint Series, no. 36 (Paris: OECD, 1992), pp. 123–126.

19. Ibid., p. 140.

20. See, for example, Rae Lesser Blumberg, Cathy Rakowski, Irene Tinker, and Michael Monteon, *Engendering Wealth and Well-Being: Empowerment for Global Change* (Boulder: Westview, 1992).

21. Lucy Creevey, *Changing Women's Lives and Work: An Analysis of Eight Microenterprise Projects* (London: IT Publications, 1996), pp. 209–219.

22. See Deborah Fahy Bryceson, "Women's Proletarianization and the Family Wage in Tanzania," in Haleh Afshar, ed., *Women, Work, and Ideology in the Third World* (London: Tavistock Publications, 1985).

23. In a survey conducted by this author in Senegal in 1991, results showed women involved in the economy in ways unimaginable during earlier research trips in the 1960s and 1970s. See Callaway and Creevey, *The Heritage of Islam.*

24. Lucy Creevey with Richard Vengroff, "Reaction to Devaluation in Senegal," *Journal of Modern African Studies* 33, no. 4 (1995): 669–683.

25. The statistics in this section are drawn from a nationwide survey in December 1990 by Assistance Technique aux Opérations Bancaires Mutualistes au Sénégal (ATOBMS). They are printed in ATOBMS, "Etude sur les Habitudes et Besoins des Populations-Cibles en Matière d'Epargne et de Crédit et sur l'Intermédiation Financière Informelle au Sénégal; Rapport Final" (Dakar: Ministère de l'Economie, des Finances et du Plan, June 1991), p. xiii.

26. Mariama Gamatié Bayard, "Impact socio-économique du système du crédit BRK dans la Région de Maradi" (Maradi: CARE, 1993).

27. Douglas Graham et al., *Finance Rurale au Niger: Une Evaluation Critique et Des Recommendations de Reforme,* Rapport Final Présenté par l'Université d'Etat du Ohio à l'USAID, Niamey, Niger (February 1987), pp. 151–165.

28. Fifty-seven percent were all women and an additional 41 percent had at least some women members.

29. Graham et al., *Finance Rurale au Niger.*

30. ATOBMS, "Etude sur les Habitudes et Besoins," especially pp. vii–xiii, 9–10; 74 percent includes both men and women.

31. Bayard, "Impact socio-économique"; interviews conducted in Maradi, 1995.

32. Added in response to a wave of international criticism that SAPs had disadvantaged the very poor and made their situation worse.

# 7

# Structural Adjustment Policies in Mexico and Costa Rica

## KIKI ANASTASAKOS

The structural adjustment programs (SAPs) undertaken by most states in Latin America and the Caribbean during the 1980s greatly affected the political, economic, and social fabric of the countries involved.[1] The policies of structural adjustment resulted in significant job reductions in the public as well as the private sectors and often led to the subsequent impoverishment of large segments of the population. Perhaps more than any other group, women were affected greatly by the structural adjustment efforts undertaken in the region. Many governments abandoned previous reforms and dramatically reduced public funding in areas such as education and health. Since a large number of women depended on such state programs for their welfare, SAPs affected them greatly and in several cases contributed to their disempowerment.

"Disempowerment" is understood to mean the lack of empowerment or a decrease in the level of empowerment among women. Central to the feminist discourse of politics, this all-important concept of empowerment is defined as a "process by which oppressed persons gain some control over their lives by taking part with others in development of activities and structures that allow people increased involvement in matters which affect them directly."[2]

An integral part of the empowerment process is economic and social well-being—the right to a livelihood and the ability to determine one's own future. Access to the tools required for economic and social progress, such as decent wages, education, and health care, is required if women are to become empowered. When facing unemployment, poor health, illiteracy, and domestic violence, women are disempowered and thus less able to participate in the political process and make claims on the state for the satisfaction of their collective needs.[3]

113

Since the state controls several of the resources affecting women's lives, the social and economic policies pursued by states may increase or diminish women's capacity to empower themselves. During the 1980s and early 1990s, SAPs in Mexico and Costa Rica reduced women's economic power and contributed to their low levels of literacy and health. Unable to exercise power within their families and communities, women became economically and politically disempowered.

The structural adjustment policies pursued in Mexico and Costa Rica during the 1980s and early 1990s were a retreat of the role of the state in managing the economy and included privatization of state enterprises and attempts to reduce budget deficits by curtailing public expenditures. In both countries, women faced increased unemployment and severe reductions in state funding for health care and education. As a result, they became largely unable to exercise any power within their families and communities. However, further comparison reveals that women became more disempowered in Mexico than in Costa Rica, where women fared somewhat better during the crisis. The findings in this study point toward the direction of the state, its institutions, and the specific policies it pursued during the period of structural adjustment.[4]

## THEORETICAL APPROACHES TO STRUCTURAL ADJUSTMENT AND WOMEN'S DISEMPOWERMENT

Among the extensive assessment studies of the SAPs that gained popularity and ideological strength during the 1980s, few have observed positive effects for women's empowerment. Diane Elson argues that SAPs were not only gender-blind but also gender-biased. She maintains that policies constrained women's ability to access paid employment and reduced state provision of public services, forcing households to pick up the slack. Thus, the cost of adjustment shifted from the paid to the unpaid economy and, as a result, to women who were the primary workers in the unpaid economy (i.e., the household).[5] According to Frances Stewart, cross-country evidence suggests that the impact of adjustment is mostly negative in terms of macroeconomic indicators as well as of poverty and basic needs. As a result, women have suffered more than men both in absolute and relative terms in several areas such as employment, social services, and prices.[6]

Henry Veltmeyer and James Petras found that during the period of structural adjustment in the 1980s women as a group faced more difficulties than men in finding work, were disproportionately affected by the historically high rates of layoffs and unemployment experienced by low-income workers, and suffered greater hardship in efforts to meet the demands of maintaining households and family life and in dealing with the rigorous conditions generated by SAPs.[7]

In 1995, the UN Commission on the Status of Women reported that one of the serious obstacles to eliminating poverty among Latin American women was the gradual decline in government spending on social programs, specifically those aimed at promoting gender equity, reflecting a broader shifting of responsibility for providing social services from the public to the private sector and civil society. The same study reported increases in unemployment, poverty, and inequality as well as increases in the number of households headed by women, most of whom worked in the informal sector without legal or social protection, and increasing female migration.[8]

The same report observed the existence of an institutional, social, and cultural structure that hindered women's empowerment at all levels, as well as the persistence of cultural patterns and stereotypes that reserved public power for men and assigned women exclusively to domestic functions. Furthermore, the same study revealed the existence, in social and political institutions, of machinery that is explicitly or implicitly discriminatory.[9]

Preliminary assessments by the UN Development Fund for Women indicate that coping responses during periods of structural adjustment may not be shared equally among members of the household. Women are reported to adopt their behavior to economic changes in an attempt to cushion the impact on their families. In what has been termed the "invisible adjustment," many women may be compelled to seek work in the informal sector or the service sector in order to maintain acceptable levels of household income. Often, leisure time or sleep is reduced to meet the demands on women's time while less time is spent with the children, with repercussions on standards of child care. Many families are forced to interrupt their children's education and send their sons out to work or keep their daughters home to take over domestic responsibilities.[10]

During the 1980s, the traditional model of the family with a head of a household who is the provider, a housewife who does the domestic work, and children who are in the educational system changed considerably and became less predominant. Woman-maintained households were more common due to migration, poverty, marital breakdown, and teenage pregnancy. Although there are methodological disagreements as to what constitutes a woman-headed household, the increase in female-led homes is estimated to be 20–30 percent.[11]

In traditional family settings, the impact of adjustment on women's empowerment must be analyzed in connection to family relations. Women are assigned to carry out the daily housework, which includes caring for children and elderly parents. The institutional support systems for the care of the very young, the elderly, and invalids were either nonexistent or very costly. With cuts in public funding for such programs, caring for elderly parents and seriously ill family members fell to the families, with women forced to carry a heavier load of domestic responsibilities.[12]

With the increase in food prices, cultural norms that encouraged unequal food distribution within families often resulted in women and girls
eating last and eating less than men and boys. This phenomenon led to
more malnourished women than men in certain communities, often leading
to protein deficiency and anemia. As the family income fell and women
asked their spouses for more money, marital conflict and domestic violence
increased as well.[13]

## THE RESEARCH METHOD

In this chapter I examine SAPs pursued by the state in Mexico and Costa
Rica and their impact on women's empowerment, particularly in the areas
of employment, education, and health. SAPs were advocated by the World
Bank and the International Monetary Fund (IMF) and were based on a liberal tradition of trade liberalization, reform of the price structure through
devaluation, reduction or elimination of subsidies, introduction of fees for
public utilities, wage freezes and higher producer incentives, particularly
for export crops, and a reduction of the role of the state not only in the
economy but also in the provision of social services.[14]

Thus, structural adjustment in the developing world during the 1980s
became synonymous with thorough experimentation in free-market economics. The rise to power of groups that espoused radical free-market
ideas, such as conservatives under Margaret Thatcher in Great Britain and
Ronald Reagan in the United States, combined with the acute debt crisis
facing many countries in the developing world, resulted in an intense pressure to adopt policies of economic restructuring.

The impact of structural adjustment on women's empowerment is ana-
lytically separated into short-, middle-, and long-term effects. Although the
short-term effects are usually contractionary through fiscal and monetary
restraint, the middle- and long-term growth effects of economic restructuring should be positive for the entire population, including women. However, the evaluation of long-term effects is extremely difficult due to our
limited ability to forecast long-term developments. Thus, this study will
center on the short- and middle-term effects of adjustment on women in
Mexico and Costa Rica for the period 1980–1990.[15]

The extent to which social institutions are gendered, promoting men's
or women's interests, varies from state to state. State responses to women's
empowerment depend on the gender construction of the family, the degree
of gender polarization in society and economy as well as the nature of state–
civil society relations, the nature of women's activism in civil society, and,
most important, the nature of the state. These factors result in diverse political and policy structures among states and largely determine state actions during structural adjustment.[16]

The economic crises in Mexico and Costa Rica during the 1980s, which prompted SAPs, were not identical. The years of recession—defined as falling per capita gross domestic product (GDP)—in Costa Rica were 1980–1983, whereas in Mexico recession occurred in 1982–1983 and again in 1986–1988. Costa Rica was more fortunate, as the contraction lasted for a shorter period of time while Mexico experienced two recessions over the decade.[17]

Nevertheless, the similarities are significant to justify a comparative study of the structural adjustment experiences of the two countries. Particularly at the beginning of the decade, both were heavily indebted and were confronted by a tremendous drop in capital inflows. When the crisis began, both had to eliminate their trade deficits (financed by foreign capital) and were confronted with the burden of finding the necessary resources to service their debts. In both cases, government budgets were under pressure while per capita income fell and poverty levels increased substantially.[18]

## STATE ECONOMIC POLICYMAKING IN
## MEXICO AND COSTA RICA DURING THE 1980S

During the course of 1982, Mexico found itself in an economic crisis of unprecedented proportions. Inflation was running at an annual rate of 100 percent, unemployment was rising, and the real minimum wage had been reduced; the government was unable to deal with the crisis. Moreover, the Mexican peso was depreciated by up to 82 percent in relation to the dollar and production declined. The public sector's fiscal deficit reached an unprecedented level, amounting to almost 16 percent of GDP.[19]

In 1982, the Miguel de la Madrid Hurtado administration adopted the IMF austerity Program (El Program Immediate de Reordenacion Economica), with emphasis on fiscal austerity, liberalization, and restructuring of the economy. Among the more important measures were public deficit reduction, price increases for goods and services provided by public agencies, and reduction by 40 percent of the number of public-sector firms.[20] Meanwhile, consumer prices practically doubled and wholesale prices rose by almost 93 percent (see Table 7.1).

Although the government raised the frequency of wage increases in 1986 to a cumulative 103 percent jump, it also increased prices and reduced subsidies on basic goods and services such as transportation and health care to make up for revenues lost from falling oil prices. The sharpest increases in controlled prices came in areas with significant impact on working families, many of which were headed by women: transportation, 117 4 percent; food and beverages, 108.7 percent; health and personal care, 113.7 percent. In addition, gasoline prices doubled while the subway fare increased from 1 peso to 20 pesos. Meanwhile, the draconian cutbacks in public-sector

**Table 7.1  Inflation of Domestic Prices in Mexico**

|                                   | 1977 | 1978 | 1979 | 1980 | 1981 | 1982 |
|-----------------------------------|------|------|------|------|------|------|
| Increase December to December     |      |      |      |      |      |      |
| Consumer price index              | 20.7 | 16.2 | 20.0 | 29.8 | 28.7 | 99.8 |
| Food                              | 21.6 | 15.4 | 20.1 | 29.4 | 24.7 | 89.8 |
| Wholesale price index             | 18.1 | 15.8 | 19.9 | 26.4 | 27.2 | 92.6 |
| Increase between annual averages  |      |      |      |      |      |      |
| Consumer price index              | 29.1 | 17.5 | 18.2 | 26.3 | 27.9 | 58.9 |
| Food                              | 28.6 | 16.5 | 18.4 | 25.0 | 26.2 | 53.5 |
| Wholesale price index             | 41.2 | 15.8 | 18.3 | 24.5 | 24.5 | 56.1 |

*Source:* ECLA, on the basis of figures supplied by the Banco de Mexico in *Economic Survey of Latin America and the Caribbean, 1982,* vol. 1 (New York: United Nations, 1982), p. 447.

expenditures, along with the sale of state enterprises, cost government employees more than 110,000 jobs from 1983 to 1985, many of which belonged to women.[21]

In Costa Rica, the economic expansion of the late 1970s gave way in the early 1980s to the deepest recession since the 1930s. Gross national product stagnated between 1979 and 1980 and then fell in 1981 and 1982. This was followed by a dramatic increase in inflation (from 18.1 percent in 1980 to 90.1 percent in 1982) and a steep decline in real earnings (35 percent from July 1980 to July 1982). The unemployment rate rose steadily from 1979 and reached a peak of 9.4 percent in July 1982. Underemployment also increased, from 4.7 percent of the labor force in 1979 to 7 percent in 1982.[22]

In 1982, the cost of living index rose at an unprecedented average rate of 90 percent. The food price index rose even more rapidly. In 1981, the average increase in the consumer price index had been 37 percent. Inflation, however, rose at a much faster rate, as the increase from December to December was 82 percent in 1982 compared with 65 percent in 1981 (see Table 7.2).

In the second half of 1982, the Costa Rican government made several major price adjustments in an effort to restore the economy. Fuel prices were increased by 92 percent and public transport rates by 100 percent. The increases in the rates of other services, such as electricity, water, and telephone, ranged from more than 60 percent for the telephone company to somewhat less than 200 percent for electricity.[23]

During the first half of 1982, real average wages and salaries suffered a new and dramatic decline of 23.6 percent, after having fallen by more than 11 percent in 1981 and by almost 3 percent in 1980. This meant a return to a level similar to that of the previous decade. Considering that inflation rose somewhat during the second half of the year, the overall drop in wages and salaries for the year was probably even greater. The drop was

Table 7.2   Inflation of Domestic Prices in Costa Rica

|  | 1977 | 1978 | 1979 | 1980 | 1981 | 1982 |
|---|---|---|---|---|---|---|
| Increase December to December |  |  |  |  |  |  |
| Consumer price index | 5.3 | 8.1 | 13.2 | 17.8 | 65.1 | 81.8 |
| Food | 8.6 | 15.9 | 14.7 | 18.8 | 70.4 | 101.1 |
| Wholesale price index | 7.4 | 9.4 | 24.0 | 19.3 | 117.2 | 79.1 |
| Increase between annual averages |  |  |  |  |  |  |
| Consumer price index | 4.2 | 6.0 | 9.2 | 18.1 | 37.0 | 90.1 |
| Food | 4 8 | 10.3 | 12.6 | 21.8 | 36.7 | 113.6 |
| Wholesale price index | 7.5 | 7.8 | 16.1 | 23.7 | 65.3 | 108.3 |

*Source:* ECLA, on the basis of official figures in *Economic Survey of Latin America and the Caribbean, 1982,* vol. 1 (New York: United Nations, 1982), p. 236.

sharpest for employees of the central government; the average minimum wages of the lower level of workers declined much less (6.3 percent) than the average.[24]

Starting in 1984, the state began a comprehensive structural adjustment program. The aim was to increase and diversify exports. In particular, "nontraditional" exports were encouraged through tax breaks, subsidies, and technical assistance. By 1986, real earnings had nearly regained 1980 levels and GDP growth reached 5.5 percent. Between 1986 and 1989, GDP growth averaged 4.5 percent and unemployment and inflation rates remained low.[25]

By 1990, the majority of Costa Rica's exports by value were labor-intensive nontraditional exports. Most successful have been agricultural goods like flowers, ornamental plants, and pineapples as well as some manufacturing, most notably textiles and electronic assembly. It is likely that women were disproportionately represented in this sector, particularly in the textile and electronic assembly industries.[26]

## THE IMPACT OF STATE POLICIES ON WOMEN'S EMPOWERMENT

In altering the structure of its economy, Mexico dismantled most trade barriers, drastically reduced state intervention, and substantially deregulated the economy. The Mexican government attempted to combat inflation and attract capital inflows while reducing wages to cheapen Mexican labor. Despite these efforts, growth and job creation did not materialize. The social costs on Mexican workers were very heavy, particularly on women: from 1984 to 1989, the ratio of female-to-male urban workers went from 77 percent to 72 percent.[27] Furthermore, women's industrial wages went down from 80 percent of men's wages to 57 percent. Meanwhile, in the public and other sectors, women's job share was reduced from 42 percent to 35 percent.[28]

As public-sector work was cut, Mexican women lost job protection as well as security and benefits. These cuts hit low-skill women the hardest, as they were concentrated in low-wage sectors and low-wage jobs within sectors. Many worked in the *maquiladoras* (large assembly industries) along the U.S.-Mexican border, thus increasing women's share in the industrial sector from 15 percent in 1984 to 18 percent in 1992. In addition, many young rural women emigrated to other countries, where they found work as domestic servants; others worked as day laborers, where they had no social benefits or social security, lived in sheds, and were easy targets for sexual abuse.[29]

Similarly, the male-female wage and earnings differentials in Costa Rica increased between 1980 and 1982. The increase in the male-female wage differential during the recession was primarily due to women entering the labor force to compensate for the falling earnings of their spouse. These women had lower levels of education than women already in the labor force and worked in low-wage jobs.[30]

However, Costa Rican women, unlike their Mexican counterparts, kept their jobs and pay in the public sector, where they were heavily concentrated. Furthermore, by 1989 the male-female wage differential was 3.5 percent for the country as a whole, down from 8.6 percent in 1987. Put differently, from 1987 to 1993, the ratio of average female wages to male wages rose from 77 percent to 83 percent in Costa Rica. Meanwhile, from 1984 to 1992, the latter being a year of economic recovery, Mexican women's total income declined from 71 percent to 66 percent of men's.[31]

Compared to Mexico, Costa Rica took a more gradual approach to restructuring its economy and had some success in doing so. The Costa Rican government increased nontraditional exports and tourism and managed to create some economic growth and employment. The export-oriented assembly firms in electronics and apparel created more jobs for women without lowering their pay.

Furthermore, the government contributed to women's social well-being by increasing maternity leave and ratifying the International Labour Organization's (ILO) convention on discrimination in 1958. In 1990, it passed its own law of equality (the Law for the Promotion of the Social Equality of Women), the most comprehensive law of its kind in Latin America. The first article of this law stated that "it is the obligation of the state to promote and guarantee the equality of rights between men and women in the political, economic, social and cultural arenas."[32]

In providing social programs related to women's economic and social welfare, the difference in state policies between Mexico and Costa Rica is evident. Although both countries were intensively adjusting in the 1980s, public expenditures on health and education in Costa Rica, although in decline from 1980 to 1990, were markedly higher than public expenditures in

Mexico during the same period. Although Costa Rica reduced its share of public expenditures from 32 percent in 1983 to 28 percent in 1986, it still far exceeded the public funds allocated by the state in Mexico for similar programs (see Table 7.3).

In Mexico, as material resources, social services, and income for family maintenance dwindled, women began to alter their consumption patterns and the amount and type of paid and unpaid labor they engaged in. Increasing numbers of women and children entered the informal and formal wage labor forces as self-provisioning of goods and services formerly purchased increased, forcing women to carry heavier domestic workloads.[33]

The decline in minimal health services resulted in poor nutritional and health conditions, as well as widespread incidence of morbidity, malaria, yellow fever, measles, and other tropical diseases among women. High incidence of malnutrition has also been observed among rural women entering the labor force. In the 1980–1992 period, the maternal mortality rate (per 100,000 live births) reached 110 in Mexico; it was only 36 in Costa Rica.[34]

The Mexican government's retrenchment in the education sector resulted in layoffs of teachers and reduced salaries, contributing to the deterioration of the general quality of education. Due to social patterns, low-income families, who could no longer afford to send their children to a university and having to make a choice between educating a son or a daughter, decided to pay for the technical education for the son.[35] The difference in rates of illiteracy among men and women in the two countries is evident Mexico has a significantly higher rate of illiteracy in the overall population than Costa Rica, as well as a larger illiteracy gap between men and women, particularly in the twenty-five and older age bracket (see Table 7.4).

Table 7.3  Expenditures on Health and Education in Mexico and Costa Rica, 1981–1990

| | H+E as Percentage of Expenditure | | H+E as Percentage of GNP | | Index of H+E Expenditure Per Capita |
| --- | --- | --- | --- | --- | --- |
| | 1981 | 1990 | 1981 | 1990 | 1990 (1981 = 1) |
| Costa Rica | 53.40 | 44.20 | 12.66 | 11.98 | 1.02 |
| Mexico | 20.10 | 15.80 | 4.18 | 2.91 | 0.61 |
| Average (intensive adjusting) | 24.27 | 20.07 | 6.10 | 5.43 | 1.17 |

Source: World Bank, World Development Reports, various years.

Table 7.4 Illiteracy Rates by Sex in Mexico and Costa Rica, 1985–1994

| | Percentage Age 15–24 Illiterate | | Percentage Age 25+ Illiterate | |
|---|---|---|---|---|
| | Women | Men | Women | Men |
| Costa Rica | 2.4 | 3.3 | 10.1 | 9.6 |
| Mexico | 5.1 | 4.0 | 20.4 | 12.7 |

*Source:* UN Secretariat, *Women's Indicators and Statistics Database* (WISTAT), Version 3, DC-ROM (New York: United Nations).

## THE ROLE OF STATE INSTITUTIONS AND WOMEN'S EMPOWERMENT

Since the state controls the resources that are required for any meaningful transformation in women's lives, its character, institutions, and policies have an undeniable impact on women's empowerment. Two features of the Mexican state are significant for the purpose of this study: (1) the fusion between the state and the Partido Revolucionario Institucional (PRI, formerly the ruling party); and (2) statism, the paramount role that the state plays in the economy and society. Political parties other than PRI have not played a crucial role in the Mexican system other than legitimating the electoral process.

In the meantime, state institutions have generally had far more prestige, resources, and influence than private, independent, or nonprofit organizations. The institution of the presidency was far more powerful than the legislative and judicial branches of government, which were ineffectual compared to the president. In addition to this ineffectiveness, a self-selecting political and technocratic bureaucracy in the state's power structure lacked any constituent responsibilities and was largely indifferent to issues of economic and social equity.[36]

Mexico's semicorporatist political system was based on the mass organizations affiliated to the ruling PRI. The three key labor organizations—the Confederacion de Trabajadores de Mexico, the Confederacion Nacional Campesina, and the Confederacion Nacional de Organizaciones Populares—played a critical role of social control and secured votes for the PRI. Members of these organizations were affiliated with the PRI, they voted for it during elections, and, in return, received government jobs and seats in Congress.[37]

Costa Rica, by contrast, is widely regarded as a model democracy, a unique case in a region where few governments have been democratically elected and have served their full terms. Since 1948, elections in Costa Rica have been supervised by the judicial branch of government, and the country's constitution renounces the maintenance of a standing army. There is a free press and vocal, responsible opposition parties. The state has enacted extensive social legislation, including universal provision of services in health and education, and family income assistance. It has also sponsored progressive experiments in areas such as nutrition, housing, and land reform. Despite the fact that Costa Rica shares with other Central American countries a heavy dependency on export agriculture, its political and economic structures have differed considerably due to a number of unique historical circumstances.

In 1943, Costa Rica became the first country in Latin America to pass modern social welfare legislation. In the following years, there was considerable institutional growth toward what is considered the "Benefactor State," focusing on state-led economic growth, social welfare guarantees, and redistributive economic policies.[38]

Although the structural adjustment crisis of the 1980s put Costa Rica's democracy to a severe test, the state maintained its focus in distributing the costs of economic stagnation. Both the governments of the Partido Liberacion Nacional and the Partido Unidad Social Cristiana continued social expenditures, although at reduced levels. Furthermore, concern over the dominance of the executive branch, as well as the extensive use of executive decree power in the early 1980s, led to the creation of the Constitutional Court, which was given the authority to determine the constitutionality of the policy process.[39]

The relatively autonomous state in Costa Rica developed formal and informal mechanisms to mediate class relations and, as a result, was responsive to the demands of the popular sectors during the economic crisis. This was facilitated by the nature of the state, which has been influenced by relatively egalitarian social relations and broad political participation.[40]

A close examination of the available data reveals that women's empowerment in both Mexico and Costa Rica suffered serious setbacks due to the overwhelming burden of the SAPs of the mid-1980s. However, in comparing the two countries, it is evident that women fared better in Costa Rica than in Mexico. There is no doubt that the problems were considerable for the Costa Rican women: many were unemployed or predominated in low-paying jobs such as domestic work while severe cuts were made in the education and health sectors. Yet the state was successful in lessening the severe impact of adjustment on women through economic and social policies, which contributed positively to women's well-being.

## CONCLUSION

During the 1980s and early 1990s, many countries in the developing world experienced a drastic reorientation in economic policies. Severe debt crises in many developing countries and the emergence of free-market ideas in countries like Britain and the United States placed the notion of structural adjustment at the center of the development debate. The new policies of structural adjustment meant a retreat of the state from managing the economy and significant reductions in state expenditures in education, health, and other social services. The impact of such drastic economic restructuring was felt by many vulnerable groups, women in particular.

In countries like Mexico and Costa Rica, women faced increased unemployment, malnutrition, poor health, and illiteracy. Their inability to meet their basic needs resulted in their increased disempowerment in both countries. However, women in Mexico became more disempowered than Costa Rican women, where the state pursued specific gender policies in an effort to lessen the burden of structural adjustment on women.

By the mid-1980s, the international community generally acknowledged the social and political implications of the SAPs. International development agencies, such as the World Bank and the IMF, began adjustment lending "with a human face" and provided "social safety nets," or emergency relief funds, to reduce the impact of adjustment measures on certain groups. Although safety net measures were meant to target "vulnerable groups," women were not the primary direct beneficiaries of such activities. Many of the state agencies and nongovernmental organizations executing these measures did not reach women because they had no specific gender policies and were generally better suited to providing relief than challenging traditional gender roles.

The structural adjustment measures pursued in the 1980s and early 1990s in countries like Mexico and Costa Rica tended to reduce the level of women's empowerment, particularly in the short and medium terms. The retrenchment of public-sector employment, the reduction in social services, and other measures contributed to the stagnation of women's empowerment. Most states did not seriously consider the social costs associated with the economic policies of adjustment and had no specific gender provisions targeting women. Often, states found themselves in a position where they had to devise their own policies to counter the impact of SAPs. Some, such as Costa Rica, performed better than others. In most cases, economic policies were pursued without consideration of the social idiosyncrasies of each society, and women's collective needs were often overlooked in favor of oversimplified prescriptions for economic development. As a result, women in many societies were disempowered; the political feasibility and success of the adjustment policies still remain under question.

## DISCUSSION QUESTIONS

1. What were the main domestic and international challenges that developing countries such as Mexico and Costa Rica were facing in the

1980s? How did structural adjustment policies come to be considered the "preferred strategy" for dealing with such challenges?

2. How does the state affect women's capacity to empower themselves? What strategies can women in developing countries utilize in their efforts to deal with gender discrimination in their social and economic domain?

3. Are all women in developing countries equally disempowered by policies of structural adjustment? Which socioeconomic groups seem to be more vulnerable to such policies?

4. In what way were Mexican and Costa Rican women disempowered as a result of the SAPs? Why were Mexican women worse off as a result of the structural adjustment policies?

5. What policy lessons can be learned from the Mexican and Costa Rican experiences? How can developing countries achieve the delicate balance of economic development and gender equality?

## NOTES

1. Many countries in Africa and Latin America pursued SAPs during the 1980s within the context of domestic economic crises, shortage of foreign capital, and tremendous debt obligations. International lending agencies such as the World Bank insisted upon economic reform, and receipt of official development aid often became dependent upon adopting adjustment measures. See Henry Vertmeyer, James Petras, and Steve Vieux, *Neoliberalism and Class Conflict in Latin America: A Comparative Perspective on the Political Economy of Structural Adjustment* (New York: St. Martin's, 1996), p. 58. They point out that conditions for structural adjustment loans usually involved some mixture of politics aimed at (1) the shrinking of the state—the cutting of central government deficits through tax reforms and expenditure reductions such as privatization, subsidy cutting, and so on; (2) sound fiscal policy and devaluation to achieve a "competitive exchange rate" for the purpose of promoting exports and discouraging imports; and (3) import liberalization—reduction of tariffs and quantitative import restrictions—to promote efficiency and competitive industry.

2. Jill M. Bystydzienski, ed., *Women Transforming Politics* (Bloomington: Indiana University Press, 1992), p. 3.

3. Leslie J. Calman, *Toward Empowerment: Women and Movement Politics in India* (Boulder: Westview, 1992), p. 192.

4. I am thankful to Richard Deeg, Gary Mucciaroni, and Ben Stavis, Department of Political Science, Temple University, for their support and intellectual guidance in preparing this chapter for publication.

5. Diane Elson, "Male Bias in Structural Adjustment," in H. Afshar and C. Dennis, eds., *Women and Adjustment Policies in the Third World* (New York: St. Martin's, 1992).

6. Frances Stewart, "Can Adjustment Programmes Incorporate the Interests of Women?" in H. Afshar and C. Dennis, eds., *Women and Adjustment Policies in the Third World* (New York: St. Martin's, 1992), p. 13.

7. Henry Veltmeyer and James Petras, *Neoliberalism and Class Conflict in Latin America* (New York: St. Martin's, 1996), p. 27.

8. UN Commission on the Status of Women, Latin America and the Caribbean, Thirty-Ninth Session, "Preparations for the Fourth World Conference on Women: Action for Equality, Development and Peace" (New York, March 15–April 4, 1995), p. 2.

9. Ibid., p. 4.

10. United Nations Development Fund for Women, "Preliminary Assessment of Impact of Stabilization and Structural Adjustment Programmes on Selected UNIFEM-Supported Projects," Occasional Paper No. 10 (New York: United Nations, 1991), p. 7.

11. Mayra Buvinic and Geeta Rao Gupta, "Women-Headed Households and Woman-Maintained Families: Are They Worth Targeting to Reduce Poverty in Developing Countries?" *Economic Development and Cultural Change* (1995).

12. Irma Arriagada, *Latin American Women at the End of the Century: Family and Work* (Instituto del Tercer Mundo, 1997), available online at socwatch@chasque.apc.org.

13. Pamela Sparr, *Feminist Critiques of Structural Adjustment* (London: Zed Books, 1994), pp. 26–27.

14. United Nations Development Fund for Women, "Preliminary Assessment," p. 9.

15. M. Quiesser, O. Larranaga, and M. Panadeiros, *Adjustment and Social Development in Latin America During the 1980s* (Munich: Wertforum Verlag, 1995).

16. United Nations Research Institute for Social Development (UNRISD), Occasional Paper No. 2, "The Politics of Integrating Gender to State Development Processes" (Geneva: UNRISD, May 1995), GE.95–01420 UNRISD/OP2, p. 4.

17. Samuel A. Morley, *Poverty and Inequality in Latin America* (Baltimore: Johns Hopkins University Press, 1991), p. 9.

18. Ibid., pp. 60–61.

19. United Nations, *Economic Survey of Latin America and the Caribbean, 1982,* vol. 1 (New York: United Nations, 1982), pp. 419–425.

20. Miguel d. Ramirez, *Mexico's Economic Crisis: Its Origins and Consequences* (Praeger: New York, 1989), pp. 98–99.

21. United Nations, *Economic Survey of Latin America and the Caribbean,* vol. 1, p. 446.

22. Ibid., p. 449.

23. George Psacharopoulos and Zafiris Tzannatos, eds., *Case Studies on Women's Employment and Pay in Latin America* (Washington, D.C.: World Bank, 1992), p. 224.

24. United Nations, *Economic Survey of Latin America and the Caribbean,* vol. 1, p. 237.

25. Ibid.

26. Ibid.

27. Ibid., p. 224.

28. United Nations, *Human Development Report 1995* (New York: United Nations, 1995), p. 40.

29. Ibid.

30. UNICEF, American and the Caribbean Regional Office, Regional Programme Women in Development, *Poor Women and the Economic Crisis: The Invisible Adjustment,* 2nd ed. (Santiago: UNICEF), pp. 66–67.

31. Psacharopoulos and Tzannatos, *Case Studies on Women's Employment,* p. 224.

32. United Nations, *Human Development Report 1995,* p. 40.

33. Psacharopoulos and Tzannatos, *Case Studies on Women's Employment,* p. 224.

34. Gerardo Otero, ed., *Neoliberalism Revisited: Economic Restructuring and Mexico's Political Future* (Boulder: Westview, 1996), p. 167.

35. United Nations, *Human Development Report 1995,* p. 54.

36. Otero, *Neoliberalism Revisited,* p. 13.

37. Ibid.

38. Otero, *Neoliberalism Revisited,* p. 14.

39. Mitchell A. Seligson, *Elections and Democracy in Central America, Revisited* (Chapel Hill: University of North Carolina Press, 1995), p. 116.

40. Laura Macdonald, *Supporting Civil Society: The Political Role of Non-Governmental Organizations in Central America* (New York: St. Martin's, 1997), pp. 36–37.

# 8

# Making Waves: Women and Development in the Caribbean

## Marian A. L. Miller

Caribbean countries experience the problems common to many developing countries. People face the challenges of declining quality of life, rising unemployment, and decreasing real incomes. Because of their neocolonial links to the global economy, their economies are being developed to satisfy external interests rather than internal needs. As a consequence, they follow a development model that places more emphasis on abstractions like gross domestic product (GDP) than it does on people's well-being. Progressive forces in the region encourage a search for alternative models of development, and Caribbean women are empowering themselves and becoming leaders in the attempt to build alternatives.

The women of the region do not make up a homogeneous group. Any analysis must therefore consider the dynamics of race, color, class, and country. Although the women are all subject to gender bias, the other factors affect the way gender bias is experienced. Class is generally a more significant variable than race, color, or country. A woman executive with a transnational corporation is likely to have priorities that are significantly different from those of her housekeeper. Consequently, although all women have to deal with socially mandated gender roles in societies historically dominated by men, poor women are particularly vulnerable.

In this chapter I examine some of the barriers faced by women in various regions of the Caribbean, and it explores how they have organized to empower themselves and address these constraints. It focuses on the Commonwealth Caribbean group of countries, which includes Antigua and Barbuda, the Bahamas, Barbados, Belize, Dominica, Grenada, Guyana, Jamaica, St. Kitts and Nevis, St. Lucia, St. Vincent, and Trinidad and Tobago.

## THE STATUS OF WOMEN

Women experience a variety of social and economic circumstances throughout the region, but their circumstances are related to pervasive gender bias. Data gathered by the United Nations Development Programme (UNDP) can be used to illustrate the status of women in the region. The UNDP's Gender-related Development Index scores a country's achievements with regard to longevity, literacy, enrollment in school, and per capita GDP and adjusts the measurement for gender inequality. The UNDP's ranking of 143 countries included the five largest countries in the Commonwealth Caribbean group—the Bahamas, Belize, Guyana, Jamaica, and Trinidad and Tobago. The Bahamas led the group, ranking thirty-second with a score of 0.842 (out of a possible score of 1.0). The others were in the middle third of the global group. Guyana, eightieth with a score of 0.698, was the lowest-ranked member of the group.[1]

The data reveal gender-related differences in some important areas. In each country men control a larger share of earned income than do women, although the difference varies significantly among the five countries: at one end, in the Bahamas the GDP per capita income for women is about 65 percent of the GDP per capita income for men; at the other end, in Belize the figure for women is 25 percent. The picture is mixed with regard to literacy rates. In Jamaica, women have a significantly higher rate of literacy than do men, whereas in Trinidad and Tobago the opposite holds true. In the other cases, the difference is less than two percentage points, with women having the advantage in the Bahamas, men having the advantage in Guyana and Belize. There is no significant difference in gross school enrollment at the primary, secondary, and tertiary levels, but a closer examination shows significant differences.[2] At the primary and secondary levels, females outperform males. This is reflected by performances in the Common Entrance Examination, which was used to determine high school places, as well as by performance in the official examination toward the end of high school.[3] A focus on the tertiary level shows that women make up the majority of students. Academic year 1994–1995 data for the University of the West Indies (UWI), the region's major university, show women making up 61.3 percent of the undergraduate population and 54.9 percent of the graduate population. Women have made inroads into such traditionally male spheres as medicine and law, but they are primarily concentrated in the faculties of arts and general studies and social sciences. The faculty of engineering is still dominated by men.[4] These differences reflect the perception by many that academic accomplishment, especially in areas such as language and literature, is effeminate.[5]

UNDP provided information on economic activity for six of the twelve countries in our group.[6] In its examination of the participation in the formal economy among women fifteen years and older, UNDP shows a wide range among these countries, from 69.1 percent in Jamaica to 26.3 percent in Belize. Only three countries—the Bahamas, Barbados, and Jamaica—show figures above 50 percent.[7] These data indicate that women's economic activity is a more significant component of the formal economy in the majority Afro-Caribbean countries, like Jamaica, the Bahamas, and Barbados, than in countries like Trinidad and Tobago and Guyana, where there is a significant Indo-Caribbean heritage, or in a country like Belize with its blend of ethnic heritages, including African, Mayan, and Hispanic influences.

Although women make up a significant part of the workforce, their decisionmaking opportunities are limited. They make up more than 50 percent of the professional and technical workforce in the Bahamas, Barbados, Jamaica, and Trinidad and Tobago, but they hold between 30 percent and 40 percent of administrative and managerial positions.[8] In addition, they very rarely hold the top management positions.

Women are also underrepresented in parliament and local government offices. An examination of the Bahamas, Dominica, Guyana, Jamaica, St. Lucia, and Trinidad and Tobago indicates that all of these countries, with the exception of St. Lucia, have at least one woman mayor. For the Bahamas, Dominica, Guyana, and Trinidad and Tobago, some 20–30 percent of the mayors are women.[9] In nine of the twelve Commonwealth Caribbean countries, women hold more than 10 percent of the seats in parliament.[10] Most of the countries exceed the world average of 13.1 percent, but this is far from satisfactory.[11] The decisions that determine the economic and social context within which women operate are still primarily made by men, inside and outside of these countries. These decisions directly affect the options that women are able to exercise in a number of arenas, including the workplace.

## WOMEN IN THE WORKFORCE

Caribbean women have always participated in the workforce. Many do this by working outside their homes: they have worked in the canefields, in factories, in other people's kitchens, as well as in technical and professional settings. Others work at home preparing crafts or food for sale. From the early sixteenth century to 1838, women slaves were required to be fully involved in the formal economy. Although slavery is no more, other informal constraints are operative, and women's contribution is still central to the region's economy, in both the agricultural and nonagricultural arenas.

### Women in the Agricultural Sector

Women have long been involved in Caribbean agriculture. During slavery, they worked alongside men in the canefields. They also worked on the land allotments given to the slaves for subsistence farming. Women worked these plots and sold the surplus in the market, beginning their role as the main producers of food crops throughout the region.

Agriculture in the Caribbean has to be understood in the context of a plantation heritage that emphasized monocrop production for export and neglected food production for local markets. This consolidation of land into large units has disadvantaged small farmers and resulted in unequal distribution of land. For example, the 1971 Barbados Agricultural Census indicated that the plantation sector controlled 87 percent of the total acreage and represented 1 percent of the number of holdings. Thirteen percent of the total acreage was divided among 99 percent of the holdings.[12]

This is the economic context in which most Caribbean women agricultural workers work today. Women make up 30–50 percent of the agricultural labor force in the region.[13] They can be placed in three principal categories: small farmers, agricultural wage laborers, and traders in farm produce.

As small farmers, they work the land by themselves or with their husbands or partners. The constraints small farmers face are particularly severe for women farmers. They typically own or rent very small plots of land and have very little access to capital or credit. Most have only a few years of schooling, and extension officers and aid agencies often do not include women farmers in programs offering training, credit, and new technologies. This is partly because women tend to focus on food production for local consumption, whereas government planners typically focus on export crops.

Scholars have identified a range of reasons for women's involvement in farming. A study of women farmers in Barbados found that the most fundamental gender distinction was relevant to people's reason for farming. "For women, farming is an integral part of social reproduction, part of being a mother or a wife; for many men it functions primarily as economically productive labour."[14] A Trinidad study found that women there farmed out of necessity, and they did not want their children to become farmers.[15] By contrast, women in Guyana[16] and St. Vincent[17] had a more positive attitude toward farming. This could be because of the differences in the levels of industrialization. Trinidad is much more industrialized than the other two countries, with significant industrial and service sectors; the industrial and service sectors may be regarded as more modern and profitable than the agricultural sector.

In the agricultural workforce, women also work as traders. Women traders, known as higglers, buy produce from small farmers and transport it to town markets or even to other countries. Some women also work as agricultural wage laborers. Although women farmers and traders work hard for little return, women who work as laborers on land owned by others are the most exploited. Wages for field hands are at the bottom of the pay scale and are usually lower for women than for men.[18]

The practice of underpaying women for their labor rests on a prevalent myth—that women are not the breadwinners. They are supported by their husbands, so their wages are merely supplemental. In other words, it is extra spending money. This has never been true for the majority of Caribbean women. A great many are single heads of households. Many others who have partners must work to supplement the men's earnings.

For many rural young women, remaining in the agricultural workforce is not a particularly attractive prospect. The hardships of rural life, combined with rising educational levels, have prompted a large-scale migration of younger women to the urban areas.

## Women in the Nonagricultural Sector

Many women leave school and migrate from the rural to the urban areas in search of work. In some areas, unemployment rates for women are twice as high as the rate for men. As a result, many women have turned to the growing informal economy, earning money as market vendors, craftswomen, and dressmakers.

Informal commercial importers (ICIs) make up a significant part of the informal economy. They go to regional destinations such as Grand Cayman, Haiti, Curaçao, and Panama and buy goods that they bring back home to sell. As this has become a more significant part of the economy, governments have moved to regulate the ICIs by means of customs and taxation, which the women find oppressive.[19]

For those in the formal economy, women earn less than men at every step along the class ladder. They are concentrated in professions thought of as being "female." Women with limited education tend to be in semiskilled, low-status, and poor-paying jobs. Domestic workers are among the most exploited, reflecting the low social value attached to housework. Because of the individual nature of domestic work and the endless stream of women needing work, it has been hard for them to organize.

Caribbean women are increasingly exploited by transnational corporations that locate their factories wherever labor costs are lowest. Corporate managers say they hire women because they are better suited to delicate work such as assembling electronic components and stitching garments. These assembly factories usually offer low pay, job insecurity, and the absence of trade unions. Workers can lose their jobs abruptly for reasons such as pregnancy, talking back to a supervisor, and refusing to work overtime. Governments that are anxious to create jobs sometimes tacitly promise corporations a nonunion workforce. Where unions do function, their power is limited by the companies' ability to shut down and leave the country on short notice rather than meet union demands.[20]

The tourism industry, as it operates in the Caribbean, perpetuates many elements of neocolonialism, with significant foreign ownership and control and significant dependence. But tourism is also an important sector, where one in six workers finds direct employment. These are largely unskilled jobs. In the hotel sector, these would include maids, security personnel, and waitresses. This is often seasonal work and can be disruptive to personal life because of changing shifts. But some women switch from domestic service to hotel work because of higher pay, regular hours, and better conditions.[21] Some women are also indirectly employed as a result of the tourism industry, working as vendors in and near resort areas. But this is an uncertain way to earn a living. In some contexts, as the vendors' numbers increase, they are perceived as nuisances, and they are either removed or required to undergo training and licensing.[22] These tensions accentuate locals' resentment of tourism and tourists.

Some women operate in the resort areas as sex workers. They often cite economic desperation as the reason for their livelihood. Sex tourism seems to be disruptive to local communities, not only because of the racialized aspects of the business but also because of the tensions caused within families.[23]

Women with more formal education have wider choices, and some of them are taking their part in the technical and professional sectors, but schools still steer women into "female" careers—as teachers, nurses, and secretaries—which tend to be lower-paying than white-collar occupations for men. A number of projects have trained women in nontraditional occupations such as auto mechanics and carpentry. Although these have been successful, they remain small-scale.[24]

## Women, Work, and the Neoliberal Development Model

Women's economic opportunities are limited by the prevailing neoliberal development model. This development model emphasizes privatization of state assets, markets unrestrained by government, and economic globalization. Consequently, what currently passes for development in the Caribbean and many other third world countries is an approach that directs resources away from the majority of the population. This situation has been exacerbated by structural adjustment programs that require governments to orient their economic policies toward a single goal: earning foreign exchange to service the debt. These programs affect the poor and women most of all. Production for domestic consumption takes second place, and emphasis is placed on tourism and cash crops for export. Structural adjustment has resulted in a range of policy measures, including currency devaluation, removal or reduction of subsidies on basic goods and services, reduction of government spending on social services, reduction of the government workforce, wage cuts in the public sector, and privatization of state enterprises. These measures have had a devastating impact on the social infrastructure of several Caribbean countries. Because structural adjustment cuts funds for social services, schools, hospitals, nutrition programs, public transportation, water, and electricity, women trying to feed families feel the impact of soaring prices acutely. As services are eliminated or become too expensive, women compensate with their own time and labor. Thus, a woman may have to carry water from a public tap after water rates rise. Or she may have to take a two-hour trip to a health clinic because the one in her neighborhood has been closed.

At the same time, these cuts in social services increase the unemployment of women, as the service categories that are cut are overwhelmingly staffed by women. Because these and other neoliberal policies affect women more than men, they limit women's ability to contribute to real national development. What is needed is a development model that is sustainable and people-centered, and Caribbean women have to play a major role in putting this alternative model in place. As the following discussion shows, they have already begun the task of organizing to change their circumstances.

## ORGANIZING FOR EMPOWERMENT

Throughout Caribbean history, women have played prominent roles in social struggles—from slave rebellions to contemporary labor protests. Although historical accounts focus on male heroes, women have acted individually and collectively to make their mark in the political, social, cultural, and economic spheres. During slavery they provided both violent and nonviolent resistance: in Jamaica, Nanny led fighting troops, and in Antigua, the Hart sisters, who were free coloreds, became antislavery activists and went against planter society by teaching enslaved children to read and write.[25] In the years after the abolition of slavery, women were involved in protests over a variety of issues, including labor, land, and taxation policies.[26] In the early to mid-twentieth century, women from all over the Caribbean increased their public and political activity via a number of venues such as the media, education, and social work. Amy Bailey of Jamaica, Louise Rowley of Grenada, Beatrice Greig of Trinidad, and Ives Heraldine Rock of St. Lucia were part of this group. Over the period of the nineteenth to the mid-twentieth century, several women's associations and organizations were formed to express women's concerns and improve their conditions. They included the Black Cross Nurses of Belize, the Jamaica Women's League, the St. Lucia Women's Association, and the Guyana Women's Political and Economic Organization.[27]

In recent decades, activities at the global level set the context for much of the regional activity involving women. These global-level activities included the United Nations Decade for Women (1975–1985) and the adoption of the Convention on the Elimination of All Forms of Discrimination Against Women in 1979. These undertakings at the global level encouraged activities already under way at the regional and national levels.

Caribbean women found that many of the development strategies popularized for women during the UN Decade for Women were inadequate. Churches and international agencies were funding programs such as sewing cooperatives. But Caribbean women had to redefine development to make it more relevant to circumstances where governments were cutting social services, freezing wages, and laying off employees. As they sought to redefine development, they found that the perspectives of European and North American feminists were not always useful. These perspectives were not always congruent with the political, social, and economic experience of many women in developing countries. As a result, Caribbean women found it useful to draw on networks in the emerging third world women's movement. One such influence has been Development Alternatives for a New Era (DAWN), a third world–based global network of women activists, researchers, and policymakers. DAWN had its beginnings in 1984. Over the life of the organization, its secretariat has been located in a number of countries, including India, Brazil, and Barbados. It has focused on the development of "alternative frameworks and methods to attain the goals of economic and social justice, peace, and development free of all forms of oppression by gender, class, race and nation."[28] From DAWN's perspective, the development process can best be viewed through the lens of poor third world women and their families.[29]

## Organizing at the Regional Level

Looking back over the period since the beginning of the UN Decade for Women in 1975, Caribbean women can identify gains, but they can also identify some important limitations. During the Decade for Women, the two governments most committed to improving the status of women were the Michael Manley government in Jamaica and the Maurice Bishop government in Grenada, but by the end of the decade both administrations had fallen from power. In spite of an increased number of women parliamentarians and even one prime minister—Eugenia Charles of Dominica—the political power structures were still dominated by men.

The establishment of the Caribbean Women's Association (CARIWA) preceded the flurry of international activity on behalf of women in the late 1970s. In 1970, this regional umbrella for nongovernmental women's groups was formed by a group of prominent women. Over the next few years, spurred by publicity surrounding the UN Decade for Women, Commonwealth Caribbean governments set up special bureaus to deal with women's affairs. Working with the women's desks and the women's program of the Caribbean Conference of Churches (CCC), nongovernmental organizations held seminars and workshops to raise awareness of the issues affecting women.[30] Several organizations were established as a result of this regional ferment. A 1977 meeting of CARIWA, CCC, and the Jamaican Women's Bureau was pivotal to the formation of the Women's Desk of the Caribbean Community Secretariat in 1980, the Women and Development Programme of the United Nations Economic Commission for Latin America and the Caribbean in 1979–1980, and the Women and Development Unit (WAND) of the University of West Indies' Extra-Mural Department in 1978.[31]

WAND was created as a part of the regional program for the UN Decade for Women. It is based in Barbados, and it supports women's initiatives through research, training, and public education. WAND coordinates and promotes women's activities in the English-speaking Caribbean. It has been successful in its outreach programs and in its efforts to use a bottom-up approach to orchestrate the integration of women in development. Essential parts of this approach are its Community Self-reliance Programme and its Sustainable Livelihoods Project. People at the community level have been empowered by their ability to influence policymakers in agricultural programs and community development. WAND has also increased awareness of women's rights among policymakers, linked government agencies with nongovernmental organizations, and helped to shape legislation on issues such as equal pay, family and reproductive rights, and domestic violence.[32] In 1990, DAWN located its secretariat at the WAND offices in Barbados.[33]

Another group involved in both research and action is the Caribbean Association for Feminist Research and Action (CAFRA), a regional grouping of feminist researchers, activists, and women's organizations. It is a facilitator of the Caribbean women's movement and encourages regional collaboration. CAFRA serves not only the English-speaking Caribbean but also the Spanish-, Dutch-, and French-speaking areas. CAFRA sees women's problems as arising from issues of race and class as well as gender. It focuses on the social factors that support exploitive relations between women and men. It wants to promote the interrelationship between research and action.[34] CAFRA's Women and Law Project has been researching the legal status of women around the region. It has held public hearings, prepared popular education materials on legal issues, and held regional meetings. It has also brought its research and action to economic issues such as export processing zones (EPZs) in Jamaica and Trinidad. Researchers reported on the substandard wages, unsanitary working environment, and inhumane labor practices that women experience in the EPZs. CAFRA was also involved in the Women in Caribbean Agriculture Project, which focused on women in farming communities in St. Vincent. It assisted with land distribution, collective farming, and livestock management techniques and provided special support for women who worked in vegetable production.[35]

The regional university system, the University of the West Indies, became involved in the change process in a major way in fall of 1986 when it launched its women's studies program on all three campuses (in Barbados, Jamaica, and Trinidad and Tobago). Although there was some resistance to this move, a strong program led by well-respected scholars overcame much of the resistance. Women and development studies (WDS) faculty from the three UWI campuses participate in the interdisciplinary women's studies program as well as in their individual disciplines. Feminist literary critics and women writers and social scientists share their scholarship and ideas in fora such as the annual International Conference of Caribbean Women Writers and the Caribbean Studies Association meeting. Feminist social scientists undertake analysis and theorizing about Caribbean women's lives under the auspices of the Institute of Social and Economic Research and the Consortium Graduate School of Social Sciences of the UWI. By adopting a woman-centered perspective, feminist historians have reconstructed a more inclusive Caribbean past. All of this has contributed to a broadening of research, teaching, and scholarship at UWI and other tertiary institutions. Some members of the WDS group have moved from the campus to the wider community. The former coordinator, Marjorie Thorpe, has represented Trinidad and Tobago in the United Nations and also served in various government positions. Additionally, former regional coordinator Lucille Mair has headed Jamaica's UN delegation.[36]

Outside of the realm of research, major regional initiatives have been undertaken to empower women and change their economic and social environment. One example of this was the Project for the Development of Caribbean Women in Trade Unions (1982–1985). This was a three-year effort to address the lack of women in leadership roles in the unions. The unions' organizational structures and social attitudes did not allow for the advancement of women. The project provided about 2,000 trade unionists with the opportunity for study, training, and self-development.[37]

Informal commercial importers have also launched a regional initiative. Their first regional conference was held in April 1991 in Dominica. ICIs underscored the fact that their "informal" sector was in fact a vital part of the formal economy and, as such, needed to be provided with training programs, incentives, and simplification of currency regulations and national restrictions. They are focusing on establishing more local traders' associations and engaging in organized lobbying.[38]

## Organizing at the National Level

In the 1970s, individual governments established women's affairs units. Most of these were established in the wake of the declaration of the International Year of the Woman in 1975. But two regional governments preceded the trend: in 1973, Guyana established the Council on the Affairs and Status of Women, and Jamaica established the Women's Bureau.[39] In the

1990s, women's affairs units tended to be less active than they were in the 1970s and early 1980s. Today they are weak and underfunded and unlikely to initiate change. Change is more likely to be initiated from outside of the government apparatus.

At the national level, the growth of the women's movement was reflected in the formation in the 1970s and 1980s of such groups as Concerned Women for Social Progress (Trinidad and Tobago), the Committee for the Development of Women (St. Vincent and the Grenadines), the Belize Rural Women's Association (DRWA), Sisi ni Dada (St. Kitts/Nevis), the Red Thread Women's Development Project (Guyana), the Women's Forum (Barbados), and Sistren (Jamaica).[40]

Caribbean women have a history of social activism through community and church groups, trade unions, and political parties. In the past, however, this seldom led to national influence or political power for women. Community groups run by women concentrated on social welfare work. In political parties and trade unions, women played a subordinate role. Every political party had its women's arm, often headed by the wife of the male party leader. Although the women's arm worked tirelessly at campaigning, fund-raising, and mobilizing members, few women rose to leadership positions within the party.[41] This is because they tended to remain in support roles instead of putting themselves forward as candidates for election. Recent elections indicate that women are putting themselves forward in larger numbers. In a constituency by-election in Jamaica in early 2001, three of the four candidates were women, and both of the two major parties had women candidates. In the December 2000 general election in Trinidad and Tobago, there was a record number of women running for parliament on major-party tickets. Sixteen women competed for seats in the legislature.[42] The number of women candidates keeps growing, but the relative percentage remains low.

In some cases, party tribalism and ideology have divided women. Some women's groups have limited effectiveness because they are closely associated with particular political parties. In some cases, the association is so close that the group does not outlive the party. One example is the National Organization for Women (NOW), which was a creation of the New Jewel Movement in revolutionary Grenada. When the New Jewel Movement ceased to exist, the NOW fell apart.

Nationally, many nongovernmental women's organizations have been limited by their middle-class base. Throughout much of the 1970s, the focus of organizing was on professional women. They made great gains during the 1970s and 1980s, working their way up to senior positions in the public and private sectors. But organizations led by professional and academic women could not always reach out successfully to working-class women. However, some attention is being given to organizing among urban and rural working-class women. Because of deteriorating economic conditions, there is a great need for this.

In Jamaica, the Women's Construction Collective (WCC) trains young women in construction skills, then secures well-paying jobs for them. The WCC was established in 1983 by the Jamaica Working Group, a group of planners, researchers, and community development specialists. In the beginning, it was part of an effort to address the high unemployment rate in some sections of Kingston, but the program has expanded to include women from middle-class backgrounds. Initially, trainees were not taken seriously, but over time contractors have recognized their reliability and are now eager to hire them.[43] The collective has also built health clinics, public sanitary facilities, and houses for flood victims. In the period since its establishment, the WCC has trained more than 1,000 women in all areas of construction work.[44]

In Belize, the Belize Rural Women's Association serves several dozen craft and food-processing cooperatives. This multiethnic group works to improve the economic and social circumstances of its members. Proceeds from fund-raising abroad were used to buy a truck to transport members' farm produce to market. BRWA and other Belizean women's organizations are working together to develop health education programs for rural women.[45]

Caribbean societies tend to be very class-conscious. But increasingly, women are holding hands across class lines in feminist solidarity. Sistren is a good example of this. The group was established in 1977 by a group of thirteen women from the Kingston ghetto. The women, who were working in an emergency jobs program as street cleaners and teachers' aides, asked a dramatist from the Jamaica School of Drama to help them produce a play for Workers' Week. The result was a play about women factory workers organizing for their rights. This small group of women became the nucleus of the Sistren Theatre Collective. Their work includes professional theater, popular education, a silkscreen project, and a magazine.[46] In 1983, they established Sistren Research to conduct research on women in Jamaica, publicize the findings, and provide support to women's groups.[47]

More than twenty years have passed since its beginning, and Sistren is still dynamic. Members have scripted and produced many plays dealing with such topics as domestic violence, teenage pregnancy, and exploitation in the workplace. They also conduct educational workshops with women agricultural workers. As a result, the women in Sistren have developed a wide range of skills, including acting, scriptwriting, teaching, graphic arts, and accounting.

Although Sistren is oriented toward the experience of working-class women, the collective has incorporated some middle-class members, defining roles for them that use their skills in fund-raising and documentation. In addition to its work in Jamaica, Sistren has sent members of the collective to assist newly formed women's groups in other Caribbean countries.

One of the groups with which Sistren has worked is the Women's Development Committee (Red Thread) in Guyana. Not only does Red Thread have to deal with the problems arising from gender bias; it also has to cross the racial divide between the Afro-Guyanese and the Indo-Guyanese women. Red Thread has focused on consciousness-raising and organization-building.[48]

Sistren was also involved with the founding of the Women's Media Watch Group. The group evolved out of a 1987 meeting of women's groups in Jamaica organized by Sistren Research.[49] This group has set up a system for monitoring the media specifically for sexist images of women that are pornographic or derogatory. The group feels that these images desensitize society to the gravity of sexual violence against women and children. This media watchdog group is involved in public education, as well as in lobbying advertisers, media people, and dramatists. Major targets have been the Association of Advertisers and the Jamaica Tourist Board. The Jamaica Tourist Board has often been criticized for using (or turning a blind eye toward the use of) negative images of women to promote Jamaica's tourist industry.

Domestic workers have also begun to organize nationally in some Caribbean territories. They belong to one of the largest working groups in the region, and they are also one of the most exploited groups. In Jamaica, they have formed the Jamaican Household Workers Association (JHWA), which pays particular attention to the issues of benefits and training.[50] The Bureau of Women's Affairs is also lobbying the Jamaican government on behalf of JHWA, seeking assistance that would give members of JHWA greater independence. This would include a training program that would provide domestic workers with alternative employment options.[51]

Some of these national groups try to coordinate their activities and learn from each other by the establishment of national umbrella groups. One example of these is the Association of Women of Jamaica (AWOJA). WDS members played a major role in the formation of this umbrella group.[52] AWOJA has a range of objectives, including the development of a common voice, pooling efforts to address common issues, creating a lobby group, and improving the condition of women in Jamaica as citizens, consumers, and women.[53]

## CONCLUSION

Economic issues continue to dominate the agenda for women in the Caribbean. As higglers, technical workers, managers, insurance sales executives, communications specialists, sidewalk vendors, informal commercial importers, nurses, teachers, clerks, domestic workers, dancers, and retirees, Caribbean women have repeatedly beaten the odds. But their choices have been made more difficult by a deteriorating social service sector, spiraling inflation, and a deregulated market.

Regional and national women's groups have attempted to address this situation by a combination of strategies intended to raise consciousness and actively initiate change, with the particular strategy or blend of strategies varying among the groups. These strategies have included undertaking research to expand the knowledge base; operating as a facilitator; taking activist, confrontational positions; disseminating information; using the theater as an educational tool; encouraging and facilitating women's participation in occupational sectors dominated by men; providing leadership training opportunities for women; and forming coalitions across class lines.

Contemporary efforts at change have embraced both research and action. Some of these efforts have benefited specific classes and groups of women. Others have benefited women more generally. Successes in the last three decades include reforms in many discriminatory laws. These include legislation mandating equal pay for equal work, as well as reforms in family law. In the aftermath of the Fourth World Conference on Women in Beijing, Antigua and Barbuda, Guyana, Jamaica, and Trinidad and Tobago adopted new legislation addressing domestic violence. The Bahamas, Barbados, Belize, and St. Vincent had legislation that predated Beijing. Dominica, Grenada, and St. Kitts do not yet have legislation on domestic violence.[54]

Women's groups in the Caribbean are experiencing small but important victories as they attempt to give women more control of their own lives and as they work toward a more people-centered development model. These victories contribute to the empowerment of women. Although many of these victories are small, they contribute to shifts in consciousness in the broader society. Small shifts in consciousness can initiate waves of change that in time can erode old, encrusted attitudes and models of development. Thus, the challenges are significant, but Caribbean women are "making waves."

## DISCUSSION QUESTIONS

1. In the Commonwealth Caribbean, how has regional-level activity supported national-level initiatives related to women?

2. There are clear differences in women's participation in the workforce between the Afro-Caribbean countries and Indo-Caribbean. Can you suggest some cultural or historical reasons for this?

3. Indicate which decade saw the most significant changes for women in the Caribbean—the 1970s, the 1980s, or the 1990s? Provide reasons for your choice.

## NOTES

1. UNDP, *Human Development Report 2000* (New York: Oxford University Press, 2000), pp. 161–164.

2. Ibid., pp. 161–162.

3. Odette Parry, "In One Ear and Out the Other: Unmasking Masculinities in the Caribbean Classroom," *Sociological Research Online* 1, no. 2 (July 1996), available online at http://www.socresonline.org.uk/socresonline/1/2/2.html (accessed May 25, 2001).

4. Patricia Mohammed, *Working Paper No. 1*, Centre for Gender and Development Studies (Mona, Kingston, Jamaica, October 1997), p. 39.

5. Parry, "In One Ear and Out the Other."

6. The six countries are the Bahamas, Barbados, Belize, Jamaica, Guyana, and Trinidad and Tobago.

7. UNDP, *Human Development Report 2000,* pp. 259–260.

8. Ibid., pp. 165–166.

9. United Nations, *The Challenge of Gender Equity and Human Rights on the Threshold of the Twenty-first Century* (Santiago, Chile: United Nations, ECLAC Women and Development Unit, 2000), p. 48.

10. United Nations, *The Challenge of Gender Equity*, p. 47; UNDP, *Human Development Report 2000,* pp. 165–167.

11. UNDP, *Human Development Report 2000,* p. 168.

12. Christine Barrow, "Small Farm Food Production and Gender in Barbados," in Janet Momsen, ed., *Women and Change in the Caribbean* (Bloomington: Indiana University Press, 1993), p. 182.

13. Catherine A. Sunshine, *The Caribbean: Survival, Strength, and Sovereignty* (Boston: South End, 1988), p. 228.

14. Barrow, "Small Farm Food Production and Gender in Barbados," p. 191.

15. Indra S. Harry, "Women in Agriculture in Trinidad," in Janet Momsen, ed., *Women and Change in the Caribbean* (Bloomington: Indiana University Press, 1993), p. 218.

16. S. Odie-Ali, "Women in Agriculture: The Case of Guyana," *Social and Economic Studies* 35, no. 2 (1986): 241–290.

17. C. Glesne, "Inclusion and Incorporation in Agricultural Production: The Case of Young Vincentians," cited in Harry, "Women in Agriculture in Trinidad."

18. Sunshine, *The Caribbean,* p. 228.

19. Patrick Smikle, "The Leaps of Letilda," *Sistren* 12, no. 1 (1990): 20–21.

20. Sunshine, *The Caribbean,* p. 229.

21. Polly Pattullo, *Last Resorts: The Cost of Tourism in the Caribbean* (London: Cassell, 1996), p. 55.

22. Ibid., pp. 57–59.

23. Beverley Mullings, "Globalization, Tourism, and the International Sex Trade," in Kamala Kempadoo, ed., *Sun, Sex, and Gold* (Lanham, Md.: Rowman and Littlefield, 1999), pp. 67, 77.

24. Sunshine, *The Caribbean,* p. 228.

25. Verene A. Shepherd, ed., *Women in Caribbean History: The British-Colonised Territories* (Kingston, Jamaica: Ian Randle, 1999), pp. 60–62.

26. Ibid., pp. 154–155.

27. Ibid., pp. 157–163.

28. Gita Sen and Caren Grown, *Development, Crises, and Alternative Visions: Third World Women's Perspectives* (New York: Monthly Review, 1987), p. 9.

29. Ibid.

30. Sunshine, *The Caribbean,* p. 231.

31. Isa Baud and Ines Smyth, *Searching for Security: Women's Responses to Economic Transformations* (London: Routledge, 1997), pp. 35–36.

32. Inter-American Development Bank, *Women in the Americas: Bridging the Gender Gap* (Washington, D.C.: Johns Hopkins University Press, 1995), p. 104.

33. Lynn A. Bolles, "Doing It for Themselves: Women's Research and Action in the Commonwealth Caribbean," in Edna Acosta-Belen and Christine E. Bose, eds., *Researching Women in Latin America and the Caribbean* (Boulder: Westview, 1993), pp. 159–161.

34. Ibid., pp. 163–164.

35. Ibid., p. 164.

36. Ibid., pp. 157–159.

37. Ibid., pp. 167–169.

38. "Caribbean ICIs Get Together," *Sistren* 13, no. 1 (July 1991): 7.

39. Baud and Smyth, *Searching for Security,* pp. 34–35.

40. Ibid., pp. 36–37.

41. These few include Eugenia Charles, who became prime minister of Dominica, and Portia Simpson, vice president of the People's National Party in Jamaica.

42. Peter Richards, "Politics—Trinidad/Tobago: Parties Field Record Number of Women," *Interpress Service,* November 27, 2000, available online at http://etextb.ohiolink.edu/bin/gate.exe?f=fulltext&state=dghp4c.2.54 (accessed April 9, 2001).

43. Alice Rogers and Mia Thompson, "Anniversary of WCC," *Sistren* 15, nos. 3–4 (1993): 16–17.

44. Barbara Calvert, "Jamaica: Women Building in a Man's World—The Women's Construction Collective," available online at http://www.c4l.org.uk/jamaica/0104.htm (accessed May 29, 2001).

45. Sunshine, *The Caribbean*, p. 232.

46. Ibid., pp. 232–233.

47. "Sistren Research Update," *Sistren* 13, no. 1 (July 1991): 26.

48. "Sistren in Guyana," *Sistren* 10, nos. 2–3 (1988): 35–37.

49. "Women's Media Watch Group: Improving the Image of Our Women in the Media," *Sistren* 10, no. 1 (1988): 16.

50. "Jamaican Household Workers Unite," *Sistren* 13, no. 1 (July 1991): 23.

51. "Women's Bureau Lobbies for Household Helpers," *Jamaica Gleaner*, February 5, 2001, available online at http://www.jamaica-gleaner.com/gleaner/20010205/news/news4.html (accessed May 30, 2001).

52. Bolles, "Doing It for Themselves," p. 159.

53. "International Women's Week: 10th Anniversary Landmark Celebration," *Sistren* 10, no. 1 (1988): 13.

54. United Nations, *The Challenge of Gender Equity,* p. 51. The report provided no information on St. Lucia.

# 9

# The Empowerment of Palestinian Women in the West Bank and Gaza Strip

## SALIBA SARSAR

> A genuine leadership does not disempower half its people, and real
> women do not accept exclusion and internal alienation. A genuine leader-
> ship draws its legitimacy from the people.
> —Hanan Ashrawi (*This Side of Peace,* 1995)

The interplay between gender and politics is crucial in itself. It is even
more crucial in a land of conflict or a land between war and peace, where
issues pertinent to women are often downplayed or ignored. Even activism
in revolutionary movements and national liberation do not assure increased
levels of empowerment or guarantee equal rights.

An example is that of Palestinian women who do not enjoy political status, access, or influence equal to their male counterparts. Despite some recent gains, gender discrimination remains an obstacle to their full participation in formal political processes and activities. Palestinian leadership is yet
to empower more women to claim their natural, rightful place in nation-
building and in society. The Palestinian Declaration of Independence of
1988—which states "governance will be based on principles of social justice, equality, and non-discrimination in public rights of men or women, on
grounds of race, religion, color, or sex"—has yet to be fully implemented.

Women's empowerment should not be regarded solely from a political
viewpoint. What is political influences other aspects of life, including the
economic, social, and cultural, and vice versa. My conceptualization of empowerment is taken from that of the United Nations Development Fund for
Women (UNIFEM). Empowerment, specifically in politics, increases
"women's control over their lives both within and outside the household so
as to enable them to improve the institutions whose governance shapes their

lives and to promote the building of stable lives."[1] UNIFEM's gender-sensitive agenda "empowers women and their organizations to challenge governments and international organizations to be accountable to women's needs and interests, increases opportunities for women to improve their leadership and managerial skills, and builds support for good governance in decision-making at all levels and in all sectors."[2] Applied to the context of Palestinian women's empowerment, it means removing obstacles to women's access to public life and economic resources as well as augmenting women's capacity to influence the direction of their society. Hence, gender-sensitive legislation and gender equity become a must for women's empowerment.

In the remainder of this chapter I will examine the Palestinian women's movement, the current status of Palestinian women, the major factors impacting their lives as expressed in informal interviews with ten ordinary Palestinian women, and the continuing struggle for their empowerment. This will be illustrated by several efforts currently under way at the governmental, grassroots, and academic levels. Empowerment, or its lack thereof, it is argued, is multidimensional, and if Palestinian women wish to actualize themselves, then they must continue to develop their voice and to formulate their demands and rights through active participation in society and public life.[3]

## PALESTINIAN WOMEN'S MOVEMENT

The successive Arab-Israeli wars; the painful experience of the Israeli military occupation, especially on the West Bank and the Gaza Strip; the intifada—a sustained general uprising, or "shaking off," during 1987–1993 among the Palestinians against Israel; and the return by the Israeli government of some land and power to the Palestinians have generated in women the need to cultivate and to value their ways of political knowing.[4] Through personal silence and hearing the voices of others, many women are listening to their own voices and searching for their own identity within the context of the national search for self-determination and human rights. From teaching to writing, from demonstrating to organizing, women are challenging opposing forces in their lives and the life of their community, thereby claiming their rightful place in society.

Historically, however, Palestinian women have been seen but not properly heard, usually acting in supportive roles to men in a patriarchal environment. Moreover, subjugation to other internal forces such as religious dogma and external forces such as military occupation over the years have disoriented their socialization process and restricted their self-actualization and political involvement.[5] By dictation or choice, most women have played traditional roles in the family and society. Some have resisted such roles by developing strategies for survival and by taking action to ameliorate their condition and that of others, such as work in the nationalist movement and in resistance.[6] Although several have been involved in Palestine's nationalist movement since its inception, very few have been taken seriously or occupied important positions of political authority.[7]

Initiated in the 1920s, the Palestinian women's movement focused its energies on the formation of charitable, philanthropic societies that carried out welfare activities and relief efforts. The leaders—middle-class, traditional, and nonpolitical in orientation—achieved recognition in Palestinian society. Their work was acceptable to and supported by the political and social power structure; it did not pose a threat to the powers that be. The Arab defeat in the 1948 war and the 1967 war especially, with the loss of life and land and the resultant dispossession and occupation, politicized the women's movement. Women became more connected to the national movement and worked more openly for the struggle. A serious question arose as to the place of women's liberation in national liberation. As Hanan Ashrawi aptly states, "The primary conflict was always defined as the national conflict, while the gender issue was relegated to the back burner and defined as obstruction of, or distraction from, the national issue."[8]

Regardless, women's organizations and cooperatives proliferated between the mid-1960s and the mid-1990s. In'ash al-Usra (the Society for the Rejuvenation of the Family) was founded in 1965. Women's work committees that are affiliated with political parties were set up in the late 1970s, including the Federation of Palestinian Women's Action Committees, the Union of Palestinian Working Women's Committees, the Union of Palestinian Women's Committees, and the Women's Committee for Social Work. Popular committees, to which men also belonged, and women's food cooperatives were active during the intifada. In the 1990s, existing women's research centers were strengthened and others were begun. Examples of specific women's organizations and initiatives are given below.

Women's organizations helped women to face the occupation and to address living in the Diaspora. More women sought education and employment, more women participated in national liberation, and more women suffered the adverse consequences of the occupation. The 1970s witnessed the development of a genuine grassroots movement among Palestinian women. The work attracted members and supporters from college students and graduates, as well as those living in villages and refugee camps. The women were mobilized to fight for ending the occupation. As such, the women's unions expanded the national role that was played by charitable societies. According to Zahira Kamal, among the several differences between the two, the women's unions presented programs that linked national liberation with the liberation of women; put forward alternative frameworks for organizing women; and drafted internal bylaws with an eye toward strengthening and sustaining a democratic atmosphere.[9]

Although women became more politically and economically aware, their attention to social issues and to their equal status in society remained minimal. Since the intifada, women have become more vocal about their rights. For them, as represented by the leaders of the Women's Affairs Technical Committee, national liberation and women's liberation go together. Both complement and supplement each other.

## THE CURRENT STATUS OF PALESTINIAN WOMEN

In this chapter I focus on Palestinian women living on the West Bank and the Gaza Strip, not those living in Israel proper (that is, within the pre–June 1967 border) or in the Diaspora. Although there are differences between conditions on the West Bank and Gaza Strip, both regions are considered as one for this analysis.

The West Bank is located between Jordan and Israel; the Gaza Strip borders the Mediterranean Sea, between Egypt and Israel. Both regions were taken by Israel from Jordan and Egypt, respectively, in the June 1967 war. According to the Israel–Palestine Liberation Organization Declaration of Principles on Interim Self-Government Arrangements, signed in Washington, D.C., on September 13, 1993, and subsequent agreements, Israel transferred certain powers and responsibilities to the Palestine National Authority in parts of the West Bank and the Gaza Strip. Permanent status is to be decided through future negotiations.

The Palestine Central Bureau of Statistics (PCBS) reports that, in 1995, Palestinians on the West Bank, including East Jerusalem, and the Gaza Strip numbered 2,890,631, with 1,467,046 (50.75 percent) being male and 1,423,585 (49.25 percent) being female.[10] As is indicated in Table 9.1, if only those between the ages of fifteen and sixty-four years (PCBS defines working age as fifteen years and over) are included, then women (50.6 percent) edge men (49.7 percent) by 0.9 percent.

Women lag behind men in most areas. This is evident in the recent gender statistics from PCBS.[11] In the area of population and family, about 14 percent of teenage girls, ages fifteen to nineteen years in 1995, were married before age seventeen, compared to less than 1 percent of teenage boys.

In employment, the women's labor force participation rate is extremely low, at 11 percent, in comparison to males, whose participation rate was 69 percent in 1996. Almost half the women in the labor force work in the service sector (e.g., education, health, and public administration), in contrast to men, who are more evenly distributed across the different economic sectors (see Table 9.2).

Table 9.1  **Women and Men in the West Bank and Gaza Strip, 1998 (percentage by age groups)**

| Age Group | West Bank | | | Gaza Strip | | | Palestinian Regions | | |
|---|---|---|---|---|---|---|---|---|---|
| | Male | Female | Total | Male | Female | Total | Male | Female | Total |
| 0–14 | 45.3 | 43.7 | 44.6 | 50.6 | 50.0 | 50.3 | 47.1 | 45.9 | 46.5 |
| 15–65 | 51.1 | 52.4 | 51.7 | 46.8 | 47.0 | 46.9 | 49.7 | 50.6 | 50.1 |
| 65+ | 3.6 | 3.9 | 3.7 | 2.6 | 3.0 | 2.8 | 3.2 | 3.5 | 3.4 |
| Total | 100 | 100 | 100 | 100 | 100 | 100 | 100 | 100 | 100 |

*Source:* Palestine Central Bureau of Statistics, "Women and Men in Palestine" (Ramallah, Palestine, 1998).

Table 9.2  **Labor Force Participation, 1996 (percentage by gender)**

| Economic Sector | Percentage in Total Economic Activity | | Percentage of Gender Composition | |
|---|---|---|---|---|
| | Female | Male | Female | Male |
| Agriculture and fishing | 29.2 | 11.6 | 29.9 | 70.1 |
| Mining and quarrying | 0.1 | 1.1 | 0.9 | 99.1 |
| Manufacturing | 15.4 | 15.9 | 14.0 | 85.9 |
| Construction | 0.7 | 19.5 | 0.6 | 99.4 |
| Commerce, hotels, and restaurants | 7.5 | 20.1 | 5.9 | 94.1 |
| Transportation and storage | 0.6 | 5.5 | 1.9 | 98.1 |
| Series of other branches | 46.5 | 26.3 | 23.1 | 76.9 |
| Total | 100 | 100 | 14.5 | 85.5 |

*Source:* Palestine Central Bureau of Statistics, "Women and Men in Palestine" (Ramallah, Palestine, 1996).

The majority of unemployed women have postsecondary education. Only a small proportion of unemployed males has higher education (see Table 9.3).

In literacy, although the overall rates are very high, women (77 percent) trail men (91.5 percent) by 14.5 percent.

In the field of education, women constitute a small portion of the teaching staff in secondary and postsecondary education.

In public life, women are utterly underrepresented. Men dominate most, if not all, essential areas. As is indicated in Table 9.4, with the exception of student councils in colleges and universities, the percentage of women in leadership positions does not reach 10 percent.

In the historic January 1996 Palestinian election campaign for the eighty-eight-member self-rule parliament or legislative council and a president, only twenty-eight of 676 candidates (4.14 percent) were women. Most ran as independents, implying a lack of financial and political support from the established parties such as Yasser Arafat's Fatah movement. Out

**Table 9.3 Unemployed Palestinian Persons by Years of Schooling, 1996**

| Years of Schooling | Women | Men |
|---|---|---|
| 0 | 2.3 | 2.4 |
| 1–6 | 6.8 | 26.0 |
| 7–9 | 11.0 | 30.0 |
| 10–12 | 23.5 | 29.6 |
| 13+ | 56.4 | 12.0 |
| Total | 100 | 100 |

*Source:* Palestine Central Bureau of Statistics, *Labor Force Survey* (Ramallah, Palestine, 1996).

**Table 9.4 Participation in Public Life of Palestinian Persons, 1996**

| Leadership Positions | Women | Men | Percentage of Women |
|---|---|---|---|
| Legislative Council | 5 | 83 | 6 |
| Palestine National Council | 56 | 688 | 8 |
| Ministers | 2 | 22 | 8 |
| Labor union members (excluding Jenin and Nablus) | 5,303 | 62,027 | 8 |
| Student councils in colleges/universities | 31 | 90 | 26 |

*Source:* Palestine Central Bureau of Statistics, "Women and Men in Palestine" (Ramallah, Palestine, 1996).

of the 52 percent of registered women voters, 42 percent voted. Five of the twenty-eight women candidates won.[12] There was a sole challenger to Arafat's bid for the presidency: Samiha Khalil, community leader and founder of In'ash Al-Usra. As was expected, she did not win. In 2000, none of the thirty-two ministers in the Palestine National Authority was a woman, and in all the local councils on the West Bank and the Gaza Strip, only one was headed by a woman, specifically in the small village of Khirbet Oeis in the Salfit area near Nablus.

Commenting on the role of women in Palestinian society, Suha Arafat—the wife of Yasser Arafat, president of the Palestine National Authority—stated that the presence of women in public life does not mean that women are fully liberated or have reached their full potential. According to her, women were often denied the right to participate actively and substantially in Palestinian institutions and, for this reason, should demand that all laws and rules pertaining to their rights be enforced.[13]

PERSONAL INTERVIEWS WITH
AND THE LITERATURE BY AND ON PALESTINIAN WOMEN

The current status of Palestinian women and the difficulties under which they are toiling are also understood by their perceptions of reality. What follows is based on interviews I conducted with Palestinian women[14] and on the literature by and on Palestinian women.[15]

It is argued that most women have faced and many still face multiple forms of oppression that have prevented them from actualizing themselves and from playing a wider role in society. Due to higher levels of education, personal initiative, experience with the national movement, and/or national crises, some have been able to exert more political influence and have national respect.[16]

The women I interviewed mentioned the June 1967 war, the resultant Israeli military occupation, and the intifada as triggers that have catapulted them into a new sphere. Although these events have created unbearable conditions for women, their families, and society (for example, imprisonment, the imprisonment of their loved ones, the tough economy, deterioration of educational levels, Israeli confiscation of land), they alerted women to the reality of their own lives and surroundings. Most saw the necessity to seek work outside the home to make ends' meet as permanent. Although they knew what was traditionally expected of them, they ventured to balance their traditional role with a modern one that often created more challenges for them.

Regardless, the war and occupation made women more socially active and more politically aware. A staff nurse I interviewed pointed to the start of the occupation as also being the start of her interest in activism. She explained how she helped to save lives or to console the bereaved. She told me not to believe the official underestimated counts of the wounded and the dead. Ashrawi relates a similar beginning in her book. Activism brought her "the meaning of organization, resistance, discipline, and self-criticism as a means of reform." Activist involvement awakened a sense of self, an understanding of being true to oneself. It awoke, too, a sense of allowing the voice of Palestine to be heard.[17]

Women began to question and challenge authority, both at home and elsewhere. Living in an atmosphere of conflict did not blind any to the problems of oppression rising from within their own society. My interviewees mentioned that women are "triply oppressed"—together with the men in society, by the men themselves, and through self-oppression. Each of these forms of oppressions has several expressions.

In terms of the first form of oppression, Samira Haj, in a study of Palestinian women and patriarchal relations, argues that "Palestinian men are also exploited, oppressed, and barred from positions of power, and therefore . . . it is not just gender but gender as a social relation and its interactions with other social relations and activities that define the perspectives, self-definition, and mutual interactions of Palestinian men and women."[18] Consequently, this oppression is transferred to women. Researchers may have pinpointed a psychological cause for much of this intracultural suppression. Suha Sabbagh, the former director of the Washington,

D.C.–based Institute for Arab Women's Studies, sees the attitude toward women as a "psychological backlash" generated primarily by the occupation. Speaking to journalist Jan Goodwin, she explained, "The Palestinian male . . . the authority figure in the house, has lost all his authority." Women who began to find a political voice through their participation in the intifada began to assert their human rights. This no doubt posed a new threat to the male ego, already shaken by the occupation.[19]

The second form of oppression relates to the patrilineal family complex of classic patriarchy—that is, the devaluation of the daughter against the son, early marriage, membership in the male-headed household of one's spouse, and the birth of a male heir and the acquisition of power that eventually attends it—which continuously reproduces female subordination and male domination.[20] One social worker stated that when her mother died she had to take care of her siblings. Although she was allowed to go to school, she was forbidden to work. Getting a job was not possible until her siblings grew and her father became old and sick. Her wish is to be recognized on her own merit. Her dream is to live "in freedom, without prison walls."

In terms of the third form of oppression, it seems that most women were conditioned to be self-regulating, doing what is expected of them rather than what they expect. Palestinian women learn to deal with the whispered gossip. In a society where even an unfounded accusation may result in harm, women suppress themselves under the threat of what may be said by others. Even those who have strength in their convictions respect the adverse powers of gossip. A journalist told me that if she is seen coming home late at night or bringing a male stranger home, much criticism follows from her neighbors or "extended family." She usually preempts their remarks by educating them about what is happening in her life. Honor killings in Palestine do occur. Several Palestinian women have been murdered by their male family members for the perceived misuse of their sexuality.[21] "Distance yourself from evil and sing for it," a businesswoman recited an Arab saying to me. Out of fear, expediency, or wisdom, maintaining the status quo seems preferable to taking risks by venturing into the unknown.

Life took on new meaning during the intifada. Palestinians discovered their national spirit amid the Israeli punitive measures and the resultant pressures from the intifada itself.[22] One school administrator spoke of how she found her voice at that time. Her life took on new meaning and challenge. She had something meaningful for which to toil.

The three forms of oppression found new expressions during the intifada. Life changed for many Palestinian women. During the first years, according to a United Nations study, women accounted for 10 percent of casualties and 23 percent of injuries.[23] Palestinian women, believed to have participated in the uprising, found themselves constantly harassed, jailed, and even tortured by their Israeli occupiers. Terry Boulata, a research assistant for the Palestinian Human Rights Information Center, was arrested and accused as a leader in the intifada on numerous occasions. "But they accuse nearly everyone they imprison of that," Boulata told journalist Goodwin.[24]

The intifada enabled many women to discover their authentic voice, often to the dismay of many men. The resurgence of Muslim extremism that emerged during this period helped counter the perceived threat of female independence. As more and more men have returned to religion, more and more women have found themselves returned to a traditional, home-based culture. Fadwah Labadi, spokeswoman for the Women's Studies Center in the West Bank, claims that "eighty-five percent of our men don't want women to rise."[25]

Fear and oppression for Palestinian women does not just come from the occupation. A hospital administrator explained to me how men use double standards by respecting the utterances of male doctors and not her own words. Requests from her and other female administrators and staff for extra assistance create a crisis. "We extended ourselves to help them, and in our hour of need, they stab us in the back. You expect it from the soldiers but not from them." A woman might tolerate any indignities heaped upon her by the occupiers because they are viewed as enemies, but she finds similar behavior by those of her own family and culture to be totally hurtful and unacceptable.

Ashrawi believes that unless afflicted by the "male postures of domination and exploitation," women in politics tended to "form a gender community without frontiers or national barriers."[26] In discussing the spirit of the Palestinian woman, she writes: "Palestinian women developed the sharp fierceness of a denied but not broken spirit." This fierceness, born under the "dual discrimination of gender and national identity," could be subdued but never extinguished.[27]

However, infighting among Palestinian women's groups did and does occur, a behavior that weakens the cause of women. Rather than unite, women found themselves at an impasse; inadvertently, "they had incorporated the same factional rivalries and disputes that had troubled the political groups from which they had evolved."[28] Sabbagh also states the position that Palestinian women are, in some ways, responsible for their oppression. Although women readily involved themselves in the intifada, the uprising's leadership failed to capitalize on the women's response. "In the focus on national liberation, the needs of women were ignored," says Sabbagh. Rather than unifying, women allowed themselves to be oppressed through threats of dishonor and even death.[29]

As for the negotiations and peace process, women are split as to the true meaning and value of these activities. Among many women whose lives have known terror and death, particularly those who have lost loved ones, there is little room for a peaceful settlement. Even the Oslo Agreement of 1993, which signaled the transition from the Palestinian struggle to autonomy, did not change their environment. Palestinian women, however, continued their activism.[30] The militant spirit that carried these women into the intifada still burns, despite what is impressed upon them by the occupation or by men. But this attitude is not universal. The search for and acceptance of peace, for some women, is the only available option. "What choice do the Palestinians have?" a student asked me. For others, it is an imperative step. "Peace must become the future of our kids."[31]

Since the coming of the Palestine National Authority to areas of the West Bank and to the Gaza Strip, women have felt less marginalized. Yet the hindrances in their way remain, including patriarchal structures, antiquated laws, and religious conservatism. A prime example is what happened in 1998 when a coalition of women, with guidance from the Women's Center for Legal and Social Counseling, wanted to secure equal rights for women. They conducted a series of seminars under the title "A Model Parliament," which was received by the religious and secular establishments with anger or coolness.[32]

The Palestinian women I interviewed are aware of their world and political surroundings. Their level of awareness, however, does not translate into total rejection of what is ailing them and their society. Few have turned their thoughts into sustained, public political action. In a conversation with a school administrator, I praised Ashrawi's work and her book. Her reply was: "Don't misunderstand what I am saying; I like Ashrawi, but she is an exceptional woman."

Some women, although somewhat aware, live at the mercy of those around them. The truth lies elsewhere. The voices of others prevail in their lives. They adhere to sex-role stereotypes. They survive and succeed by playing by the rules set by others. Their leadership is external to the self.

Other women's images of reality are colored by their need to live and let live. They are active socially and financially, but politically they are silent. There is no authentic voice, and there is little awareness of a central self. As one interviewee posed it to me, "How do you expect women to have an integrative voice whey they have to fend for themselves and survive to see tomorrow?"

Still others know the truth and what it takes to survive but do not have the proper tools to express themselves and convince others to listen to them. They have not developed the ability yet to reframe their reality and to integrate rational and emotive thought and objective and subjective knowing.

Very few women are "really talking." Their authentic voice—heard or unappreciated—is, however, loud and clear. It extends beyond the self. It aspires. It influences. It transforms. It elevates.

## THE CONTINUING STRUGGLE
## FOR PALESTINIAN WOMEN'S EMPOWERMENT

Women's empowerment does not happen on its own or haphazardly. Concerted efforts are needed to put forward practical policies and programs to advance and sustain its development. Such efforts are under way in several corners of Palestinian society, particularly at the governmental, grassroots, and academic levels, or a combination thereof. *PASSIA Diary 2000,* a publication of the Palestinian Society for the Study of International Affairs, lists some eighty-four women's organizations, with sixty-four found in East Jerusalem and the major cities of the West Bank and twenty in the Gaza Strip.[33] What follows will highlight six organizations, programs, and projects.

### Directorate of Gender Planning and Development

The Directorate of Gender Planning and Development (DGPD) was established by the Ministry of Planning and International Cooperation in 1996 to ensure that "Palestinian policies, legislation, decrees, plans, and programs are gender sensitive."[34] A strong commitment is given to enhancing the status of women and their capabilities and access to resources at all levels. This includes women's participation in decisionmaking and in all aspects of life. Thus far, DGPD has been successful at institutional capacity-building through the attendance of relevant training workshops and the creation of a documentation center; at strengthening the women's offices within ministries; and at increasing awareness of executive leadership of gender planning. DGPD has ambitious objectives. Among them are increasing the awareness of legislative, political, and executive leadership of the important role of gender planning for sustainable development; establishing a data clearinghouse to support differentiating gender needs assessment, identification of constraints, and assessment of progress; and raising women's representation in high decisionmaking levels.

### Women's Affairs Technical Committee

The Women's Affairs Technical Committee (WATC), created in 1992, is a recognized and well-respected nongovernmental organization.[35] It brings together a coalition of women who represent the main political parties, women's associations, human rights institutions, as well as independent professions. They cooperate to abolish all types of discrimination against women. Their ultimate goal is to achieve equality and social justice in a Palestinian democratic state.

WATC's aims are reached through several paths, including networking; lobbying and campaigning; training in communication skills and administrative and managerial competence; integrating gender and human rights in education and promoting a gender-sensitive educational system; and informing the public about women's issues and activities and challenges and accomplishments.

WATC's efforts paid many dividends in 1996. Through lobbying the Palestine National Authority, the following was accomplished:

- Women are no longer required to have the permission of their male guardians to receive a travel document;
- Women can keep their maiden names after marriage;
- Women are no longer required to have a male chaperone while taking driving lessons;
- Women are permitted to open a bank account in their children's name, a right that was open only to men; and
- Women are now able to give their nationality to their children.

According of WATC, obstacles in the way of women's empowerment abound. The occupation continues to dehumanize and impoverish women. Also, with Palestine being an integral part of the Arab world, the limitations on Arab women generally retard Palestinian women's progress. Suheir Azzouni, director of WATC, though optimistic about women's potential and power, is realistic about the future. She writes:

> Palestinian women remain to be the fruits of a revolution. Many are their achievements in a short period. Their unity around women's issues gives them power. The creation of statehood from scratch also carries within it the hope of more social justice. To what degree this social justice will be reflected within the emerging Palestinian state will only be revealed by time.[36]

### The Jerusalem Center for Women

The Jerusalem Center for Women (JCW) is a nongovernmental women's organization working to advance the cause of women's rights in Palestinian society, in addition to the cause of Palestinian rights in Israel and the world at large.[37] Established in 1994 as an outgrowth of an ongoing dialogue between Palestinian and Israeli women, JCW is committed to "the principles of equality, reciprocity, and parity in human rights and fundamental freedoms." Its activities include training and empowerment seminars and workshops, monitoring women's rights, public education lectures, and defending Jerusalem. JCW and Bat Shalom, the Jerusalem Women's Action Center in Israel, hold joint programs through Jerusalem Link, the coordinating body. The goal of Jerusalem Link is "to promote women's political, social, and cultural activities and leadership in the service of women's rights and the realization of peace on the basis of justice and equality."[38]

In this connection, Palestinian women within or outside Jerusalem Link have dialogued with Israeli women.[39] Others, such as Eileen Kuttab, Islah Jad, and Rima Hammami, have joined some of their male counterparts in signing a communiqué calling on Israelis to agree to a just solution that is based on a Palestinian state set within the 1967 borders or a national state.[40]

## Women's Studies at Birzeit University

The struggle to ensure gender equity and to help the development of gender-sensitive policies is also undertaken in academe, at such institutions as Birzeit University.[41] An excellent example is the work of the Women's Studies Program. Established in 1993, the program provides teaching, training, research, and community outreach. The focus is not only on the political or the national struggle but also on social issues, thus making visible the contributions of women. *Palestinian Women: A Status Report,* published by the program, examines a variety of topics, including population, family, labor and the economy, education, law, health, and gender and development. This ten-section report is introduced by a thoughtful chapter on Palestinian society, written by Lisa Taraki, a member of the Women's Studies Program and an associate professor in the Department of Sociology and Anthropology.[42]

## The Palestinian Coalition for Women's Health

The work to advance gender equity and gender-sensitive policies is also undertaken in the area of women's health. This is illustrated by the work of the Palestinian Coalition for Women's Health (PCWH), a professional platform consisting of representatives of the major institutions working in the health field.[43] PCWH members include faculty, practitioners, and others working for governmental and nongovernmental departments, including international agencies. These include individuals from the Department of Community and Public Health at Birzeit University, the Department of Women's Health and Development at the Ministry of Health of the Palestine National Authority, the United Nations Development Programme, and the United Nations Children's Fund. PCWH enriches national level policies regarding women's health; produces prototype training materials on women's health that reflect a holistic life-cycle to the understanding of women's health; and monitors developments in women's health programs.

## Women's Empowerment Project

An exemplary program that combines elements of the above efforts is the Women's Empowerment Project (WEP), which is part of the Gaza Community Mental Health Program.[44] WEP's main goal is "to improve the quality of life of women victims of violence, their families and community, through strengthening of local rehabilitation, education and training facilities." Its facilities enable women "to be trained in vocational and income generating skills, while at the same time providing psychological and legal counseling, and education in self-development, women's health, and social and legal issues." In addition to lectures, workshops, public meetings, and support groups are organized on a regular basis.

## Other Efforts

In addition, Palestinian women have joined hands to draft the Declaration of Principles on Palestinian Women's Rights, a document based on the Palestinian Declaration of Independence, the United Nations Conventions, the Universal Declaration of Human Rights, and other such statements relating to political, civil, economic, social, and cultural rights.[45] Palestinian women have also made their case clear in front of international conferences such as the Fourth World Conference on Women, which was held in Beijing in September 1995. Funds to support women's initiatives have come from several sources, particularly from abroad. These include the European Commission, the European Union, the U.S. Agency for International Development, Canada Fund, Ford Foundation, Norwegian Human Rights Fund, and the U.S., Australian, Danish, and Swedish governments.

## CONCLUSION

Palestinian women have too many demands placed upon them. They should not be expected to sacrifice with the men but not reap the full benefits. They need not make sense of their experiences through a male prism. They need not keep their silence. Although conflict, nationalism, activism, and peace have a multiplicity of meaning for women, as they do for men, women must continue to develop their own voice, make themselves heard, and author their own becoming.

For political and civic participation to be meaningful for women and men alike, it has to be an integral part of how both women and men receive, translate, and produce meaning. Palestinian empowerment should extend beyond the self or the few supporters to include the ability to appropriate those aspects of Palestinian life that provide the basis for knowing, communicating, healing, and transforming the social order and the structures of common life. It should be based on connecting past and present traditions and vision for the future. It should involve legitimate ways by which individuals, social movements, and political parties express themselves, interact with each other, influence others, negotiate power, and act.

This empowerment is a must not only to fulfill some legal code but also to advance what is right. This mode of thinking ought to make more coherent inner truth and outward behavior. It ought to advance self-interest and the collective interest, personal liberation, and national liberation.

## DISCUSSION QUESTIONS

1. What must Palestinian women do today in order to assure increased levels of empowerment for themselves in the future?

2. How has the Palestinian women's movement enhanced or distracted from the empowerment of Palestinian women?

3. Compare the current conditions of women to that of men in the West Bank and the Gaza Strip.

4. Examine a major event in Palestinian-Israeli history (e.g., the June 1967 war, military occupation, the Palestinian intifada) and analyze its impact on the lives of Palestinian women.

5. Analyze the different forms of oppression from which Palestinian women suffer. How can these be eliminated or minimized?

6. Select any Palestinian woman's organization, program, or project and discuss its approach and struggle for women's empowerment.

7. Critically evaluate two of the following:

    a. Palestinian women are trapped; their oppression is too pervasive to be overcome.

    b. Gender discrimination in Palestinian society will continue regardless of the strengthening of Palestinian public institutions.

    c. National liberation is a must for personal liberation.

    d. It is in the best interest of Palestinian men to assist Palestinian women in acquiring their equal and legitimate rights.

## NOTES

1. See United Nations Development Fund for Women, "Political Empowerment: Strengthening Women's Leadership," available online at http://www.gopher. undp (accessed March 3, 1998).

2. Ibid.

3. Research for this chapter was completed in summer 2000. Israeli occupation of Palestinian lands, the failure of the Israeli-Palestinian peace process, and the resultant second Palestinian intifada, which began on September 29, 2000, have worsened and made more complicated the conditions of Palestinian women's lives.

4. See Suha Sabbagh, ed., *Palestinian Women of Gaza and the West Bank* (Bloomington: Indiana University Press, 1998); Simona Sharoni, *Gender and the Israeli-Palestinian Conflict: The Politics of Women's Resistance* (Syracuse: Syracuse

University Press, 1995); and Tamar Mayer, ed., *Women and the Israeli Occupation* (London: Routledge, 1994).

5. For an analysis of the conditions and challenges that Palestinian women face in their patriarchal society as influenced by the Israeli military occupation, see Samira Haj, "Palestinian Women and Patriarchal Relations," *Signs: Journal of Women in Culture and Society* 17, no. 4 (1992): 761–777. For an examination of the personal texture of the individual lives of Palestinian women, see Michael Gorkin and Rafiqa Othman, *Three Mothers, Three Daughters: Palestinian Women's Stories* (Berkeley: University of California Press, 1996).

6. For analyses of Palestinian women's nationalist work and resistance, see Amal Kawar, *Daughters of Palestine: Leading Women of the Palestinian National Movement* (Albany: State University of New York Press, 1996); Sharoni, *Gender and the Israeli-Palestinian Conflict*, esp. chap. 4; and Philippa Strum, *The Women Are Marching: The Second Sex and the Palestinian Revolution* (Brooklyn, N.Y.: Lawrence Hill Books, 1992).

7. For an examination of the history of leading women's involvement in the Palestinian National Movement from the mid-1960s to the early 1990s, see Kawar, *Daughters of Palestine*.

8. Ashrawi in Dima Zalatimo, "An Interview with Hanan Mikhail Ashrawi: The History of the Women's Movement," in Sabbagh, *Palestinian Women of Gaza and the West Bank,* p. 185.

9. Zahira Kamal, "The Development of the Palestinian Women's Movement in the Occupied Territories: Twenty Years After the Israeli Occupation," in Sabbagh, *Palestinian Women of Gaza and the West Bank.*

10. Palestine Central Bureau of Statistics, "Population and Family," in *Statistics of Women and Men in Palestine* (Gender Pamphlet in Arabic) (Ramallah, Palestine: Palestine Central Bureau of Statistics, March 1998).

11. The language and data are taken from *Statistics of Women and Men in Palestine.*

12. Cited in "Women Want More Stake in Palestinian Council," *Reuters News Service,* January 26, 1996, available online at http://burn.ucsd.edu/~archive/riot-1/1996.Jan/0291.html (accessed July 30, 1997).

13. Cited in Ala' Mashharawi, "Mother to the Nation," *Jerusalem Times,* November 11, 1996, available online at http://www.amin.org/biladi2/pal1.htm (accessed November 12, 1996).

14. Informal interviews or conversations were conducted with ordinary Palestinian women in Jerusalem and the West Bank starting in summer 1995. They include a journalist, a teacher, a school administrator, two social workers, an activist, a hospital administrator, a nurse, a graduate student, and a businesswoman.

15. See Saliba Sarsar, "Bibliography on Palestinian Women," available online at http://www.columbia.edu/cu/libraries/indiv/area/MiddleEast/palwomen.html (accessed December 12, 1998).

16. These include Hanan Ashrawi, the former minister of higher education with the Palestine National Authority and a member in the Palestine Legislative Council; Zahira Kamal, the highest-ranking woman in the Democratic Front for the Liberation of Palestine (prior to its split) in the Occupied Territories and the director of gender planning and development in the Ministry of Planning and International Cooperation with the Palestine National Authority; and Intisar El Wazir, minister of social affairs with the Palestine National Authority.

17. Hanan Ashrawi, *This Side of Peace: A Personal Account* (New York: Simon and Schuster, 1995), pp. 107, 26–27.

18. Haj, "Palestinian Women and Patriarchal Relations," p. 765.

19. Cited in Jan Goodwin, *Price of Honor: Muslim Women Lift the Veil of Silence on the Islamic World* (Boston: Little, Brown, 1994), pp. 299–300.

20. Haj, "Palestinian Women and Patriarchal Relations," p. 764.

21. For a discussion of women's honor in the Palestinian context, see Kawar, *Daughters of Palestine*, pp. 20–26. For a discussion of honor killings, see Suzanne Ruggi, "Honor Killings in Palestine," *Middle East Report* (spring 1998), available online at http://www.merip.org/ruggi.htm (accessed November 4, 1998).

22. For more on the intifada, see Sabbagh, *Palestinian Women of Gaza and the West Bank;* Strum, *The Women Are Marching;* Don Peretz, *Intifada: The Palestinian Uprising* (Boulder: Westview, 1990); and Zachary Lockman and Joel Beinin, eds., *Intifada: The Palestinian Uprising Against Israeli Occupation* (a MERIP book) (Boston: South End, 1989).

23. Quoted in Goodwin, *Price of Honor,* p. 294.

24. Ibid., p. 295.

25. Ibid., p. 292.

26. Ashrawi, *This Side of Peace,* p. 201.

27. Ibid., p. 228.

28. Ibid., p. 60.

29. Quoted in Goodwin, *Price of Honor,* p. 301.

30. See Palestinian Society for the Protection of Human Rights and the Environment (Jerusalem), "Failed Hopes: The Life of Palestinian Women After the Signing of the Oslo Accords," available online at http://www.lawsociety.org/reports/1997/v0mliv.html (accessed November 12, 1998).

31. For an analysis of the political environment after Oslo and Palestinian women's reaction to it, see Amal Kawar, "Palestinian Women's Activism After Oslo," in Sabbagh, *Palestinian Women of Gaza and the West Bank.*

32. See Daoud Kuttab, "The View from the East: Palestinian Women Move Out of Shadow," available online at http://www.amin.org/pages/dkuttab/april_1698.htm (accessed June 16, 1998); and Dahlia Scheindlin, "Democrats or Devils? A Women's Model Parliament," available online at http://www.geocities.com/Wellesley/3321/win11a.htm (accessed March 10, 2000).

33. The Palestinian Academic Society for the Study of International Affairs (Jerusalem), "PASSIA Diary 2000," pp. 110–114.

34. For a synopsis of the work of the Directorate of Gender Planning and Development, see http://www.pna.net/reports/dgpd.htm (accessed March 2, 1998).

35. For a good description of the work of the Women's Affairs Technical Committee, see its homepage, available online at http://www.pal-watc.org/ (accessed June 16, 1998).

36. Suheir Azzouni, "Palestinian Women and Equal Status in Society," available online at http://www.pal-watc.org/women.htm (accessed June 16, 1998).

37. See the Jerusalem Center for Women homepage, available online at http://www.j-c-w.org/ (accessed November 13, 1998).

38. For the goals, background, activities, and declaration of the Jerusalem Link, see the homepage of the Jerusalem Center for Women or the homepage of Bat Shalom, available online at http://www.batshalom.org/JerusalemLink.htm (accessed November 13, 1998).

39. See Eileen F. Babbit and Tamra Pearson D'Estrée, "An Israeli-Palestinian Women's Workshop: Application of the Interactive Problem Solving Approach," in Chester A. Crocker and Fen Osler Hampson with Pamela Aall, eds., *Managing Global Chaos: Sources of and Responses to International Conflict* (Washington,

D.C.: United States Institute of Peace Press, 1996), pp. 521–529; and Galia Golan and Zahira Kamal, "Bridging the Abyss: Palestinian-Israeli Women's Dialogue," in Harold H. Saunders, ed., *A Public Peace Process: Sustained Dialogue to Transform Racial and Ethnic Conflicts* (New York: St. Martin's, 1999), pp. 197–220.

40. For a copy of the communiqué that was signed by about 120 Palestinian intellectuals and addressed to the Israeli and Jewish public, both in English and Hebrew, see *Haaretz* (March 13, 2000).

41. See Roula el-Raifi, "Laying the Foundations of a Democratic Palestine: The Women's Studies Program at Birzeit University," available online at http://www.idc.ca/books/reports/1997/11-01e.html (accessed March 2, 1998)

42. See Lisa Taraki's chapter on Palestinian Society, available online at http://www.birzeit.edu/ourvoice/society/sept/Lisa998.html#top (accessed October 30, 1998).

43. See the Palestinian Coalition for Women's Health homepage, available online at http://www.birzeit.edu/chd/whycoal.html (accessed October 30, 1998).

44. For more information on the Women's Empowerment Project and some of its stories of success, see its homepage, available online at http://www.gcmhp.net/women.htm (accessed April 5, 2000).

45. For an analysis of and the full text of the Declaration of Principles on Palestinian Women's Rights, see Sabbagh, *Palestinian Women of Gaza and the West Bank,* chap. 15 and appendix.

# 10

# Conclusion: Assessing Women and Empowerment

## Rekha Datta & Judith Kornberg

The chapters in this book analyze women's empowerment at the international, national, and local levels. The role of international institutions—their legal regimes, and the political, economic, and social efforts on behalf of women by these institutions—is only one part of this analysis. State policies, and how the intersection of state policies with traditional political, economic, and social structures determine the course of women's empowerment, are also examined. Women's efforts to organize themselves on the grassroots level to further their political, economic, and social participation in society are another important focus of these chapters.

Each of these areas of investigation—multilateral approaches to improving women's rights; changes in the nation-state and its laws and policies governing women; and women taking charge by forming alliances to promote their issues—has been the subject of scholarly analysis. Rarely, however, has the empowerment of women been analyzed simultaneously on all three levels.

In this volume, the authors seek to extend their discipline by studying women's empowerment within a far broader context than that traditionally used by political scientists. And by doing so, they shatter preconceived notions and also discern commonalities across national boundaries.

At the international and national levels, women are participating actively in empowerment processes. In this regard, they are successfully shaping international and national policies and institutions and mobilizing women who have become aware of their rights and gained valuable resources and skills. International conferences bring women together across national barriers, and successful models developed in one nation are shared with others.

In Chapter 2, Charlotte Graves Patton commends the United Nations (UN) for setting standards for empowerment of women and for providing the international fora for discussion of women's empowerment. She argues, however, that for women's empowerment to progress, the United Nations must look beyond its focus on international administrative units and national political institutions. UN efforts to increase empowerment in the twenty-first century, Patton argues, must incorporate a far greater understanding of women's' political, social, and economic issues on local and regional levels.

Kathleen Suneja in Chapter 3 also commends UN efforts to create an international legal regime that protects women, particularly with respect to female genital mutilation, the sex trade, and rape as a war crime. She is in agreement with Charlotte Patton that the United Nations' macro-level efforts are not enough. International legal norms must be incorporated into national and local policy through the efforts of women within their own societies. The United Nations can provide a framework, but women can more effectively shape the debate and effect legal changes within their own countries.

Both China and India—one a communist nation in transition to a market economy and greater political openness, the other a capitalist democratic nation of tremendous diversity—have longstanding commitments to improving women's status. Mao Tse-tung famously said that women hold up half the heavens, and the Indian constitution of 1950 specifically addressed the status of women. Yet in both China and India, women's political, economic, and social gains have been limited and in some cases even receded due to changes in economic structure, religious pressures on political institutions, and the like. Kellee Tsai (Chapter 4) and Rekha Datta (Chapter 5) agree that despite national policies and ideologies committed to equality for women and men, patriarchal frameworks preventing women's empowerment still prevail in both China and India. Both authors see positive signs in women's successes that are occurring often on a local level, with those working for empowerment bringing to their efforts an understanding of international discussions of women's empowerment and the frameworks that national governments must establish.

The economic policies of global economic institutions and of national governments, when they participate in the global economy as well as when they are internally focused, generally contribute to women's disempowerment. Women's economic situations usually worsen as a result of structural adjustment programs (SAPs). At the same time, the resources and services that women need to alleviate their traditional responsibilities, thereby allowing upward mobility, generally have been curtailed. Upward mobility for women therefore becomes all the more difficult. Yet even within the context of patriarchal social structures and SAP-induced government cutbacks and economic challenges, the extent of women's disempowerment varies across and within countries.

Lucy Creevey (Chapter 6) and Kiki Anastasakos (Chapter 7), examining the results of SAPs in Niger and Senegal, and Mexico and Costa Rica, respectively, reach remarkably similar conclusions. Their field research indicates that SAPs have in many cases resulted in the disempowerment of women—but not uniformly. How much women were disempowered differed markedly from country to country. In West Africa, Mexico, and Costa Rica, women's economic and social status is so complex that more than structural adjustment is at play in the recent reverses in their economic status. Both authors argue that further research is needed to better understand why SAPs have had a divergent effect on women. This research, they agree, must then be used by international agencies advocating structural adjustment, as well as by national governments, to ensure that women's collective needs are not overlooked in any prescription for economic development.

"Self-empowerment" is equally a theme in Marian Miller's discussion of women in the Caribbean (Chapter 8) and Saliba Sarsar's discussion of Palestinian women (Chapter 9). Women in these regions are initiating "waves" of social consciousness and protest to improve their socio-economic status and overall empowerment and leadership in the community. Rather than seeking broad changes in their political, economic, and social status, Caribbean and Palestinian women have focused on "making waves" through small steps. These small waves will lead to societal changes that will eventually lead to the further empowerment of women in the Caribbean and in the West Bank and the Gaza Strip.

The chapters in this volume thus approach the multilevel and complex nature of empowerment by looking at the international, national, and subnational levels and the various strategies of empowerment used at these levels. They highlight the different implications of empowerment for women in unique contexts of development and social change. International organizations take a broader perspective to address systematic gender violence issues. Although they may or may not generate economic development, these laws and policies enable women to have greater self-confidence and freedom from violence and oppression and therefore empower them to take leadership in other spheres of their life as well.

Thus, this book does not seek to offer a definition or meaning of empowerment that will be effective and applicable globally. The case studies provide an opportunity to recognize the differences in empowerment experiences in different regions of the world and the levels at which they occur. They recognize the effect of scholarship as well as policies, laws, regulations, and movements that affect the status of women. "To succeed, women must become active both at the level of discovering strategies and implementing them at the level of national politics. They must continue to fight to maintain the language of equality and translate it into practicable measures."[1]

We hope to reinforce the emerging notions of assessing empowerment in all its richness, variety, and complexity. The meaning of empowerment for this book is therefore broad, inclusive, and flexible. In order to understand empowerment, we must recognize the unique experiences of women in developing countries. Likewise, the strategies and policies that bring empowerment will vary in different contexts. The vicissitudes of the development process are already established. Volumes such as the current one will underscore the complex and varying degrees and nature of empowerment as well.

The current research, including research by the authors in this book, does not allow us to gauge the extent to which the processes of women's empowerment—women's activism at the international and national and local levels—are altering the disempowering effects of current national and international policies and of gender-biased traditions, social structures, and governmental and corporate institutions. We come away from these studies knowing that we need to learn far more about how women become empowered in their own societies. Rather than relying on assumptions based on the empowerment of women in the developed world, or on narrow discipline-specific areas of study, the study of the empowerment of women in the third world must take place on all levels and through cooperation among scholars from different disciplines.

NOTE

1. Haleh Afshar, ed., *Women and Empowerment: Illustrations from the Third World* (New York: St. Martin's, 1998).

# GLOSSARY

*ACC:* United Nations Administrative Committee on Coordination

*ACWF:* All China Women's Federation

*CCP:* Chinese Communist Party

*CEDAW:* UN Committee on the Elimination of Discrimination Against Women. Composed of twenty-three independent experts, the Committee reviews the reports of state parties (currently 156) on the implementation of the Convention on the Elimination of All Forms of Discrimination Against Women and evaluates the progress made. Convened for the first time in 1982, CEDAW is the treaty-monitoring body for the Convention.

*Chipko movement:* Women's movement, also an environmental movement in the 1970s in northern India when village women literally hugged trees to protect them from logging companies. Also known as the "tree huggers" movement. "Chipko" in Hindi means "to attach to" and refers to the women hugging or attaching themselves to the trees to prevent deforestation.

*CPPCC:* Chinese People's Political Consultative Conference

*CSW:* UN Commission on the Status of Women. Prepares recommendations and reports to the UN Economic and Social Council (ECOSOC) on promoting women's rights and monitors within the UN system and the implementation of the Beijing Platform for Action. Created in 1946 as a subsidiary body of ECOSOC, the Commission first met in 1947. The Commission, an intergovernmental body, has forty-five members, each elected for four years.

*DAW:* UN Division for the Advancement of Women. Acts as a focal point for coordination and mainstreaming of gender issues in the UN system. It has been the Secretariat of the four UN world conferences on women and is responsible for servicing the CSW and the CEDAW. It carries out gender analysis in the twelve critical areas of the Platform for Action and on emerging issues. It also has a mandate for gender mainstreaming in the UN system in support of the Special Adviser to the UN Secretary-General on Gender Issues and the Advancement of Women.

*ECOSOC:* UN Economic and Social Council. Oversees systemwide coordination in the implementation of the Beijing Platform for Action and makes recommendations in this regard.

*FGM:* female genital mutilation

*FWCW:* Fourth World Conference on Women (Beijing, September 4–15, 1995)

*GDI:* Gender-related Development Index

*GEM:* Gender Empowerment Measure

*General Assembly (United Nations):* The highest intergovernmental body in the United Nations, the General Assembly is the principal policymaking and appraisal organ on matters relating to the follow-up to the FWCW.

*GIDP:* Gender in Development Programme

*HRS:* Chinese household responsibility system

*human development:* A wider and more comprehensive concept of development. It includes the process of enlarging people's choices in the areas of education, longevity, and economic power.

*Human Development Index:* A composite index that measures human development. It measures longevity by life expectancy; knowledge by examining adult literacy and mean years of schooling; and standard of living by purchasing power based on real GDP per capita adjusted for the cost of living.

*ICPD/Cairo:* International Conference on Population and Development held in Cairo, Egypt, in 1994.

*INSTRAW:* International Research and Training Institute for the Advancement of Women. Stimulates and assists, through research, training, and the collection and dissemination of information, the advancement of women and making women's contribution to development more visible. It assists the efforts of intergovernmental, governmental, and nongovernmental organizations in this regard. The Institute began operations in 1980 and is based in the Dominican Republic.

*Maitree:* Umbrella organization coordinating the activities of various organizations to support women against domestic violence and other abuses of women's rights. Based in Kolkata, India.

*national machineries:* Government-established national mechanisms to plan, advocate for, and monitor progress in the advancement of women.

*NGO:* Nongovernmental organization

*NPC:* Chinese National People's Congress

*PoA:* The twenty-year Programme of Action of the International Conference on Population and Development (ICPD) held in Cairo, Egypt, in 1994 was adopted by 179 countries; the ICPD Programme of Action underscores the integral and mutually reinforcing linkages between population and development and endorses a new rights-based strategy that focuses on meeting the needs of individual women and men rather than on achieving demographic targets.

*PRC:* People's Republic of China

*SEWA:* The Self-Employed Women's Association, a trade union, cooperative, and women's movement in India. SEWA has been at the forefront of empowering self-employed women since 1972. Headquarters in Ahmedabad, India.

*UNDP:* United Nations Development Programme

*UNESCO:* UN Educational, Scientific, and Cultural Organization. In promoting gender equality, the self-empowerment of women, and their full citizenship, UNESCO is guided by the following principles: (1) mainstreaming a gender perspective in all policy-planning programming, implementation, and evaluation activities; (2) promoting the active and broad participation of women at all levels and fields of activity, with particular attention to women's priorities, perspectives, and contributions to the rethinking of both the goals and means of development; and (3) developing specific programs, special projects, and activities for the benefit of girls and women.

*UNFPA:* United Nations Population Fund. Guided by and promotes the principles of the Programme of Action of the International Conference on Population and Development (1994). In particular, UNFPA affirms its commitment to reproductive rights, gender equality, and male responsibility, as well as to the autonomy and empowerment of women everywhere.

*UNICEF:* United Nations Children's Fund. Aims to promote the equal rights of women and girls and to support their full participation in the political, social, and economic development of their communities. Supports the equality and advancement of girls in infancy, childhood, and adolescence.

*UNIFEM:* United Nations Development Fund for Women. Promotes women's empowerment and gender equality, working primarily at the country level. It works to ensure the participation of women in all levels of development planning and practice and acts as a catalyst, supporting efforts that link the needs and concerns of women to all critical issues on the national, regional, and global agendas. Established in 1976 as the Voluntary Fund for the UN Decade for Women, the Fund became UNIFEM in 1985, an autonomous body in association with the United Nations Development Programme.

*WHO:* World Health Organization

*WID:* Women in development

# UN Conventions and Declarations of Particular Importance to Women's Rights

The Declaration on the Elimination of Violence Against Women (1993) cites violence against women as "one of the crucial mechanisms by which women are forced into a subordinate position compared with men." The United Nations has appointed a Special Rapporteur on Violence Against Women to collect data and recommend measures to eliminate such violence and its causes.

The Convention on the Elimination of All Forms of Discrimination Against Women (1979), described as the international bill of rights for women, prohibits any distinction, exclusion, or restriction made on the basis of sex that impairs or nullifies human rights and fundamental freedoms of women in all areas. A UN committee regularly monitors progress in implementing the Convention and holds hearings on reports submitted by state parties. An optional protocol to the Convention has been adopted.

The Declaration on the Protection of Women and Children in Emergencies and Armed Conflicts (1974).

The Declaration on the Elimination of Discrimination Against Women (1967) affirms that "discrimination against women, denying or limiting as it does their equality of rights with men, is fundamentally unjust and constitutes an offence against human dignity."

The Convention on Consent to Marriage, Minimum Age for Marriage, and Registration of Marriages (1962) decrees that no marriage can occur without the consent of both parties.

The Convention Against Discrimination in Education adopted by the General Conference of the United Nations Educational, Scientific, and Cultural Organization (December 14, 1960) paves the way for equal educational opportunities for girls and women.

The Discrimination (Employment and Occupation) Convention (1958) promotes equality of rights between men and women in the workplace.

The Convention on the Political Rights of Women (1952) commits member states to allow women to vote and hold public office on equal terms with men.

The ILO Equal Remuneration Convention (1951) establishes the principle and practice of equal pay for work of equal value.

The Convention for the Suppression of the Traffic in Persons and of the Exploitation of the Prostitution of Others (1949) calls for the punishment of those procuring others for prostitution.

# BIBLIOGRAPHY

Afshar, Haleh, ed. *Women and Empowerment: Illustrations from the Third World.* New York: St. Martin's, 1998.

———. *Women, Work, and Ideology in the Third World.* London: Tavistock Publications, 1985.

Afshar, Haleh, and Carolyne Dennis, eds. *Women and Adjustment Policies in the Third World.* New York: St. Martin's, 1992.

Agarwal, Bina, ed. *Structures of Patriarchy: The State, the Community, and the Household.* London: Zed Books, 1988.

Andors, Phyllis. *The Unfinished Liberation of Chinese Women.* Bloomington: Indiana University Press, 1983.

Ashrawi, Hanan. *This Side of Peace: A Personal Account.* New York: Simon and Schuster, 1995.

Barrett, Richard E., William P. Bridges, Moshe Semyonov, and Xiaoyuan Gao. "Female Labor Force Participation in Urban and Rural China." *Rural Sociology* 56, no. 1 (spring 1991): 1–21.

Baud, Isa, and Ines Smyth. *Searching for Security: Women's Responses to Economic Transformations.* London: Routledge, 1997.

Benerìa, Lourdes, ed. *Women and Development: The Sexual Division of Labor in Rural Societies.* New York: Praeger, 1982.

Benerìa, Lourdes, and Shelley Feldman, eds. *Unequal Burden: Economic Crisis, Persistent Poverty.* Boulder: Westview, 1992.

Bhasin, Kamla, et al., eds. *Against All Odds: Essays on Women, Religion, and Development from India and Pakistan.* Delhi: Deep and Deep, 1996.

Blumberg, Rae Lesser, Cathy Rakowski, Irene Tinker, and Michael Monteon. *Engendering Wealth and Well-Being: Empowerment for Global Change.* Boulder: Westview, 1992.

Bolles, A. Lynn. "Doing It for Themselves: Women's Research and Action in the Commonwealth Caribbean." In Edna Acosta-Belen and Christine E. Bose, *Researching Women in Latin America and the Caribbean.* Boulder: Westview, 1993, pp. 153–174.

Boserup, Ester. *Woman's Role in Economic Development.* New York: St. Martin's, 1970.

Brydon, Lynne, and Sylvia Chant. *Women in the Third World.* New Brunswick, N.J.: Rutgers University Press, 1989.

Bystydzienski, Jill M. *Women Transforming Politics: Worldwide Strategies for Empowerment.* Bloomington: Indiana University Press, 1992.

Callaway, Barbara, and Lucy Creevey. *The Heritage of Islam: Religion and Politics in West Africa.* Boulder: Lynne Rienner Publishers, 1994.

Calman, Leslie J. *Toward Empowerment: Women and Movement Politics in India.* Boulder: Westview, 1992.

Cohen, Cathy, et al., eds. *Women Transforming Politics: An Alternative Reader.* New York: New York University Press, 1997.

Conners, Jane. "Legal Aspects of Women as a Particular Social Group." *International Journal of Refugee Law* (special issue, August 1997): 114–128.

Cook, Rebecca J. "Human Rights and Reproductive Self-Determination." *American University Law Review* 44 (spring 1995): 975–1016.

———. *Human Rights of Women: National and International Perspectives.* Philadelphia: University of Pennsylvania Press, 1994.

Cook, Rebecca J., and Deborah Maine. "Spousal Veto over Family Planning Services." *American Journal of Public Health* 77, no. 39 (1987).

Cothran, Dan A. *Political Stability and Democracy in Mexico: The "Perfect Dictatorship?"* Westport, Conn.: Praeger: 1994.

Creevey, Lucy. *Changing Women's Lives and Work: An Analysis of Eight Microenterprise Projects.* London: IT Publications, 1996.

———. *Women Farmers in Africa: Rural Development in Mali and the Sahel.* New York: Syracuse University Press, 1986.

Croll, Elisabeth. *Chinese Women Since Mao.* Armonk, N.Y.: M. E. Sharpe, 1983.

Dalla Costa, Mariarosa, and Giovanna F. Dalla Costa. *Paying the Price: Women and the Politics of International Economic Strategy.* London: Zed Books, 1995.

Davin, Delia. *Women-Work, Women, and the Party in Revolutionary China.* Oxford: Clarendon, 1976.

Dominguez, Jorge I., and James A. McCann. *Democratizing Mexico: Public Opinion and Electoral Choices.* Baltimore: Johns Hopkins University Press, 1996.

Dwyer, Daisy, and Judith Bruce, eds. *A Home Divided: Women and Income in the Third World.* Stanford: Stanford University Press, 1988.

Evans, Peter B., D. Rueschemeyer, and T. Skocpol. *Bringing the State Back In.* Cambridge: Cambridge University Press, 1985.

Frieden, Jeffry A. *Debt, Development, and Democracy: Economic Policy and Political Participation in Latin America, 1965–1985.* Princeton: Princeton University Press, 1991.

Furlong, Marlea, and Kimberly Riggs. "Women's Participation in National-Level Politics and Government—The Case of Costa Rica." *Women's Studies International Forum* 19, no. 6 (1996): 63–64.

Ghai, Dharam, ed. *The IMF and the South: The Social Impact of Crisis and Adjustment.* London: Zed Books, 1991.

Ghorayshi, Parvin, and Claire Belanger, eds. *Women, Work, and Gender Relations in Developing Countries: A Global Perspective.* Westport, Conn.: Greenwood, 1996.

Gindling, T. H., and A. Berry. "The Performance of the Labor Market During Recession and Structural Adjustment: Costa Rica in the 1980s." *World Development* 20 (1993): 1599–1617.

Gonzalez de la Rocha, Mercedes. *The Resources of Poverty: Women and Survival in a Mexican City.* Cambridge: Blackwell Publishers, 1994.

Goodwin, Jan. *Price of Honor: Muslim Women Lift the Veil of Silence on the Islamic World.* Boston: Little, Brown, 1994.

Gorkin, Michael, and Rafiqa Othman. *Three Mothers, Three Daughters: Palestinian Women's Stories.* Berkeley: University of California Press, 1996.

Haj, Samira. "Palestinian Women and Patriarchal Relations." *Signs: Journal of Women in Culture and Society* 17, no. 4 (1992): 761–777.

Hartstock, Nancy. *Money, Sex and Power: Towards a Feminist Historical Materialism.* Boston: Northeastern University Press, 1985.

Herrick, Bruce, and Barclay Hudson. *Urban Poverty and Economic Development: A Case Study of Costa Rica.* New York: St. Martin's, 1981.

Hodgson, Dennis, and Susan Cotts Watkins. "Feminists and Neo-Malthusians: Past and Present Alliances." *Population and Development Review* 23, no. 3 (September 1997): 469–523.

Inter-American Development Bank. *Women in the Americas: Bridging the Gender Gap.* Washington, D.C.: Johns Hopkins University Press, 1995.

Jacka, Tamara. *Women's Work in Rural China: Change and Continuity in an Era of Reform.* New York: Cambridge University Press, 1997.

Johnson, Kay Ann. *Women, the Family, and Peasant Revolution in China.* Chicago: University of Chicago Press, 1983.

Kabeer, Naila. *Reversed Realities: Gender Hierarchies in Development Thought.* New York: Verso, 1994.

Kahne, Hilda, and Janet Z. Giele, eds. *Women's Work and Women's Lives.* Boulder: Westview, 1993.

Katzenstein, Peter, ed. *Between Power and Plenty.* Madison: University of Wisconsin Press, 1978.

Kawar, Amal. *Daughters of Palestine: Leading Women of the Palestinian National Movement.* Albany: State University of New York Press, 1996.

Kissling, Frances. "The Challenge of Christianity." *American University Law Review* 44 (1994): 1345–1349.

Leahy, Margaret E. *Development Strategies and the Status of Women.* Boulder: Lynne Rienner Publishers, 1986.

Lentner, Howard H. *State Formation in Central America: The Struggle for Autonomy, Development, and Democracy.* Westport, Conn.: Greenwood, 1993.

Levy, Marion J. *The Family Revolution in China.* New York: Octagon, 1971.

Lockman, Zachary, and Joel Beinin, eds. *Intifada: The Palestinian Uprising Against Israeli Occupation.* Boston: South End, 1989.

Lycklama A Nijeholt, Geertje, Virginia Vargas, and Saskia Wieringa, eds. *Women's Movements and Public Policy in Europe, Latin America, and the Caribbean.* New York: Garland Publishing, 1998.

Macdonald, Laura. *Supporting Civil Society: The Political Role of Non-Governmental Organizations in Central America.* New York: St. Martin's, 1997.

Maher, Robin M. "Female Genital Mutilation: The Struggle to Eradicate This Rite of Passage." *Human Rights* 23, no. 4 (fall 1996): 12.

March, Kathryn, and Rachelle Taqqu. *Women's Informal Associations in Developing Countries.* Boulder: Westview, 1986.

Mayer, Tamar, ed. *Women and the Israeli Occupation.* London: Routledge, 1994.

McConnell, Moira L. "Violence Against Women: Beyond the Limits of the Law." *Brooklyn Journal of International Law* 21 (1996): 899.

McIntosh, Alison, and Jason L. Finkle. "The Cairo Conference on Population and Development: A New Paradigm?" *Population and Development Review* 21, no. 2 (June 1995): 223–260.

Meron, Theodor. "Rape as a Crime Under International Humanitarian Law." *American Journal of International Law* 87 (July 1993): 424–428.

Momsen, Janet, ed. *Women and Change in the Caribbean.* Bloomington: Indiana University Press.

Momsen, Janet H., and Vivian Kinnard, eds. *Different Places, Different Voices: Gender and Development in Africa, Asia and Latin America.* London: Routledge: 1993.

Morley, Samuel A. *Poverty and Inequality in Latin America: The Impact of Adjustment and Recovery in the 1980s.* Baltimore: Johns Hopkins University Press, 1991.

Morton, Ward M. *Woman Suffrage in Mexico.* Gainesville: University of Florida Press, 1962.

Moser, Caroline. *Gender Planning and Development: Theory, Practice, and Training.* New York: Routledge, 1993.

Mullings, Beverley. "Globalization, Tourism, and the International Sex Trade." In Kamala Kempadoo, ed., *Sun, Sex, and Gold.* Lanham, Md.: Rowman and Littlefield, 1999, pp. 55–80.

Nash, June, and Maria Patricia Fernandez-Kelly, eds. *Women, Men, and the International Division of Labor.* Albany: State University of New York Press, 1983.

Nelson, Barbara J., and Najma Chowdhury, eds. *Women and Politics Worldwide.* New Haven: Yale University Press, 1994.

Oi, Jean. *State and Peasant in Contemporary China: The Political Economy of Village Government.* Berkeley: University of California Press, 1989.

Ong, Aihya. *Spirits of Resistance and Capitalist Discipline: Factory Women in Malaysia.* Albany: State University of New York Press, 1987.

Oppong, Christine. *Seven Roles of Women: Impact of Education, Migration, and Employment.* Geneva: International Labour Office, 1987.

Otero, Gerardo, ed. *Neoliberalism Revisited: Economic Restructuring and Mexico's Political Future.* Boulder: Westview, 1996.

Parish, William L., and Martin K. Whyte. *Village and Family in Contemporary China.* Chicago: University of Chicago Press, 1978.

Parpart, Jane L., ed. *Women and Development in Africa: Comparative Perspectives.* Lanham, Md.: University Press of America, 1989.

Parry, Odette. "In One Ear and Out the Other: Unmasking Masculinities in the Caribbean Classroom." *Sociological Research Online* 1, no. 2 (July 1996). Available online at http://www.socresonline.org.uk/socresonline/1/2/2.html.

Patel, Krishna R. "Recognizing the Rape of Bosnian Women as Gender-Based Persecution." *Brooklyn Law Review* 60 (fall 1994): 929–958.

Pattullo, Polly. *Last Resorts: The Cost of Tourism in the Caribbean.* London: Cassell, 1996.

Peretz, Don. *Intifada: The Palestinian Uprising.* Boulder: Westview, 1990.

Philip, George, ed. *The Mexican Economy.* New York: Routledge, 1988.

Pietila, Hilkka, and Jeanne Vickers. *Making Women Matter: The Role of the United Nations.* Atlantic Highlands, N.J.: Zed Books, 1990.

Psacharopoulos, George, and Zafiris Tzannatos. *Case Studies on Women's Employment and Pay in Latin America.* Washington, D.C.: World Bank, 1992.

Queisser, Monika, O. Larranaga, and M. Panadeiros. *Adjustment and Social Development in Latin America During the 1980s.* Munich: Weltforum Verlag, 1992.

Qweb. Empowerment of Women Links. Available online at http://www.qweb.kvinnoforum.se/empowerment/links.html.

Ramirez, Miguel D. *Mexico's Economic Crisis: Its Origins and Consequences.* New York: Praeger, 1989.

Rogers, Barbara. *The Domestication of Women: Discrimination in Developing Societies.* New York: St. Martin's, 1979.

Rottenberg, Simon, ed. *Costa Rica and Uruguay: The Political Economy of Poverty, Equity, and Growth.* Washington, D.C.: World Bank and Oxford University Press, 1993.

Sabbagh, Suha, ed. *Palestinian Women of Gaza and the West Bank.* Bloomington: Indiana University Press, 1998.

Samarsinghe, Vidyamali. "Puppets on a String: Women's Wage Work and Empowerment Among Female Tea Plantation Workers of Sri Lanka." *Journal of Developing Areas* 27, no. 3 (April 1993): 329–340.

Sarsar, Saliba. "Bibliography on Palestinian Women." Available online at http://www.columbia.edu/cu/libraries/indiv/area/MiddleEast/palwomen.html (accessed December 12, 1998).

Seligson, Mitchell A., and John A. Booth, eds. *Elections and Democracy in Central America, Revisited.* Chapel Hill: University of North Carolina Press, 1995.

Sen, Gita, and Caren Grown. *Development, Crises, and Alternative Visions: Third World Women's Perspectives.* New York: Monthly Review, 1987.

Sen, Gita, and Noeleen Heyzer, eds. *Gender, Economic Growth, and Poverty.* New Delhi: International Books, 1994.

Sen, Gita, et al., eds. *Population Policies Reconsidered: Health Empowerment and Rights.* Cambridge: Harvard University Press, 1994.

Shager, Michael D. *Winners and Losers: How Sectors Shape the Developmental Prospects of States.* Ithaca: Cornell University Press, 1994.

Sharoni, Simona. *Gender and the Israeli-Palestinian Conflict: The Politics of Women's Resistance.* Syracuse: Syracuse University Press, 1995.

Shepherd, Verene A., ed. *Women in Caribbean History: The British-Colonised Territories.* Kingston, Jamaica: Ian Randle, 1999.

Shue, Vivienne. *The Reach of the State.* Stanford: Stanford University Press, 1988.

Singer, Morris. *Growth, Equality, and the Mexican Experience.* Austin: University of Texas Press, 1969.

Sparr, Pamela, ed. *Mortgaging Women's Lives: Feminist Critiques of Structural Adjustment.* London: Zed Books, 1994.

Stacey, Judith. *Patriarchy and Socialist Revolution in China.* Berkeley: University of California Press, 1983.

Stewart, Frances. *Adjustment and Poverty: Options and Choices.* London: Routledge, 1995.

Stichter, Sharon, and Jane L. Parpart, eds. *Women, Employment, and the Family in the International Division of Labour.* Philadelphia: Temple University Press, 1990.

Strum, Philippa. *The Women Are Marching: The Second Sex and the Palestinian Revolution.* Brooklyn, N.Y.: Lawrence Hill Books, 1992.

Sunshine, Catherine A. *The Caribbean: Survival, Struggle, and Sovereignty.* Boston: South End, 1988.

Tickner, J. Ann. "You Just Don't Understand: Troubled Engagements Between Feminists and IR Theorists." *International Studies Quarterly* 41, no. 4 (December 1997).

Tinker, Irene, ed. *Persistent Inequalities: Women and World Development.* New York: Oxford University Press, 1990.

UNHCR Division of International Protection. "Gender-Related Persecution. An Analysis of Recent Trends." *International Journal of Refugee Law* (special issue, autumn 1997).

United Nations. *The UN Internet Gateway on the Advancement and Empowerment of Women.* Avalable online at http://www.un.org/womenwatch/.

Veltmeyer, Henry, and James Petras with Steve Vieux. *Neoliberalism and Class Conflict in Latin America: A Comparative Perspective on the Political Economy of Structural Adjustment.* New York: St. Martin's, 1996.

Winslow, Anne, ed. *Women, Politics, and the United Nations.* Westport, Conn.: Greenwood, 1995.

Witke, Roxane, and Margery Wolf, eds. *Women in Chinese Society.* Stanford: Stanford University Press, 1975.

World Bank Group. *Gender Net.* Available online at http://www.worldbank.org/gender/.

# THE CONTRIBUTORS

Kiki Anastasakos is a member of the Department of Political Science at Temple University. She has done extensive research on the impact of internationalization on women and labor. She has been a visiting researcher at the Max Planck Institute for the Study of Societies, Cologne, Germany.

Lucy Creevey is professor of political science at the University of Connecticut and has worked as a consultant for various institutions, including the World Bank, UNIFEM, and USAID on studies of women and empowerment.

Rekha Datta is associate professor of political science at Monmouth University in West Long Branch, New Jersey. She is the author of *Why Alliances Endure: The United States–Pakistan Alliance, 1954–1971* (1994) and of articles about South Asia in the post–Cold War era.

Judith Kornberg is director of the School of Continuing Education and Professional Development at Purchase College of the State University of New York and is a lecturer in the college's Asian Studies Program. She coauthored, with John Faust, *China in World Politics* (1995).

Marian A. L. Miller is associate professor of political science at the University of Akron. She has written extensively on women's issues and environmental issues in the Caribbean.

Charlotte Graves Patton is adjunct assistant professor in the Department of Political Science at York University of the City University of New York.

She serves as the alternate nongovernmental organization representative of the International Studies Association to the United Nations.

Saliba Sarsar is associate professor of political science at Monmouth University.

Kathleen Suneja is research scholar at the Library of Congress in Washington, D.C. She has been a consultant to the United Nations High Commission for Refugees Project on the Causes of Refugee Formation and Flows, to the U.S. Agency for International Development Task Force on the Newly Independent States of Eastern Europe and the Soviet Union, and to the American Bar Association's Section for International Law. She has served as adjunct faculty at American University in Washington, D.C.

Kellee S. Tsai is assistant professor of political science at Johns Hopkins University. She received her Ph.D. in political science from Columbia University and spent two years as Academy Scholar at the Harvard Academy for International and Area Studies. Her publications include *Banking Behind the State: Private Entrepreneurs and Informal Finance in China* (forthcoming) and articles in *Journal of International Affairs, China Quarterly,* and *China Journal.*

# INDEX

Abortion, and China's population policy, 57–58. *See also* Reproductive health
Abzug, Bella, 17
Agricultural sector: Caribbean women in, 131–133; Chinese women in, 54, 61; Sengalese women's activities in, 106–107, 108; women's declining activity in, 81
AIDS, 25
All-China Women's Federation (ACWF), 51
Alma Alta Conference, Declaration on the Right to Health for All and the Safe Motherhood Initiative, 17
Annan, Kofi, 15
Arafat, Suha, 150
Arafat, Yasser, 149–150
Association of Women of Jamaica (AWOJA), 141
Azzouni, Suheir, 156

Bahamas: Gender-related Development Index and, 130; women's economic and political activity in, 131
Barbados, 137; women's economic activity in, 131; women's movement in, 139
Belize: Rural Women's Association, 140; women's education in, 130
Bhutto, Benazir, 86

Birzeit University, Women's Studies Program, 157
Bosnian conflict: sexual violence against women in, 33, 39
Boulata, Terry, 153

CARE BRK, 109
Caribbean Association for Feminist Research and Action (CAFRA), 137
Caribbean Community Secretariat, Women's Desk of, 137
Caribbean Conference of Churches (CCC), 136–137
Caribbean women: development policies and, 136; economic activity of, 130–131, 141–142; education and training of, 130, 134; health education programs for, 140; as informal commercial importers, 133, 138; and legislative reforms, 142; national organizations for, 138–141; organizing of domestic workers in, 141; political participation of, 131, 139; regional initiatives for, 136–138; as sex workers, 134; as small farmers, 131–132; social activism of, 135–141; and social service cuts, 134–135; in tourism industry, 133–134; as traders, 132; transnational corporations and, 133; underpayment and exploitation of,

# ABOUT THE BOOK

For decades, researchers and policymakers have examined the impact of development programs on women—and evidence of sustained gender discrimination has inspired local, national, and international policy reforms. But has the empowerment movement increased women's control of resources? Has it had the desired effect on gender relations traditionally defined by patriarchal ideology and institutions?

Addressing these questions, this book explores international, national, and local empowerment efforts in Africa, Asia, Latin America, and the Middle East. The result is a nuanced account of empowerment goals and strategies at all levels of initiative.

**Rekha Datta** is associate professor of political science at Monmouth University. **Judith Kornberg** is director of the School of Continuing Education and Professional Development at Purchase College, SUNY. She is coauthor (with John Faust) of *China in World Politics*.